Financial Accounting

For LCCI, 'A' level and intermediate professional examinations

GEOFF BLACK, FCA, FBIM

Woodhead-Faulkner · Cambridge

Published by Woodhead-Faulkner Ltd
Fitzwilliam House, 32 Trumpington Street, Cambridge CB2 1QY, England

First published 1986

British Library Cataloguing in Publication Data
Black, Geoff
    Financial accounting.
    1. Accounting
    I. Title
    657'.48   HF5635

    ISBN 0-85941-336-5

Library of Congress Cataloging in Publication Data
Black, Geoff
    Financial accounting.

    Includes index.
    1. Accounting.   2. Accounting—Great Britain.
    I. Title.
    HF5635.B662   1986   657'.48   86-11050
    ISBN 0-85941-336-5 (pbk.)

Designed by Ron Jones

Typeset by Tradespools Ltd, Frome, Somerset

Printed in Great Britain by
St Edmundsbury Press Ltd, Bury St Edmunds, Suffolk

Preface

'They cannot thrive, who have not an exact Account of their Expences and Incoms.' Hugh Audley (d.1662)

These words, written in the seventeenth century, have an obvious relevance to a textbook devoted to the study of accountancy. This book, whilst explaining how the 'exact Account' should be kept, allows the reader to learn how a business not only records and presents its accounting information but also how the information can be analysed and interpreted. This volume concentrates on financial accounting, which explores, inter alia, the financial relationships which exist between the business entity and the outside world (e.g. shareholders, customers, suppliers and the Government). There is another branch of accountancy, cost and management accounting, which is covered by a companion volume, *Cost and Management Accounting* by Trevor Daff, also published by Woodhead-Faulkner.

This book has been written primarily for examinations of an 'intermediate' level, including 'A' level, LCCI (Intermediate and Higher), Accounting Technicians and the first examinations of professional bodies such as Certified Accountants and Chartered Secretaries. It will also be of benefit to those who wish to attain a good general background to accounting procedures without necessarily taking examinations.

The first chapter of the book is devoted to a consideration of basic double-entry book-keeping principles. This provides an introduction for the complete newcomer to the subject whilst providing a refresher course for those who may have some knowledge of such procedures. Readers who propose entering for specific examinations are advised to check an up-to-date syllabus to confirm the range of topics to be covered. No two accountancy syllabuses are identical, and if readers are in any doubt then they should be guided by the principle that there is no such thing as 'surplus knowledge'! The author has tried to make the text as easy to understand as possible, and has borne in mind the fact that more candidates for UK accountancy examinations live outside the UK than within it. Any suggestions, from lecturers or students, which might serve to improve such understanding will be gratefully received and possibly incorporated into future editions.

The author is indebted to the following examining bodies for granting permission to use their recent examination questions:

Associated Examining Board (AEB)
Association of Accounting Technicians (AAT)
Certified Diploma in Accounting and Finance (CDAF)
Chartered Association of Certified Accountants (ACCA)
Institute of Bankers (IOB)
Joint Matriculation Board (JMB)
London Chamber of Commerce and Industry (LCCI)
University of London Schools Examining Board (ULSEB)
Welsh Joint Examination Committee (WJEC)

Company account formats contained within the Companies Act 1985 have been reproduced by kind permission of the Controller of Her Majesty's Stationery Office.

In all cases, answers given to examination questions are the responsibility of the author and have neither been provided nor approved by the examining body concerned.

In conclusion, the author would like to express his gratitude to his father, Robert Black, for painstakingly reviewing draft material, and providing much useful help and comment, to Linda Bradshaw, for the prompt and efficient typing of the manuscript, to Trevor Daff, for help and encouragement, and to John Blanchfield of the computer department of CCAT, for help in compiling the index.

Geoff Black
Cambridge, July 1986

Contents

CHAPTER 1

Basic Accounting Procedures

1.1 How does accounting differ from book-keeping?

Students commencing a course in accounting may have spent some time in a study of book-keeping. It is advisable, therefore, at the outset to establish the ways in which accounting differs from book-keeping, and the following definitions can be considered.

Book-keeping: The analysis, classification and recording of financial transactions in books of account.

Accounting: The analysis, classification and recording of financial transactions *and the ascertainment of how such transactions affect the perform-ance and financial position of a business.*

Accounting, according to these definitions, takes over where book-keeping leaves off, and throughout this book it shall be seen that the end use of the accounting information by 'non-accountants' is as important, if not of greater importance, as the provision by accountants of the 'means of production' via the book-keeping system. However, we must not lose sight of the fact that the accounting information will only be useful if the underlying book-keeping system can be relied upon to produce accurate and relevant data. Consequently, we shall use this chapter to revise some of the basic principles of book-keeping, and then look in detail at certain aspects which cause particular difficulties.

The study of accounting presupposes a good understanding of the double-entry system, and students who are in any doubt concerning the adequacy of their knowledge are advised to pay particular attention to the revision of basic principles which now follows.

1.2 The book-keeping system

The financial transactions of the business are methodically recorded in various books of account, collectively known as the 'double-entry book-keeping system'. This system has evolved over many centuries and has undergone comparatively few changes since the Middle Ages. The major change in recent years obviously concerns the word 'book', as the widespread use of computers by businesses of all sizes has meant a movement away from traditional pen and paper to the entries appearing on visual display units and computer print-outs. The underlying book-keeping system remains basically unaltered, but the speed with which the information can be processed and made available for interpretation has increased dramatically. In this volume (as in accounting examinations) the word 'book' is retained for convenience, but is used as a collective noun to include not only handwritten accounting records, but also mechanically and electronically processed systems.

1.3 Books of prime entry

As the name implies, 'double-entry' book-keeping involves entering each financial transaction systematically in *two* locations within the records of the business. This is due to the recognition that there is a 'dual aspect' to each transaction; that the business both receives and gives value. For example, a business buying stock will not only receive goods, but will also have to pay cash to the supplier. Similarly, when the business makes a sale, it not only receives cash from its customer, but also has to give goods or services in return.

The record of 'receiving' and 'giving' is the essence of the double-entry system. As a general rule, entries on the debit (abbreviated DR) side of an account record value received, whilst entries on the credit (abbreviated CR) side record value given.

To be confident that all aspects of the business's financial life are fully recorded within the books, one must ensure that a system exists which is flexible enough to cope with the various types of transactions which occur. Figure 1.1 shows how information from various sources is processed at the first stage of the book-keeping

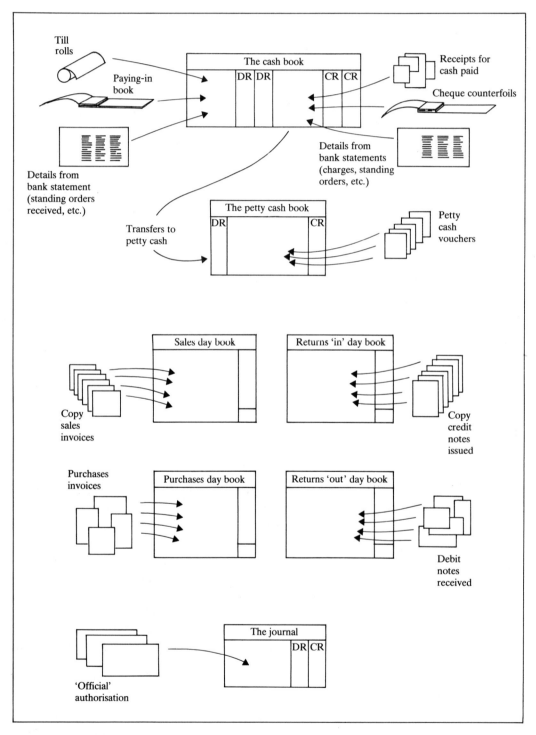

Fig. 1.1 The books of prime entry.

Table 1.1

Name	Contents	Type of transactions	Source documents	How entered	Posted to:
1. Cash book	Cash account Bank account	Cash sales Cash from debtors Standing orders received Other cash receipts	Till rolls Sales summary sheets Bank statements Paying-in books	Debited	Credit of accounts in ledger
		Cheques paid Cash paid Standing orders paid	Cheque books Receipts for cash Bank statements	Credited	Debit of accounts in ledger
2. Petty cash book	Petty cash account	'Float' received from main cash account	Cashier's receipt	Debited	Credit of cash book
		Petty cash expenditure	Petty cash vouchers and accompanying receipts	Credited	Debit of ledger accounts
3. Sales day book	*No* accounts, only a list of sales	Sales made on 'credit' terms	Copies of sales invoices	Listed and totalled at intervals	Individual invoices to DR of customer's account in sales ledger, totals of invoices to CR of sales account in general ledger
4. Returns in day book	*No* accounts, only a list of values of goods returned by customers	Goods returned by customers (previously sold on 'credit' terms)	Copies of credit notes issued	Listed and totalled at intervals	Individual credit notes to CR of customer's account in sales ledger, totals of credit notes to DR of returns in account in general ledger

Table 1.1 (*continued*)

Name	Contents	Type of transactions	Source documents	How entered	Posted to:
5. Purchases day book	*No accounts, only a* list of purchases	Purchases (of goods or services, etc.) made on 'credit' terms	Purchases invoices received	Listed and totalled at intervals	Individual invoices to CR of supplier's account in purchases ledger, total of invoices to DR of relevant accounts in general ledger
6. Returns out day book	*No accounts, only a* list of values of goods returned to suppliers	Goods returned to suppliers, previously bought on 'credit' terms	Debit notes received	Listed and totalled at intervals	Individual debit note to DR of supplier's account in purchases ledger, totals of debit notes to CR of returns out account in general ledger
7. The journal	Descriptions of book-keeping entries required for transactions	Any transaction (or transfer between ledger accounts, or correction of errors) not listed in any other book of prime entry	Official authorisation, e.g. signed by owner	Accounts to be debited and credited are shown for each transaction	DR and CR of ledger accounts as analysed in journal

system, by means of being entered in a 'book of prime entry', prior to being posted to the ultimate destination of a ledger account. Table 1.1 gives a detailed explanation of the function of each book.

In addition to providing the first link in the chain of accounting entries, books of prime entry are also used extensively by management as sources of reference, whether for purposes of day-to-day control, or for dealing with queries which may arise from customers or suppliers.

1.4 The ledger

This is a collective title given to three separate books: the sales ledger, the purchases ledger and the general ledger. These act as 'books of secondary entry', taking information from the books previously listed in section 1.3. Figure 1.2 illustrates the main routes of entries progressing from the books of prime entry into the ledger, and Table 1.2 is a summary of the contents of the three books which make up the ledger.

Table 1.2

Name	Contents	Entries posted from:	
		(Debit entries)	*(Credit entries)*
1. The sales ledger	The personal accounts of debtors, i.e. customers to whom the business sells on 'credit' terms	Sales invoices from sales day book	Returns in from returns in day book Cash from cash book
2. The purchases ledger	The personal accounts of creditors, i.e. suppliers of goods and services from whom the business buys on 'credit' terms	Returns out from returns out day book Cash paid, from cash book	Purchases invoices from purchases day book
3. The general ledger	'Impersonal' accounts of assets, liabilities, capital, income and expenditure*	Cash paid, from cash book Purchase and expense invoice totals from purchases day book Returns in totals from returns in day book	Cash received, from cash book Sales invoice totals from sales day book Returns out totals from returns out day book

* Three impersonal accounts are contained within the cash book and petty cash book: the cash account, the bank account and the petty cash account. The cash book and petty cash book are therefore technically part of the general ledger, as well as being 'books of prime entry'.

1.5 'Final' accounts

The definition of book-keeping given earlier referred to the 'analysis, classification and recording of financial transactions'. Whilst this is of course essential to ensure the efficient management of the day-to-day operations of the business, a further stage must now be considered which enables the owner to have an 'overview' of the business's affairs. This is achieved by the preparation of accounting summaries (known, albeit inaccurately, as 'the accounts') at regular intervals. These intervals, or 'financial periods', need not be of twelve months' duration, but each business will have to produce 'final accounts' covering the whole financial year for the purpose of taxation assessment.

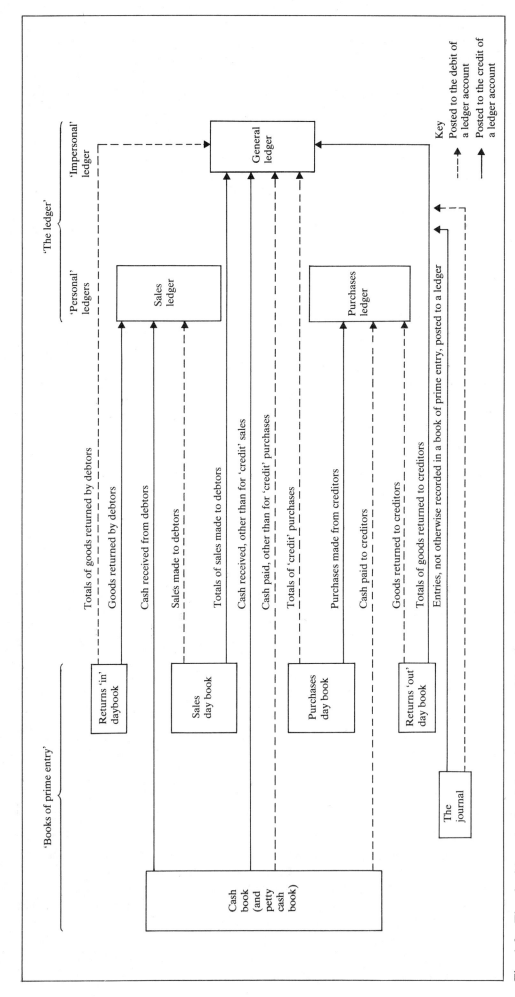

Fig. 1.2   The double-entry book-keeping system (showing main 'routes' of entries).

THE TRIAL BALANCE

When the business wishes to summarise the book-keeping records for the purpose of calculating its profit or loss or establishing its value according to its books, then an essential preliminary step is the extraction of a 'trial balance'. Although not an integral part of the double-entry system, the trial balance acts as a check on the arithmetical accuracy of the system by proving that the total of the debit entries equals the total of the credit entries. The trial balance is simply a list of all the balances which exist at the date on which the check is being made, distinguishing between 'debit' balances and 'credit' balances. Balances fall under the following four major categories:

	Debit balances	*Credit balances*
1. Assets (e.g. plant, stock, debtors, cash)	X	
2. Expenses (e.g. purchases, wages)	X	
3. Capital and liabilities (e.g. capital, creditors)		X
4. Income (e.g. sales)		X
	X = equals =	X

Even though the trial balance agrees arithmetically, errors may still be present within the book-keeping system due to one or more of the following.

(a) Errors of commission, where the wrong person's account has been posted with the correct amount.
(b) Errors of omission, where a transaction has been completely omitted.
(c) Errors of principle, where the wrong type of account has been posted (e.g. rent posted to buildings account).
(d) Compensating errors, where two or more errors cancel each other.
(e) Errors of original entry, where the incorrect amount has been posted to the correct accounts.
(f) Reversed entries, where debit entries have been credited and vice-versa.

Despite the possibility of errors remaining, a 'balanced' trial balance still represents an invaluable check on the overall arithmetical accuracy of the entries, and previously undetected errors are often brought to light in the course of its preparation.

TRADING AND PROFIT AND LOSS ACCOUNTS AND THE BALANCE SHEET

The summary of the financial position of the business is divided into two distinct statements, the trading and profit and loss accounts, which show the 'income' or 'revenue' position over the entire financial period, and the balance sheet, which shows the 'capital' position (total net assets) of the business as at the last day of the financial period.

'Income' or 'Revenue' Statement *(Trading and Profit and Loss Accounts)*				*'Capital' Statement* *(the Balance Sheet)*			
Trading Account	Cost of sales x	Sales	x	Capital	x	Fixed assets	x
	Gross profit x						
	X		X	Current liabilities x		Current assets	x
Profit and Loss Account	Overheads x	Gross profit	x				
	Net profit x						
	X		X		X		X

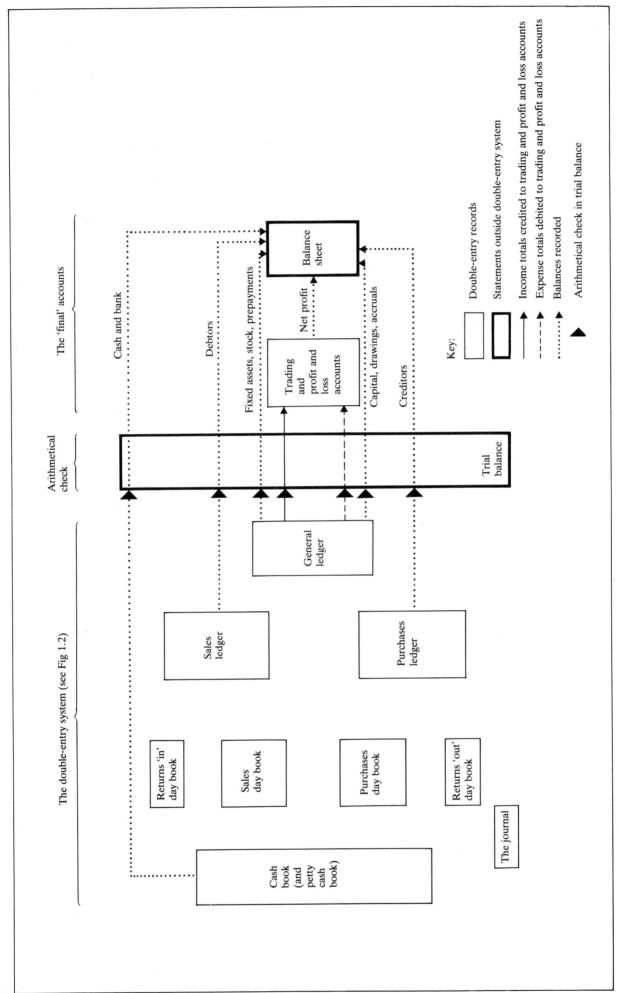

Fig. 1.3   The production of final accounts from the double-entry system.

Note that the trading and profit and loss accounts are part of the double-entry system, but the balance sheet, like the trial balance, is merely a statement extracted from the system. Figure 1.3 illustrates the sources of entries in the 'final accounts'.

Example 1 provides an opportunity for students to study in detail not only the production of 'final accounts' from an agreed trial balance, but also the extent of the underlying book-keeping information from which the trial balance is compiled. The solution has been shown in a 'horizontal' format, which is the method that is likely to be most familiar to students at this stage.

Example 1

Jean Knight is in business as a clothing wholesaler, trading under the name 'Jean's Jeans'. Her financial year ends on 30 November, and the trial balance of her business as at 30 November 1984 is shown below.

	Debit £	Credit £
General Ledger		
Accountancy	350	
Advertising	285	
Bad debts	60	
Bank charges	74	
Capital		23,261
Discount allowed	129	
Discount received		230
Drawings	7,500	
Fixtures and fittings, at cost	11,400	
Light and heat	1,030	
Motor expenses	518	
Motor van, at cost	8,900	
Postage, printing and stationery	390	
Provision for depreciation on fixtures and fittings, 1 December 1983		3,400
Provision for depreciation of motor van, 1 December 1983		3,200
Provision for doubtful debts, 1 December 1983		350
Purchases	49,600	
Rent and rates	3,100	
Repairs	810	
Sales		75,972
Stock, 1 December 1983	7,224	
Telephone and insurance	619	
Wages of assistants	11,460	
Sales ledger: Total debtors	7,384	
Purchases ledger: Total creditors		8,140
Cash book: Bank balance	3,600	
Cash balance	120	
	£114,553	£114,553

Notes:
1. Stock at 30 November 1984 is valued at £12,400.
2. Wages owing at the year-end amounts to £130.
3. Rent prepaid totals £200 at the year-end.
4. Depreciation is to be charged on fixtures, on the reducing balance basis, at a rate of 10 per cent per annum.
5. The motor van is to be written off over five years by the straight line depreciation method, assuming a residual value of £900.
6. The provision for doubtful debts is to be increased to £450.

Required:

Trading and profit and loss accounts for the year ended 30 November 1984 and the balance sheet as at that date.

Solution:

Jean Knight
Trading as 'Jean's Jeans'

Trading and Profit and Loss Accounts for the year ended 30 November 1984

Opening stock	7,224	Sales	75,972
Purchases	49,600		
	56,824		
Less: Closing stock	12,400		
Cost of goods sold	44,424		
Gross profit c/d	31,548		
	£ 75,972		£ 75,972
Wages	11,590	Gross profit b/d	31,548
Light and heat	1,030	Discount received	230
Postage, printing, etc.	390		
Advertising	285		
Telephone and insurance	619		
Rent and rates	2,900		
Repairs	810		
Motor expenses	518		
Bank charges	74		
Accountancy	350		
Discount allowed	129		
Bad debts written off	60		
Provision for doubtful debts	100		
Depreciation:			
on fixtures and fittings	800		
on motor van	1,600		
	21,255		
Net profit	10,523		
	£ 31,778		£ 31,778

Balance Sheet as at 30 November 1984

Capital					
Opening balance, 1 Dec 1983	23,261	*Fixed assets*			
Add: Net profit	10,523	Fixtures and fittings,			
	———	at cost		11,400	
	33,784	*Less:* Provision for			
Less: Drawings	7,500	depreciation		4,200	
	———			———	
	26,284			7,200	
		Motor van, at cost		8,900	
		Less: Provision for			
		depreciation		4,800	
				———	
					4,100
					———
					11,300
Current liabilities		*Current assets*			
Creditors	8,140	Stock		12,400	
Accruals	130	Debtors	7,384		
	———				
	8,270	*Less:* Provision			
		for doubtful			
		debts		450	
				———	6,934
		Prepayments		200	
		Bank		3,600	
		Cash		120	3,920
				———	———
					23,254
	———				———
	£ 34,554				£ 34,554
	———				———

COMMENTARY

The student will recognise that the entries in the final accounts are derived from the balances which appear in the trial balance at the end of the financial period, as adjusted for accruals, prepayments, movements on provisions, and the closing stock valuations. As an aid to a thorough revision of the book-keeping system, the (summarised) ledger accounts which gave rise to the trial balance entries are listed below, together with explanatory notes thereon. The accounts have been 'closed off' at 30 November 1984, i.e. 'income' and 'expenditure' account balances have been posted to the trading account or profit and loss account (P & L a/c), whilst asset, liability and the capital account balances have been carried down within the account, to give the opening figures for the next financial year as well as providing the information required for the balance sheet at the year-end.

When studying these accounts, it will prove helpful to refer to Fig. 1.3, which shows the main routes of book-keeping entries.

General ledger

	Debit		Credit		Notes
Accountancy					
30 Nov 1984 (Total)	350	30 Nov 1984	Profit and loss a/c	350	An 'expense' account, showing the total transferred to the profit and loss account at the year-end.
Advertising					
30 Nov 1984 (Total)	285	30 Nov 1984	Profit and loss a/c	285	As 'Accountancy'.
Bad debts					
30 Nov 1984 Transfers from sales ledger	60	30 Nov 1984	Profit and loss a/c	60	Bad debts are irrecoverable sales ledger balances which must be 'written off' to profit and loss account.
Bank charges					
30 Nov 1984 (Total)	74	30 Nov 1984	Profit and loss a/c	74	As 'Accountancy'.
Capital					
30 Nov 1984 Transfer drawings Account	7,500	1 Dec 1983	Opening balance b/f	23,261	This account shows the book value of the owner's interest in the business. The net profit increases that value, but as the owner has drawn £7,500 out of the business during the year, the capital has increased by only just over £3,000 between the start and end of the year.
30 Nov 1984 Closing balance c/d	26,284	30 Nov 1984	Net profit from Profit and loss a/c	10,523	
	33,784			33,784	
		1 Dec 1984	Opening balance b/d	26,284	
Discount allowed					
30 Nov 1984 (Total)	129	30 Nov 1984	Profit and loss a/c	129	An 'expense' account, showing the discount allowed by the business to 'credit' customers in return for prompt payment.
Discount received					
30 Nov 1984 Profit and loss a/c	230	30 Nov 1984	(Total)	230	An 'income' account showing the value of discount received by the business as a reward for paying suppliers promptly.

Drawings

30 Nov 1984	(Total)	7,500	30 Nov 1984	Transfer to capital a/c	7,500

The total value drawn from the business by the owner, transferred at the year-end to the debit of capital account.

Fixtures and fittings

30 Nov 1984	(Total)	11,400	30 Nov 1984	Closing balance c/d	11,400
1 Dec 1984	Opening balance b/d	11,400			

Fixtures and fittings are 'fixed assets', i.e. assets not held for re-sale but to be used within the business over a long period.

Light and heat

30 Nov 1984	(Total)	1,030	30 Nov 1984	Profit and loss a/c	1,030

As 'Accountancy'

Motor expenses

30 Nov 1984	(Total)	518	30 Nov 1984	Profit and loss a/c	518

As 'Accountancy'

Motor van

30 Nov 1984	(Total)	8,900	30 Nov 1984	Closing balance c/d	8,900
1 Dec 1984	Opening balance b/d	8,900			

As 'Fixtures and fittings'

Postage, printing and stationery

30 Nov 1984	(Total)	390	30 Nov 1984	Profit and loss a/c	390

As 'Accountancy'

Provision for depreciation of fixtures and fittings
Provision for depreciation of motor van
Provision for doubtful debts

[See section 1.6 for an explanation of these three accounts.]

Purchases

30 Nov 1984	(Total)	49,600	30 Nov 1984	Trading account	49,600

The total of goods, *bought for re-sale*, tranferred to the trading account.

Rent and rates

30 Nov 1984	(Total)	3,100	30 Nov 1984	Profit and loss a/c	2,900
		———		Prepayment c/d	200
		3,100			———
					3,100
1 Dec 1984	Prepayment b/d	200			

As 'Accountancy', but £200 of the total debited to the account was 'prepaid', i.e. related to the next financial year. For example, a cheque for £200 paid in November may have been for December's rent.

Repairs

30 Nov 1984	(Total)	810	30 Nov 1984	Profit and loss a/c	810

As 'Accountancy'.

Sales

30 Nov 1984	Trading account	75,972	30 Nov 1984	(Total)	75,972

The total of sales of goods made during the year, transferred to the trading a/c.

Stock

1 Dec 1983	Opening balance b/f	7,224	30 Nov 1984	Trading account	7,224
30 Nov 1984	Trading account	12,400		Closing balance c/d	12,400
		19,624			19,624
1 Dec 1984	Opening balance b/d	12,400			

The opening and closing values of unsold goods, transferred to the trading account. Stocks are usually valued at the lower of 'cost and net realisable value'.

Telephone and insurance

30 Nov 1984	(Total)	619	30 Nov 1984	Profit and loss a/c	619

As 'Accountancy'.

Wages of Assistants

30 Nov 1984	(Total)	11,460	30 Nov 1984	Profit and loss a/c	11,590
	Accrual c/d	130			
		11,590			
			1 Dec 1984	Accrual b/d	130

As 'Accountancy', but an additional £130 had been incurred for wages at the year-end but not paid for until some time after the year-end.

Sales ledger (example of one account)

A. Customer

14 June 1984	Invoice	5,800		19 Aug 1984	Cheque	5,800
22 Oct 1984	Invoice	1,740		30 Nov 1984	Closing balance c/d	1,740
		7,540				7,540
1 Dec 1984	Opening balance b/d	1,740				

The trial balance shows the total of all debtors' balances at the year-end.

Purchases ledger (Example of one account)

A. Supplier

5 Feb 1984	Cheque	840		12 Jan 1984	Purchase invoice	840
10 June 1984	Cheque	298		19 May 1984	Purchase invoice	308
	Discount	10		20 Sept 1984	Purchase invoice	660
30 Nov 1984	Closing balance c/d	660				
		1,808				1,808
				1 Dec	Opening balance b/d	660

The trial balance shows the total of all creditors' balances at the year-end.

Cash book

		Cash	Bank			Cash	Bank
30 Nov 1984	(Totals)	3,250	79,170	30 Nov 1984	(Totals)	3,130	75,570
					Closing balances c/d	120	3,600
		3,250	79,170			3,250	79,170
1 Dec 1984	Opening balances b/d	120	3,600				

The trial balance shows the cash balance and the bank balance at the end of the year.

Notes: 1. Abbreviations used are: a/c Account b/f Brought forward b/d Brought down c/d Carried down

2. Where the word 'total' appears, this represents the sum of the individual entries posted to the account from one or more books of prime entry.

15

1.6 Specific difficulties

CAPITAL OR REVENUE?

We referred earlier to the trading and profit and loss accounts as the 'revenue' statement, and the balance sheet as the 'capital' statement. Why is this distinction between capital and revenue so important? The answer lies in understanding the meaning of the two terms.

1. *Revenue expenditure* is the cost incurred in the day-to-day running of the business, e.g. raw materials, wages, motor expenses, advertising.
2. *Capital expenditure* relates to the purchase of fixed assets, i.e. those assets which are bought in order to be used by the business over several accounting periods, e.g. land and buildings, motor vehicles, computers.

All expenditure treated as 'revenue' has been debited (accountants often use the expression 'written off') either to the trading account or to the profit and loss account, thereby directly reducing the level of profit. If it had been incorrectly treated as 'capital' expenditure (e.g. petrol bills being added to the cost of a vehicle), then the effect is to both overstate the fixed assets on the balance sheet and also to overstate the net profit, due to expenses being understated. Not only is this misleading, but it may also lead to financial difficulties if the business believes that it is more profitable than it really is.

As the capital expenditure is used in the business, it usually loses value (with the exception of freehold land) by reason of the increasing age of the fixed assets, or the gradual obsolescence caused by new technology. This loss of value is known as *depreciation*, and must be reflected in the revenue statement in the same way that other losses (expenses) are shown.

METHODS OF PROVIDING FOR DEPRECIATION

There are two main methods, the *straight line basis* and the *reducing balance basis*. In the example of 'Jean's Jeans', the motor van was depreciated using the former method whilst the fixtures were depreciated using the latter.

Straight line method

This assumes that the loss in value of the fixed asset is spread evenly over the life of the asset. The annual depreciation is therefore calculated by using the following formula:

$$\frac{\text{Cost} - \text{'residual' value}}{\text{Estimated life in years}}$$

and using the figures from Example 1 relating to the motor van:

$$\frac{£8,900 - £900}{5} = £1,600$$

Therefore £1,600 is 'written off' the value of the van each year for five years. The ledger account for the year ended 30 November 1984 is shown as follows:

Provision for depreciation on motor van

30 Nov 1984	Closing balance c/d	4,800	1 Dec 1983	Opening balance b/f	3,200
			30 Nov 1984	Profit and loss a/c	1,600
		4,800			4,800
			1 Dec 1984	Opening balance b/d	4,800

From this account, we know that the van has been owned by the business for three years by 30 November 1984 (£4,800 ÷ £1,600 p.a. = 3).

The van will continue to be depreciated until its 'book life' has elapsed. If further motor vans are purchased in later years, the depreciation on these will also appear in the provision account, and it is usual to maintain a separate 'fixed assets register' (not part of the book-keeping system), to keep track of the amounts of depreciation provided on individual assets.

Reducing balance method (also called 'diminishing' balance method)

This method assumes that more depreciation is lost in the early years of the asset's life than in the later years. The calculation of the annual depreciation is made by applying a given percentage* to the 'net book value' (cost less accumulated depreciation to the start of the year). In Example 1 depreciation on fixtures was to be charged at the rate of 10% on the reducing balance. The ledger account for the year ended 30 November 1984 would be as follows:

Provision for depreciation on fixtures

30 Nov 1984	Closing balance c/d	4,200	1 Dec 1983	Opening balance b/f	3,400
			30 Nov 1984	Profit and loss a/c	800
		4,200			4,200
			1 Dec 1984	Opening balance b/d	4,200

The depreciation for the year has been calculated at 10% on:

	£
Cost	11,400
Less: Opening provision b/f	3,400
	8,000
Depreciation at 10% =	800

Assuming that fixtures were neither bought nor sold in the following year, the amount to be transferred to profit and loss account for depreciation in the year to 30 November 1985 would be: $10\% \times (11,400 - 4,200) = £720$.

Note that depreciation does not necessarily set aside sufficient funds to provide for the eventual replacement of the asset. That is not the prime purpose of depreciation, as we are only reflecting the decline in value, rather than attempting to retain profits to buy new assets at the end of their useful lives. (See Chapter 10 for a more detailed explanation of how companies can adjust depreciation in line with inflation.)

Example 2

Kimberley and Co. commenced business on 1 January 1980 and purchased vehicles costing £50,000 and equipment costing £20,000.

It was decided to depreciate vehicles over five years using the straight line method, assuming no residual values. Equipment was to be depreciated at 30% per annum, using the reducing balance method.

Required:
Prepare a schedule showing the depreciation for vehicles and equipment for each of the years ended 31 December 1980, 1981 and 1982.

*Although examination candidates are not normally required to calculate the exact percentage required to 'write off' the asset under this basis over a specific number of years, it is possible to ascertain the rate by use of the following formula:

$$r = 100 \left(1 - n\frac{RV}{P} \right)$$

where r = % rate of depreciation
   n = number of years' life
   RV = residual value
   P = principal (i.e. original cost)

Solution:

	Vehicles £	Equipment £
Year ended 31 December 1980		
Cost	50,000	20,000
Depreciation	10,000	6,000
(written down value)	40,000	14,000
Year ended 31 December 1981		
Depreciation	10,000	4,200
(written down value)	30,000	9,800
Year ended 31 December 1982		
Depreciation	10,000	2,940
(written down value)	20,000	6,860

COMMENTARY

In practice, each individual vehicle or item of equipment would be shown in a separate column, rather than being amalgamated into overall headings. This aids the calculation of total depreciation which is necessary when a fixed asset is sold (see section 1.7).

OTHER PROVISIONS

The titles of the ledger accounts which record depreciation include the word 'provision', as the business is 'providing for' the loss in value of its fixed assets. Depreciation is an estimate, as no one really knows the true decline in value until the asset is sold. The business is being *prudent* (see Chapter 5) by reducing its profit to allow for the loss in value. Fixed assets are not however the only assets where a loss in value may take place. For example, losses (or reduced profits) may be incurred in one or more of the following circumstances.

(a) Customers failing to pay all or part of their sales ledger balances.
(b) Debtors taking advantage of discounts, thereby paying less into the business than the total of debtors disclosed on the balance sheet.
(c) Future, unquantifiable expense, due to commitments under guarantees or warranties given by the business to customers.

In each of these cases, the most appropriate course of action is for the business to 'make provision' for the potential loss. Provisions can be either specific or general, the former being used where the source of the potential losses can be fairly accurately identified (e.g. 'doubtful' debtors, customers entitled to deduct discounts), the latter where this is not possible (e.g. future commitments under guarantees).

In the example of 'Jean's Jeans', the only provision, apart from depreciation, was in relation to 'doubtful debts'. The trial balance showed an opening provision of £350 on 1 December 1983, whilst note 6 gave the instruction for this to be increased to £450. We are not told whether this is a specific or a general provision; if the former, then the owner has been able to identify a number of customers, with debts totalling £450, who have given cause for concern regarding their ability to pay. If a general provision, then the owner has estimated that, from past experience, approximately 6% of total debtors never pay their bills, so it is reasonable to maintain a provision at this level ($6\% \times £7,384 = £443$, 'rounded up' to £450). In either case, the ledger account would appear as follows:

Provision for doubtful debts

		1 Dec 1983	Opening balance b/f	350
30 Nov 1984	Closing balance c/d	450	30 Nov 1984 Profit and loss account	100
		450		450
		1 Dec 1984	Opening balance b/d	450

Future increases or decreases in provisions are adjusted in a similar way; increases by being debited to profit and loss account, decreases by the 'excess' provision no longer required being credited to profit and loss account (i.e. added back to gross profit).

ACCRUALS AND PREPAYMENTS

The trading and profit and loss accounts summarise the revenue position over a particular period, usually a year. However, problems frequently arise in their compilation due to the following.

1. Revenue expenditure 'consumed' in the financial period but not invoiced (or wages earned but not paid) until after the end of the period (e.g. an electricity account for the final three months of the financial year, not invoiced until six weeks after the year-end). Items falling within this category are referred to as 'accruals', and are current liabilities at the balance sheet date. The book-keeping entries are as shown in the 'wages' account in Example 1.

2. Payments made *during* the financial period, which relate to revenue expenditure either wholly or partly 'consumed' in the following financial period or periods (e.g. a payment for twelve months' insurance cover, only part of which relates to a period prior to the year-end, the remainder being related to the following financial year). These items are referred to as 'prepayments' and represent current assets at the balance sheet date. The 'rent' account in Example 1 explains the book-keeping treatment of prepayments.

3. Income received either in advance or in arrears (e.g. a tenant paying three months' rental prior to the financial year-end of the landlord, for a period following the financial year-end). Subscriptions paid to clubs and associations often 'overlap' the year-end and appropriate adjustments should be made to relate the receipts to the relevant years. (See next chapter.) Any income in advance is included as a current liability on the balance sheet, whilst income in arrears (i.e. due but not yet received) is shown as a current asset.

Example 3

A business with a year-end on 31 December has the following information concerning 'motor expenses':

1 January 1984	Amount owed for petrol	£280
	Motor insurance paid in advance	£145
31 December 1984	Cash and cheques for motor expenses	£3,390
	Amount owed for petrol	£193
	Motor insurance paid in advance	£173

The business carried a small stock of engine oil, valued at £95 on 1 January 1984, and £133 on 31 December 1984.

Required:
Show the general ledger account for motor expenses for the year ended 31 December 1984, and the relevant extracts from the final accounts.

Solution:

Motor expenses account

1 Jan 1984	Prepayment b/f	145	1 Jan 1984	Accrual b/f	280
	Stock of engine oil b/f	95			
31 Dec 1984	(Total of)				
	Cash and cheques	3,390	31 Dec 1984	Profit and loss a/c	3,237
	Accrual c/d	193		Prepayment c/d	
	(Petrol)			(Insurance)	173
				Stock of engine oil c/d	133
		3,823			3,823

1 Jan 1985	Prepayment b/d	173	1 Jan 1985 Accrual b/f	193
	Stock of engine oil			
	b/d	133		

Profit and Loss account (extract) year ended 31 December 1984

Motor expenses   3,237

Balance Sheet (extract) as at 31 December 1984

Current liabilities (include):		*Current assets* (include):	
Accruals	193	Repayments and sundry stocks	306

COMMENTARY

Accruals are liabilities, prepayments are assets. The former are therefore shown as credit balances in the ledger account whilst the latter are shown as debit balances. Stocks of 'sundry' items such as engine oil or stationery are the equivalent of prepayments, since the expenditure has been incurred, but the use of the item is deferred to a future period. The accounting treatment of such items is identical with that for prepayments.

1.7   Disposals of fixed assets

The fixed assets and provision for depreciation accounts in the general ledger contain details of all fixed assets owned by the business, together with the depreciation charged over their lifetime. When a fixed asset is sold (or scrapped) we must ensure that the original cost and the total depreciation charged is removed from those accounts, and also make a calculation to show if the depreciation charged over its life was too much or too little when compared with the actual value when sold or scrapped. A transfer will be made to profit and loss account in the year of disposal to adjust for this 'over' or 'under' depreciation.

The book-keeping procedure to be adopted falls into two sections.

1. *At the date of disposal*
   Preliminary: Open a disposal of (named) fixed asset account
   (a)   Enter the sale proceeds (DR cash a/c or debtor's a/c CR disposal a/c).
2. *At the end of the financial period*
   (b)   Transfer the original cost (DR disposal a/c CR fixed asset a/c).
   (c)   Transfer the *total* depreciation over the asset's life (DR provision for depreciation a/c CR disposal a/c).
   (d)   Transfer the balance on the disposal account as follows:
      (i)   A credit balance is transferred to the credit of profit and loss account, and represents an *overprovision* for depreciation in previous years (often erroneously referred to as a 'profit on sale').
      (ii)   A debit balance is posted to the debit side of profit and loss account and represents an *underprovision* for depreciation in previous years (often erroneously referred to as a 'loss on sale').

The result of the above entries is to acknowledge that the asset no longer belongs to the business, and that both the fixed assets total and the provision for depreciation must be reduced accordingly. The amount of net profit is either increased or decreased dependent upon whether too much depreciation had been written off the asset (i.e. the 'book value' at the date of sale was lower than the 'real value') or too little depreciation had been written off (i.e. the 'book value' was greater than the 'real value').

Example 4

The balance sheet of a trader as at 31 January 1982 showed the following information concerning plant and machinery.

	£	£
Cost	39,000	
Less provision for depreciation	16,000	23,000

Plant and machinery is depreciated at the rate of 20% per annum on the cost of assets owned at the year-end. On 1 February 1982 a machine costing £7,000 was purchased. A machine bought on 1 February 1980 for £4,000 was sold on the same day, the proceeds being £1,900.

Required:

(a) The plant and machinery account, the provision for depreciation on plant and machinery account, and the disposal of plant and machinery account for the year ended 31 January 1983.

(b) Balance sheet extracts relating to plant and machinery as at 31 January 1983.

Solution:

(a)

Plant and machinery account

1 Feb 1982	Balance b/f	39,000	31 Jan 1983	Transfer disposal	4,000
	Addition	7,000		Balance c/d	42,000
		46,000			46,000
1 Feb 1983	Balance b/d	42,000			

Provision for depreciation on plant and machinery account

31 Jan 1983	Transfer Disposal*	1,600	1 Feb 1982	Balance b/f	16,000
	Balance c/d	22,800	31 Jan 1983	Profit and loss a/c† (provision for year)	8,400
		24,400			24,400
			1 Feb 1983	Balance b/d	22,800

Disposal of plant and machinery account

31 Jan 1983	Transfer cost from plant & machinery a/c	4,000	1 Feb 1982	Proceeds of sale	1,900
			31 Jan 1983	Transfer depreciation	1,600
				profit and loss a/c (= under-provision in previous years)	500
		4,000			4,000

(b) Extract from balance sheet as at 31 January 1983

Plant and machinery

	£	£
Cost	42,000	
Less provision for depreciation	22,800	19,200

COMMENTARY

The under-provision of £500 arose because the net book value at the date of sale was (£4,000 − £1,600), which was £500 greater than the *true* value of £1,900.

1.8 The journal

The day books referred to earlier in the chapter are also often referred to as 'journals', but there is a separate book of prime entry, specifically called 'the journal' which has a very specialised function within the double-entry system.

Whilst the vast majority of a business's transactions follow one of the 'conventional' routes into the ledger, via the cash book or a day book (see Figure

*Workings. Cost of machine sold £4,000: Owned for two full years ∴ Total depreciation = 2 × £800 = £1,600.
†Workings. Calculated at 20% × £42,000 (balance on plant and machinery account at year-end).

1.2), there is a small number of transactions which cannot follow these routes. These include the following:

   i   Transfers between accounts.
   ii Correction of errors.
  iii Creation of, and alterations to, reserves and provisions.
  iv Adjustments for accruals and prepayments.
   v Any other 'non-routine' transactions, e.g. the entries required on the disposal of fixed assets.

The journal simply provides a summary of the book-keeping entries required to record the transaction, together with a brief statement by way of explanation, known as a 'narration'.

Example 5

Show the journal entries required to record the following:
(a) £100 debited to stationery account instead of telephone account.
(b) A balance of £80 on J. Robinson's sales ledger account to be written off as bad, due to Robinson's bankruptcy.
(c) Wages accrued at the year-end, totalling £3,160.

Solution:

	Journal	Folio reference	DR £	CR £
(a)	DR telephone account	G.L. 84	100.00	
	CR stationery account	G.L. 73		100.00
	—Correction of misposting to the stationery account			
(b)	DR bad debts account	G.L. 12	80.00	
	CR J. Robinson's account	S.L. 351		80.00
	—Bad debt written off due to customer's bankruptcy			
(c)	DR wages account	G.L. 94	3,160.00	
	CR accruals account	G.L. 12*		3,160.00
	—Wages owing but unpaid at the year-end.			

COMMENTARY

The debit entries are always shown before the credit entries, and a short 'narration' is given to explain the reason for making the entries. Folio references are simply a cross-reference to aid location of the precise page in the ledger. For example, the bad debts account will be found on page 12 of the general ledger, whilst J. Robinson's account appears on page 351 of the sales ledger. In practice, folio references are shown against all entries within the cash book and the ledger, but students are not usually required to provide them. Consequently, they were omitted from the ledger entries shown in the solutions in Examples 1 and 4.

1.9 Vertical presentation of accounting statements

It is perhaps understandable that many accountancy students are so immersed in 'debits and credits' that they fail to grasp one of the most important features of the accountant's work; that the information which is produced from the book-keeping system should be capable of being understood by non-accountants.

    Nowhere is this better illustrated than in the presentation of 'final' accounts. As we have seen, these are the summaries of the business's 'revenue' and 'capital position. As such they should be presented in a manner which is logical and easy to read, because they are read not only by those well-versed in accounting procedures, but also by important people (notably the owners of the business!) who may not have the benefit of such knowledge.

*There are two ways of treating the 'double-entry' for accruals (and prepayments). If desired, separate accounts can be opened (as in the above journal entry) to record them within the financial year. The entries are then 'written back' to the individual expense accounts at the start of the next year. The alternative (and simpler) treatment is to carry down the balances within the various expense accounts to the start of the next year. This method was adopted in Example 1.

The method most widely used for the presentation of the 'final' accounts is known as the 'vertical' or 'columnar' style. Whilst obviously derived from the same information which appears in the traditional or 'horizontal' method, the statements are no longer split into two halves conforming to the conventional account lay-out, but are compiled with the emphasis on logical presentation, rather than strict adherence to double-entry principles. For instance, the final accounts of 'Jean's Jeans' (see Example 1) would be shown as in Example 6, if a 'vertical' presentation were to be used.

Example 7

Jean Knight
Trading as 'Jean's Jeans'
Trading and Profit and Loss Accounts for the year ended
30 November 1984

		£	£
Sales			75,972
Less:	Cost of goods sold:		
	Opening stock	7,224	
	Purchases	49,600	
		56,824	
Less:	Closing stock	12,400	
			44,424
Gross profit			31,548
Add:	Discount received		230
			31,778
Less:	Expenses:		
	Wages	11,590	
	Light and heat	1,030	
	Postage, printing, etc.	390	
	Advertising	285	
	Telephone and insurance	619	
	Rent and rates	2,900	
	Repairs	810	
	Motor expenses	518	
	Bank charges	74	
	Accountancy	350	
	Discount allowed	129	
	Bad debts written off	60	
	Provision for doubtful debts	100	
	Depreciation on fixtures and fittings	800	
	Depreciation on motor van	1,600	
			21,255
Net profit			£ 10,523

Balance Sheet as at 30 November 1984

	£	£	£
Fixed assets			
Fixtures and fittings, at cost		11,400	
Less: Provision for depreciation		4,200	7,200
Motor van, at cost		8,900	
Less: Provision for depreciation		4,800	4,100
			11,300
Current assets			
Stock		12,400	
Debtors	7,384		
Less: Provision for doubtful debts	450	6,934	

Prepayments		200
Bank		3,600
Cash		120
		23,254
Less: Current liabilities		
Creditors	8,140	
Accruals	130	
		8,270
Working capital (net current assets)		14,984
		£ 26,284
Financed by:		
Jean Knight's capital account		
Opening balance, 1 December 1983		23,261
Add: Net profit		10,523
		33,784
Less: Drawings		7,500
		£ 26,284

Examination questions often specifically ask for final accounts to be drawn up in a *vertical* style, and students must ensure that they are fully conversant with this style of presentation.

Exercises

1.1. Mark Drayton is in business as a retail tailor. His financial year ends on 31 December, and the trial balance of his business as at 31 December 1985 is shown below:

	Debit £	Credit £
General ledger		
Accountancy	390	
Advertising	3,860	
Bad debts	1,120	
Bank charges	310	
Capital		35,700
Carriage out	510	
Discount received		680
Drawings	8,700	
Light and heat	1,570	
Motor expenses	2,120	
Motor vans (at cost)	31,500	
Postage, telephone and insurance, etc.	4,860	
Provision for depreciation of motor vans, 1 Jan 1985		14,400
Provision for depreciation of shop fittings 1 Jan 1985		11,700
Provision for doubtful debts, 1 Jan 1985		4,350
Purchases	139,700	
Rent and rates	14,470	
Sales		205,860
Shop fittings (at cost)	20,500	
Stock 1 Jan 1985	24,560	
Sundry expenses	7,380	
Wages of assistants	9,670	
Sales ledger balances	37,560	
Purchases ledger balances		31,370
Cash book: Cash in hand/bank overdraft	1,080	5,800
	£309,860	£309,860

Notes:
1. Stock at 31 December 1985 is valued at £22,500.
2. Light and heat owing at the year end amounts to £360, and a telephone accrual of £230 is to be provided for.
3. Rent totalling £1,200 is prepaid at the year-end.
4. Depreciation is charged on motor vans at 40% on the diminishing balance basis. Shop fittings are depreciated on the straight line basis over five years, assuming a total residual value of £1,000.
5. The provision for doubtful debts is to be adjusted to equal 5% of the total debtors.

Required:
(a) Trading and profit and loss accounts for the year ended 31 December 1985 and the balance sheet as at that date.
(b) If your answer to (a) has been presented in a 'horizontal' format, re-draft the final accounts into a 'vertical' (columnar) style.

1.2. From the information given below, show:
(a) The provision for doubtful debts account for each of the three years ended 31 December 1981, 1982 and 1983.
(b) Extracts from the final accounts for each year, relating to debtors, bad debts and the provision for doubtful debts.

	Year to:		
	31 Dec 1981	31 Dec 1982	31 Dec 1983
	£	£	£
Debtors (before adjustments)	26,180	33,100	28,200
Bad debts to be written off	807	400	433
Doubtful debts at the year-end	670	2%*	500

Note: The balance on the provision for doubtful debts account at 1 Jan 1981 was £475.

1.3. On 31 December 1983 the balance sheet of R. Thomas, a retail trader, was as follows:

	£		£	£
Capital	15,679	Fixtures & fittings		4,950
		Motor vehicle		2,920
				7,870
Creditors	2,825	Stock in trade	8,930	
Accrued rent	420	Debtors	280	
		Prepaid rates	390	
		Prepaid insurance	194	
		Bank	1,260	11,054
	18,924			18,924

During the year ended 31 December 1984, the following cash payments were made:

	£
Rent	1,380
Rates	1,796
Insurance	228

In addition, during the year, Thomas had supplied goods with a sales value of £310 to his landlord. No invoice was raised for this transaction, the amount being set against Thomas's rent liability. The insurance amount was paid on 31 October 1984, and was the premium for one year from 1 November 1984. The rates payment was made in two equal instalments of £898 on 1 April 1984 and 1 October 1984,

*A general provision on debtors, less bad debts.

these being the due dates. At 31 December 1984, rent due but unpaid amounted to £540.

Required:
(a) Prepare Journal entries (without narrations) to deal with the 31 December 1984 adjustments for rent, rates and insurance.
(b) Prepare a Ledger Account for *each* expense showing the transfer to the Profit and Loss Account for 1984.

(LCCI – Intermediate)

1.4. A property of a business was rented at £250 per month payable monthly. The rent was three months in arrears on 31 December 1988 and five months in arrears on 31 December 1989. The rates were £1,200 per annum payable half yearly in advance on 1 April and 1 October in each year. At 31 December 1988 the rates for the half year to 31 March 1989 had not been paid, but these arrears were cleared and rates for 1989 were paid when due.

Required:
From the information above prepare the combined rent and rates account for the year ended 31 December 1989 showing the figures that would appear for rent and rates in the profit and loss account and the figures in the balance sheet at 31 December 1989.

1.5. Shortly after the end of May 1981 James Brothers received a statement of account from their suppliers, Hardware Manufacturing Co. The statement was as follows:

May		£	£
1	Balance brought forward		1,916
7	Goods	268	
10	Goods	172	
15	Goods	356	
17	Correction	20	
20	Goods	87	
25	Goods	214	
30	Goods	386	1,503
May			3,419
11	Credit note	28	
18	Credit note	47	75
May			3,344
12	Cash	887	
12	Discount	23	
14	Contra account	52	962
			2,382

Notes:
i Two invoices dated 17 April and 23 April for £114 and £97 respectively, which were included in the balance brought forward on the statement, had not been passed and entered in James Brothers' books until May.
ii A debit note for £28 had been passed through James Brothers' books during April, in respect of the same item shown on the statement as May 11.
iii An invoice dated 16 May for £213 had been correctly passed through James Brothers' books, but wrongly posted in Hardware Manufacturing Co's books to Jones Brothers' account.
iv The item Correction refers to an invoice in April for £123, which had been correctly entered in James Brothers' books, but wrongly posted in Hardware Manufacturing Co's books as £103.
v The Contra item on 14 May of £52 refers to goods purchased by Hardware

Manufacturing Co from James Brothers, but not transferred in their books to Hardware Manufacturing Co's account in the purchase ledger.
vi The invoice of 30 May for £386 had not been passed through James Brothers' books.

Required:
(a) Show the entries in Hardware Manufacturing Co's account in James Brothers' ledger for the month of May, assuming that all entries had been properly made apart from those referred to in the above notes.
(b) Prepare a statement reconciling the balance of £2,382 shown on Hardware Manufacturing Co's statement with the balance of the account prepared in answer to part (a) above.
Show your calculations adjacent to your answer.

(WJEC)

1.6. Bridge Manufacturing Company commenced business on 1 January 1979 and purchased machinery costing £100,000 and fittings and equipment costing £50,000.
It was decided to depreciate machinery at the rate of 15% per annum on cost, and fittings and equipment at 10% per annum on cost. Profits were as follows:

	£
Year ended 31 December 1979	79,120
Year ended 31 December 1980	88,262
Year ended 31 December 1981	105,533

Early in 1982 depreciation policy was reconsidered. There had been no further purchases of machinery or fittings and equipment, but further purchases were under consideration and it was decided to change to the diminishing balance method of calculating depreciation, using a rate of 25% per annum for machinery and 20% per annum for fittings and equipment.

Required:
(a) Prepare a schedule showing the depreciation, under the original method, for machinery and fittings and equipment and the written down values, for each of the years 1979, 1980 and 1981.
(b) Prepare a statement showing what the amount of profit would have been in each of the years 1979, 1980 and 1981 if the diminishing balance method of depreciation had been in use.

(WJEC)

1.7. The balance sheet of Needle Ltd as at 30 April 1980 showed the following information concerning motor vehicles.

	£	£
Fixed assets		
Motor vehicles at cost	23,000	
Less: Provision for depreciation	14,000	9,000

It is company policy to depreciate motor vehicles at the rate of 15% on the cost of assets held at the end of each year.
The company purchased on 1 January 1981 a motor van for £4,000. A motor van purchased on 1 January 1979 for £3,000 was traded in for the new vehicle, and £1,800 cash was paid in full settlement.
In addition a motor car purchased on 1 January 1978 for £3,500 was involved in an accident during March 1981 and has been declared a write-off. The company's insurers have agreed to pay £1,800 as compensation for the loss.

Required:
(a) (i) The motor vehicles disposals account for the year ended 30 April 1981.
    (ii) The provision for depreciation of motor vehicles account for the year ended 30 April 1981.
    (iii) The appropriate figures relating to motor vehicles in the balance sheet at 30 April 1981.

(b)   A discussion of the relationship between depreciation and the replacement of fixed assets.

(AEB)

1.8   The managing director of a medium-sized limited company has written to you as follows:

'In order to keep full financial control over the day-to-day operations of my company, I need up-to-date knowledge of the cash position, the debtors and the creditors. I can obtain this from the bank statements, my sales invoices and statements, and my suppliers' invoices and statements. Why then does my company need to incur the large expense of employing accountants to maintain a full double-entry book-keeping system?'

Prepare a reasoned answer to the managing director's question.

(ULSEB)

CHAPTER 2

Further Accounting Procedures (1)

2.1 Additional methods of depreciation

Most businesses* use either the straight line or reducing balance methods of providing for depreciation on their fixed assets (see section 1.6). However, there are occasions when neither of these is appropriate, owing perhaps to the specialised nature of the asset, or the desire of the business to link the depreciation to the actual usage of the asset.

THE REVALUATION METHOD

This is a very straightforward method to use, as the depreciation charge for the year is simply the difference between the estimated values of the asset at the start and end of the year, as adjusted for purchases or sales of assets during the year. The method is most often used for loose tools, i.e. where there are large numbers of relatively small items (hammers, drills, grinders, etc.) which would be difficult to record and depreciate individually. The estimate of value is usually made by a responsible official of the business, e.g. a foreman, and is subject to an independent check by an auditor in the case of a limited company.

Example 1

During the year to 31 August 1985, U-Bend Plumbers bought hand tools at a cost of £780. The stock of loose tools on 1 September 1984 was estimated at £4,300, whilst the foreman estimated the year-end stock at £4,600. No loose tools had been sold during the year. Calculate the depreciation on loose tools for the year to 31 August 1985.

Solution:
The depreciation on loose tools was £480, calculated as follows:
   (Opening value + Additions) − Closing value
   (£4,300 + £780) − £4,600 = £5,080 − £4,600 = £480

COMMENTARY

The £480 does not just represent 'wear and tear' on the tools; it also reflects the sad fact that tools will inevitably get lost, stolen or simply 'disappear' during the course of a year!

THE MACHINE-HOUR METHOD

This is a 'usage-linked' calculation which depends upon a reasonably accurate record being kept of the hours worked by each machine which is being depreciated, together with an estimate of its total working life in hours.

The formula to calculate the annual depreciation is as follows:

$$\frac{\text{'Machine-hours' worked in year}}{\text{Total estimated life in 'machine-hours'}} \times (\text{Cost} - \text{residual value})$$

* A recent survey of 300 industrial and commercial companies showed that 259 used the straight line method exclusively, whilst most of those remaining used a combination of the straight line and other methods.

The advantage claimed for this method is that the expense disclosed in the profit and loss account will reflect more accurately the *actual* depreciation of the asset compared with the 'main two' methods. Critics would argue that as the method relies upon estimates (as do all methods!) it is just as prone to error. In addition, the costs of maintaining detailed hourly records may be deemed prohibitive.

Example 2

A printing company keeps a record of the hours worked by its four offset-litho machines. During the year to 31 December 1979, they were used as follows:

Machine	Hours
1	2,120
2	1,860
3	2,175
4	1,342

Other relevant details relating to the machines are:

Machine	Cost (£)	Estimated scrap values (£)	Estimated lives (machine-hours)
1	3,900	400	12,500
2	4,400	300	10,000
3	2,600	300	10,000
4	1,700	150	8,000

Required:
A calculation of the depreciation of each machine for the year to 31 December 1979, using the machine-hour method of calculation.

Solution:

Machine	Depreciation £
1	594
2	763
3	500
4	260

Workings:

Machine

1 $\quad \dfrac{2,120}{12,500} \times (3,900-400) = £594$

2 $\quad \dfrac{1,860}{10,000} \times (4,400-300) = £763$

3 $\quad \dfrac{2,175}{10,000} \times (2,600-300) = £500$

4 $\quad \dfrac{1,342}{8,000} \times (1,700-150) = £260$

COMMENTARY

The depreciation for each machine is the proportion which the actual usage for the period bears to the total estimated usage. The machine is therefore fully depreciated when the hours of actual usage are equal to the total estimated hours of usage. If the machine continues in use beyond that total, no further depreciation will be charged, unless the company decides to reassess the estimated residual value to a lower figure than that originally set.

THE SUM OF THE DIGITS METHOD

This is a variation on the 'reducing balance' method, and writes off more depreciation in the earlier years of the asset's life than in the later years. The procedure is very simple.

1. Decide upon the estimated life in years.
2. Starting with the number as in (1) above, list each year separately in a column, and total the column.
3. Depreciation is calculated in each year by the following formula:-

$$\frac{\text{Number for the year}}{\text{Column total}} \times (\text{Cost} - \text{Estimated scrap value})$$

Example 3

As asset costs £12,500 and at the end of its anticipated life of five years is expected to have a scrap value of £500. Calculate the annual depreciation, using the 'sum of the digits' method.

Solution:

Year	Depreciation calculation	Annual depreciation
1	$5/15 \times (12,500 - 500)$	£4,000
2	$4/15 \times (12,500 - 500)$	£3,200
3	$3/15 \times (12,500 - 500)$	£2,400
4	$2/15 \times (12,500 - 500)$	£1,600
5	$1/15 \times (12,500 - 500)$	£ 800

Workings:

List of 'digits'	Fraction to be applied
5	$5/15$
4	$4/15$
3	$3/15$
2	$2/15$
1	$1/15$
15 = sum of the digits	

COMMENTARY

It is interesting to compare the above figures with a 'reducing balance' calculation. A rate of 47% must be used for the latter method in order to write off the asset to approximately £500 in five years. The year by year comparison is shown in Table 2.1.

Table 2.1

Year	Depreciation per reducing balance method £	Depreciation per 'sum of the digits' method £
1	5,875	4,000
2	3,114	3,200
3	1,650	2,400
4	875	1,600
5	463	800

The 'sum of the digits' method gives a more even spread of depreciation as compared with the 'reducing balance' method.

SINKING FUNDS

If depreciation were not provided on fixed assets, then the result would be an overstatement of profits and a concurrent overvaluation of fixed assets. When depreciation is provided, profits are lowered, and the fixed assets are given a more realistic value, recognising the effect of 'wear and tear' and other similar factors.

However, profits which have been 'set aside' in the provision account have not left the business and are therefore still available for use within the business in the normal way. Eventually, the problem of asset replacement arises, and also that cash must be paid in order to buy new assets in substitution for the old, worn-out ones. The problem is made worse when one realises that, due to inflation, the new assets are likely to cost far more than the price paid originally for the old assets.

One way around this problem is the setting up of a 'sinking fund', whereby cash equal to the depreciation provision is invested *outside* the business in 'safe' forms of interest-bearing deposits or securities. The intention is, therefore, that the sums set aside, plus the interest thereon, will be readily available to be drawn upon in the future when the new assets need to be purchased. In practice, however, few firms use this method other than for leasehold property (see below), as they can usually gain a higher return by using funds *within* the business and so generate greater profits.

AMORTISATION

This term is synonymous with depreciation, but is particularly used to describe the gradual loss in value of *leasehold* property. It is usually calculated in the same way as for the 'straight-line' method of depreciation seen in Chapter 1, with the period of the lease being used as the 'estimated life of the asset'.

Amortisation is frequently linked to a sinking fund, as the lease, being a 'wasting' asset with a fixed time limit, may be re-negotiated at a higher cost (or 'premium') at its expiration. The sinking fund would consequently ensure the availability of the necessary funds at the appropriate time.

Example 4

On 1 January 1978 Discount Traders Ltd took out a five-year lease on some premises at a cost of £90,000. The directors decided to set up a sinking fund to help provide for the renewal of the lease when it expired and £15,000 was invested each year, commencing on 31 December 1978, for this purpose. The investment earned interest at the rate of 10% per annum. A new lease was purchased for £100,000 immediately upon expiry of the old lease.

Required:
Show the entries in the Lease Account, Sinking Fund Account and the Sinking Fund Investment Account, for the five-year life of the lease, necessary to record the above transactions, and for the purchase of the new lease. (WJEC)

Solution:

Lease Account

1 Jan 1978 Cash	90,000	31 Dec 1978 c/d	90,000
1 Jan 1979 b/d	90,000	31 Dec 1979 c/d	90,000
1 Jan 1980 b/d	90,000	31 Dec 1980 c/d	90,000
1 Jan 1981 b/d	90,000	31 Dec 1981 c/d	90,000
1 Jan 1982 b/d	90,000	31 Dec 1982 Sinking fund a/c	90,000
31 Dec 1982 Cash	100,000	c/d	100,000
	190,000		190,000
1 Jan 1983 b/d	100,000		

Sinking Fund Account

31 Dec 1978 c/d	15,000	31 Dec 1978 P&L a/c	15,000
		1 Jan 1979 b/d	15,000
		31 Dec 1979 Bank: Interest	1,500
31 Dec 1979 c/d	31,500	P&L a/c	15,000
	31,500		31,500
		1 Jan 1980 b/d	31,500
		31 Dec 1980 Bank: Interest	3,150
31 Dec 1980 c/d	49,650	P&L a/c	15,000
	49,650		49,650
		1 Jan 1981 b/d	49,650
		31 Dec 1981 Bank: Interest	4,965

31 Dec 1981 c/d	69,615	P&L a/c	15,000
	69,615		69,615
		1 Jan 1981 b/d	69,615
		31 Dec 1982 Bank: Interest	6,961
31 Dec 1982 Lease			
a/c	90,000	P&L a/c*	13,424
	90,000		90,000

Sinking Fund Investment Account

31 Dec 1978 Cash	15,000	31 Dec 1978 c/d	15,000
1 Jan 1979 b/d	15,000		
31 Dec 1979 Cash†	16,500	31 Dec 1979 c/d	31,500
	31,500		31,500
1 Jan 1980 b/d	31,500		
31 Dec 1980 Cash	18,150	31 Dec 1980 c/d	49,650
	49,650		49,650
1 Jan 1981 b/d	49,650		
31 Dec 1981 Cash	19,965	31 Dec 1981 c/d	69,615
	69,615		69,615
1 Jan 1982 b/d	69,615		
31 Dec 1982 Cash	20,385	31 Dec 1982 Cash from sale of investments	90,000
	90,000		90,000

OTHER METHODS

Whilst the depreciation methods used by the vast majority of businesses have now been dealt with, there is a small number of other methods available, which are considered to be outside the scope of this textbook. They include:

(a) The annuity method, and
(b) The depletion unit method.

2.2 Final accounts: variations on the basic model

As outlined in Chapter 1, the final accounts of a sole trader will normally consist of the statements shown in Figure 2.1.

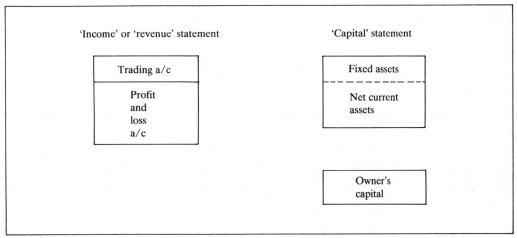

Fig. 2.1 The final accounts of a sole trader.

*The transfer from profit and loss account in the year to 31 December 1982 has been adjusted so that the total in the fund is exactly £90,000.
†The 'cash' debits in the sinking fund investment account are the annual sums of £15,000, plus the amount of interest earned on the investments in the preceding year.

THE APPROPRIATION ACCOUNT

If the business organisation is either a partnership or a limited company, the ownership is, by definition, in the hands of more than one person. Consequently, the revenue statement must be extended to include an 'appropriation account' which shows the ways in which the profits of the business are divided between the partners or, in the case of a limited company, divided between the company and shareholders. In later chapters both partnerships and limited companies will be described in detail, but it is necessary to know at this stage the basic form which the appropriation account takes (see Figure 2.2).

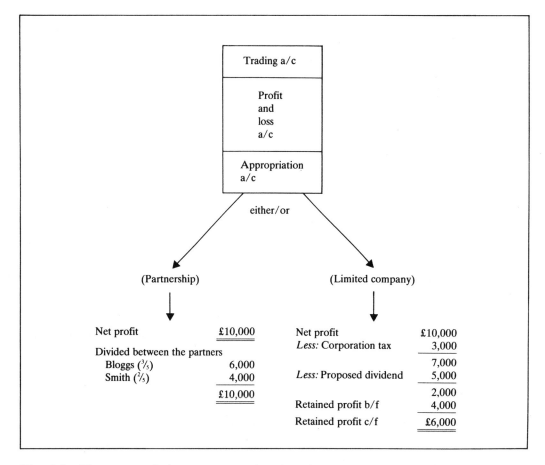

Fig. 2.2 The appropriation account – its place in the revenue statement and simple examples of a partnership and limited company's appropriation account.

CAPITAL STATEMENTS OF PARTNERSHIPS AND LIMITED COMPANIES CONTRASTED WITH THOSE OF A SOLE TRADER

The appropriation account is the main difference to be observed when contrasting the revenue statement of a sole trader with that of a partnership or a limited company. The capital statement will also contain certain different items dependent on the type of business organisation, and these are summarised in Figure 2.3. As with appropriation accounts, it is important to grasp the basic differences at this stage, although a more detailed study of these topics is made in Chapters 4 and 6.

2.3 'Service only' businesses

A sole proprietor who provides a service as opposed to trading (i.e. 'buying and selling') goods does not need a 'trading' account, and consequently the revenue statement will only contain a profit and loss account. The balance sheet will be virtually identical with that of a trading business, although there will be no 'stock of goods on hand' at the year-end (see Figure 2.4).

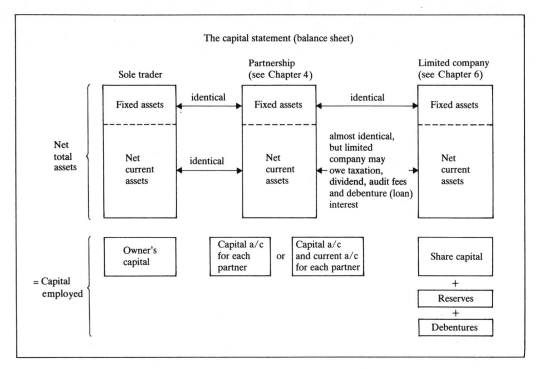

Fig. 2.3   Comparison of the contents of the capital statements of sole traders, partnerships and limited companies (simplified).

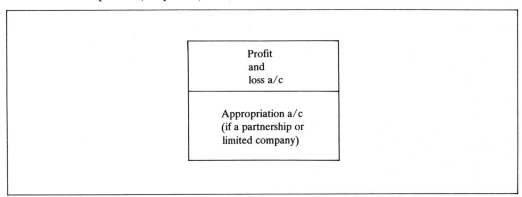

Fig. 2.4   The revenue statement of a 'service only' business.

2.4   'Manufacturing' businesses

Any business which makes the products which it sells will need to show more information in its final accounts than one which merely buys in products from other manufacturers. Consequently, a 'manufacturing account' is provided at the start of the revenue statement, which itemises all the factory costs associated with the production process. This 'factory production cost' is divided into 'direct' and 'indirect' expenses, the former (also known as 'variable' expenses) being those which can be specifically related to the product being made, e.g. raw materials, wages of 'production' workers, the latter (indirect) being other costs incurred within the factory, but of a more general nature, e.g. a supervisor's wages, factory insurance.

The collective term for all direct expenditure is the 'prime cost' of production, and this is clearly shown in the manufacturing account. Marginal costing is dealt with in *Cost and Management Accounting* by Trevor Daff.* It explains in detail the importance of identifying direct (variable) expenses. Here, it is sufficient to recognise that as production increases, so do the direct expenses. For example, if a bakery producing wrapped loaves bakes 1,000 loaves in a week, then it is reasonable to assume that 1,000 plastic bags will be needed to put them in. If

*Published by Woodhead-Faulkner Ltd.

production increases to 10,000, then 10,000 plastic bags will be needed. However, the rent of the bakery will remain the same, regardless of whether the production level is 1,000 or 10,000. The plastic bags therefore represent a direct cost, and are part of the prime cost of production, whilst the rent is an indirect expense.

STOCKS IN A MANUFACTURING BUSINESS

There are usually three separate types of stock:

1. Stocks of raw materials, i.e. quantities of 'ingredients' as yet unused in the production process. The opening and closing stocks of raw materials are incorporated within the 'prime cost' section of the manufacturing account.
2. Stocks of work-in-progress, i.e. quantities of products which have not completed all stages of the production process. The opening and closing stocks of work-in-progress are usually shown after all the factory costs have been listed. The only (rare) exception is when the information is given that the work-in-progress has been valued at *prime cost*, in which case the adjustment is made within the prime cost section of the manufacturing account.
3. Stocks of finished goods, i.e. goods which have completed the production process but have not yet been sold. These are adjusted in exactly the same way as the stocks of a non-manufacturing business, being incorporated within the 'cost of goods sold' section of the trading account.

Note that all three closing stock figures must be shown on the balance sheet.

Example 5

William Boot owns a factory which manufactures waterproof footwear. The following is a summary of the transactions of the company during the financial year ended 31 May 1984.

Value of opening stocks or raw materials:
Rubber   £16,225
Linings   £2,950
Glue   £325

Purchases of raw materials:
Rubber   £162,120
Linings   £14,025
Glue   £800

Factory expenses:
Wages of production workers, 6,300 man-hours at £3 per man-hour.
Hire of special moulds (a direct expense), £1,500.
Rent and rates, £14,501 (three-seventeenths of this total is for an office building).
Non-productive labour, £16,480.
Light, heat and power, £18,500 (this includes a payment of £700 which relates to the following year).
Depreciation is calculated at £2.50 per machine-hour. (Records show that six machines have been used for six hours per day for 250 days during the year.)
Sundry factory expenses, £9,400.

At 31 May 1984 raw materials stocks were:
Rubber   £30,880
Linings   £3,135
Glue   £150

Work in progress was valued at £24,500 at the start of the year and £35,302 at the end of the year.

47,500 pairs of boots were sold in the year for a total of £750,000. The opening stock of finished boots was valued at £40,000 (12,000 pairs) and the closing stock at £90,000 (27,000 pairs).

(a) You are required to prepare:
    i   A manufacturing account and trading account for the year to 31 May 1984.
    ii A calculation of the production cost of one pair of boots.
(b) A footwear retailer has offered Mr Boot a special order for 20,000 pairs. Mention two matters that should be considered before deciding whether to accept the order.

(ULSEB)

Solution:
(a) i

William Boot

Manufacturing and Trading Account for the year ended 31 May 1984

Raw materials:					Factory production cost c/d 250,000

	Rubber	Linings	Glue		
Op. Stock	16,225	2,950	325	19,500	
Purchases	162,120	14,025	800	176,945	
	178,345	16,975	1,125	196,445	
Less Cl. Stock	30,880	3,135	150	34,165	
	147,465	13,840	975	162,280	

Direct expenses:

Productive labour	18,900	
Hire of moulds	1,500	20,400
PRIME COST		182,680

Indirect expenses:

Wages	16,480	
Rent and rates	11,942	
Light, heat and power	17,800	
Depreciation	22,500	
Sundries	9,400	78,122
		260,802

Work-in-progress

Add Opening	24,500	
Less Closing	35,302	10,802
		250,000

		250,000	250,000
Opening stock of finished goods		40,000	Sales 750,000
Factory cost of production b/d		250,000	
		290,000	
Less closing stock of finished goods		90,000	
Cost of goods sold		200,000	
Gross profit		550,000	
		750,000	750,000

ii Number of pairs of boots produced (47,500 − 12,000 + 27,000) = 62,500
£250,000 ÷ 62,500 = £4 per pair.

(b) Answer should include:

i Will the acceptance of the order disrupt existing production schedules?
ii Any extra capital equipment required?
iii How does the selling price for the special order compare with the existing average selling price of £15.79 per pair?

COMMENTARY

If a question is 'silent' as to whether the work-in-progress has been valued at prime cost, then you must assume that it is valued on a 'total cost' basis. If the question had asked for an extract from the balance sheet as at 31 May 1984, showing how stocks are shown, this would have appeared as follows:

Current assets	£
Stock of raw materials	34,165
Stock of work-in-progress	35,302
Stock of finished goods	90,000
	159,467

'SPLITTING THE PROFIT'

The gross profit disclosed in William Boot's trading account in Example 5 was £550,000. What is not disclosed, however, is the relative profitability of the factory, compared with the 'retailing' side of the business. If such information were available to management, they may find that their factory is relatively inefficient, whilst the success of their sales personnel is being understated. In extreme cases, they may decide to buy in from an outside manufacturer rather than make their own products. To establish the gross profit derived from manufacturing, the 'market value' of the goods produced needs to be calculated, either by reference to the prices quoted by competitors for similar goods, or by making a reasoned estimate based on market conditions. For example, if the 62,500 pairs of boots manufactured by William Boot in Example 5 could have been bought by the company from a rival manufacturer for £420,000, then the manufacturing, trading and profit and loss accounts could be re-drafted to show a breakdown of the gross profit earned:

Example 6

(Summarised) Manufacturing Account

	£		£
Factory production cost	250,000	Market value of finished goods c/d	420,000
Gross profit from manufacturing c/d	170,000		
	420,000		420,000

Trading Account

	£		£
Opening stock of finished goods	40,000	Sales	750,000
Market value of finished goods b/d	420,000		
	460,000		
Less closing stock of finished goods	90,000		
Cost of goods sold	370,000		
Gross profit on trading c/d	380,000		
	750,000		750,000

(Extract from:) *Profit and Loss Account*

Gross profit on manufacturing b/d	170,000
Gross profit on trading b/d	380,000
	550,000

COMMENTARY

The management can, prima facie, be reasonably content with both sections of the business. As with all accounting analysis, however, a comparison must be made with the figures of previous years or anticipated results before we can decree that a healthy position is shown.

Note: 'provision for profit on stock'

Where a company has computed a separate 'gross profit on manufacturing', it is usual to find that the stocks of finished goods are valued on a 'cost plus notional profit' basis, so that the amount shown for 'gross profit from trading' is as realistic as possible. The proportion of notional profit included in the stock valuation must be deducted in the balance sheet, otherwise unearned profit would be included. This is achieved by creating a 'provision for profit on stock' which is adjusted annually by reference to the total of such unrealised profit included in the stock valuation.

2.5 Departmentalised businesses

If a business has several distinct departments, then it is vital for management purposes to establish the results of each one. This can be achieved in the final accounts by giving the revenue statement as many 'columns' as there are departments, and splitting income and expenditure accordingly. The way in which expenses can be apportioned between departments is fully dealt with in *Cost and Management Accounting** by Trevor Daff, but, for example, the total rent paid might be split on the basis of cubic area; the wage bill, by the personnel employed within the respective departments; and depreciation on fixtures, by the value of the assets contained within each department, etc.

The balance sheet of a departmentalised business will be virtually identical to that of a non-departmentalised one, although a breakdown of the assets and liabilities of each department could be provided if adequate records exist.

Example 7

Andrew and Susannah are the joint owners of a store which is divided into three departments: Clothing (C), Electrical goods (E) and Furniture (F).

The following balances have been extracted from the partnership books as at 30 November 1983.

	DR £	CR £
Purchases (C)	49,580	
(E)	44,630	
(F)	42,500	
Wages (C)	16,200	
(E)	12,050	
(F)	10,000	
General office salaries	12,000	
Rent and rates	3,800	
Buildings insurance	700	
Repairs to premises	170	
Lighting and heating	1,070	
Sales (C)		81,750
(E)		79,300
(F)		62,100
Telephone	740	
Sundry expenses	4,500	
Opening stocks (C)	7,500	
(E)	6,250	
(F)	4,800	

Notes:
1. Closing stocks are: (C) 19,700, (E) 10,800, (F) 12,400.
2. There is an accrued expense of £200 in respect of light and heat at 30 November 1983.
3. General office salaries and sundry expenses are to be divided equally between the departments. Other expenses are to be divided according to floor area, as follows:
    (C) six-tenths
    (E) three-tenths
    (F) one-tenth
4. Andrew and Susannah share profits in the proportion 3:2 respectively. The partnership agreement provides for interest on their capitals at 5% per annum. The capital accounts are as follows:

*Published by Woodhead-Faulkner Ltd.

	Andrew £	Susannah £
Opening balances 1 December 1982	12,000	10,000
Capital introduced 1 June 1983	4,000	—
	16,000	10,000

(a) Prepare the departmental trading and profit and loss accounts (in columnar form) for the year to 30 November 1983.

(b) Prepare the partnership appropriation account for the year to 30 November 1983.

(c) The owners of the store are considering whether or not to open a cafe in the store. Preliminary budgets indicate that a loss of £10,000 may occur in the first year of operation.

What other factors may influence the owners when deciding whether or not to open the cafe?

(ULSEB)

Solution:

(a)
Andrew and Susannah
Trading and Profit and Loss Accounts
for the year to 30 November 1983

		Clothing Dept £	Electrical Dept £	Furniture Dept £	Total £
Sales	(A)	81,750	79,300	62,100	223,150
Opening stock		7,500	6,250	4,800	
Purchases		49,580	44,630	42,500	
		57,080	50,880	47,300	
Less: Closing stock		19,700	10,800	12,400	
Cost of goods sold	(B)	37,380	40,080	34,900	112,360
Gross profit (A–B)		44,370	39,220	27,200	110,790
Wages		16,200	12,050	10,000	38,250
General office salaries		4,000	4,000	4,000	12,000
Rent and rates		2,280	1,140	380	3,800
Buildings insurance		420	210	70	700
Repairs to premises		102	51	17	170
Lighting and heating		762	381	127	1,270
Telephone		444	222	74	740
Sundry expenses		1,500	1,500	1,500	4,500
		25,708	19,554	16,168	61,430
Net profit		18,662	19,666	11,032	49,360

(b)
Appropriation Account for the year to 30 November 1983

		£	£
Net profit			49,360
Deduct: Interest on capital (see workings)			
	Andrew	700	
	Susannah	500	1,200
			48,160
Divided as follows:			
	Andrew (three-fifths)	28,896	
	Susannah (two-fifths)	19,264	
			48,160

(c) Factors which may influence the owners when deciding whether or not to open the cafe include:

i   Whether an overall increase in turnover may result, due to more customers being attracted to the store.

ii Whether the preliminary budgets have written off 'setting-up' costs entirely in the first year, and if so, whether they should be spread over several years.

iii Has adequate market research been undertaken to establish the need for a cafe?

iv If marginal costing techniques are applied, is the *contribution* positive or negative? If the former, then it may prove financially acceptable to open the cafe.

Workings:

Interest on capitals:

Andrew:	5% × £12,000 for six months	= £300
	5% × £16,000 for six months	= £400
		£700
Susannah:	5% × £10,000 for twelve months	= £500

COMMENTARY

The lay-out of part (a) is of prime importance, and students should note the use of 'boxes' around the lists of expenses. These are often used when setting out accounts in a columnar form, in order to improve the general readability of the information.

2.6   'Non-trading' organisations

Clubs, societies and associations require a different form of 'final accounts' compared with a trading concern, as their main function is neither trading nor profitmaking, but the provision of, for example, social, sporting or cultural activities for their members. One of the main handicaps from which such organisations suffer is the lack of accounting expertise amongst its members. Because of this, the financial statements are often very rudimentary, perhaps consisting of a 'receipts and payments account' which is merely a summary of the cash and bank transactions of the period. Whilst this is better than nothing, it has very limited value as it does not show the club's liabilities, and only shows assets bought during the period, without disclosing those assets bought in previous years. It fails to show whether the club had 'broken even' or whether expenditure was running at a higher level than income. The absence of a balance sheet could result in assets being sold without the club's knowledge, or liabilities being amassed without proper financial provision being made to meet them.

Whilst a 'receipts and payments account' might suffice where there are only a handful of members and very few financial complications, more sophisticated control must be exercised in other circumstances. This is achieved by producing an 'income and expenditure account' and a balance sheet, which conforms with all usual book-keeping principles in order to give a true picture of the affairs of the organisation.

Particular features relating to income and expenditure accounts are as follows.

1. If the club has a bar, it is usual to show its finances in a separate 'bar account' within the income and expenditure account. This enables the members to see what surplus the bar has contributed to the overall finances of the club.

2. Membership subscriptions are subject to adjustments for amounts in arrear or paid in advance at the start and end of the period. These calculations can be relatively complex (particularly in examination questions) and the use of an 'account' format is recommended for your workings (see Example 8 below).

3. An 'honorarium' (a 'gift' of cash) is often paid to the secretary or treasurer of the club in recognition of the time they spend engaged in club activities.

The balance sheet of the club follows the familiar pattern, with the only exception being that 'capital' is replaced by an 'accumulated fund', to which surpluses of income over expenditure are added (or excesses of expenditure over income deducted). The calculation of the opening balance on the fund is a simple matter of adding together all the opening assets of the club, and deducting the opening liabilities.

Example 8

The treasurer of the Trees Sports and Social Club has prepared the following receipts and payments account for the year ended 30 September 1981.

1980	£	1981	£
1 October		30 September	
Balance b/d	6,000	Bar purchases	2,960
Subscriptions	4,400	Dance expenses	2,000
Bar receipts	4,500	General expenses	4,750
Miscellaneous receipts	1,450	Groundsman's salary	5,700
Dance receipts	4,100	Resurfacing of snooker tables	1,800
		Repairs	370
		Balance c/d	2,870
	20,450		20,450

1981	
1 October	
Balance b/d	2,870

The following information is also available.

	30 Sept 1980 £	30 Sept 1981 £
Premises at cost	15,000	15,000
Bar stocks at cost	480	550
Bar purchases owing	310	420
Subscriptions owing	20	100
Subscriptions prepaid	60	80
General expenses owing	170	210
Equipment, cost £5,000, depreciated by 10% on cost per annum	2,000	?

The snooker tables are resurfaced regularly every five years and were resurfaced on 1 October 1980. The cost of resurfacing is treated as capital expenditure. The club has been in existence for some time and, although once flourishing, membership has declined in recent years. At present the membership is 221 and it has been agreed to renovate the premises at a cost of £5,000 in an attempt to attract new members. In addition members have agreed not to increase membership fees as a result of the proposal and two alternative sources of finance for the scheme are being considered.

Alternative A

To accept an offer of sponsorship from a local company who will donate £5,000 for the scheme in return for the free use of club facilities for its workers.

The treasurer estimates that the membership of the club will increase by fifty and that bar takings will increase by 20%. However, there will be a reduction of £700 in miscellaneous revenue as a result of the free use of facilities by company employees.

Alternative B

To accept an interest-free loan from a local brewery for £5,000, repayable in equal annual instalments over five years, in return for providing the club with its bar stock. As a consequence it is expected that gross profit as a percentage of bar sales will fall to 20%. However, the treasurer estimates that membership will increase by 100 and that bar takings will increase by 40%.

Required:
(a) The club's income and expenditure account for the year ended 30 September 1981 showing clearly the profit on bar sales.
(b) A balance sheet as at 30 September 1981.
(c) Advice to the treasurer, on financial grounds, as to which of the alternative methods of finance the club should accept.

(AEB)

Solution:

(a)

Trees Sports and Social Club
Income and Expenditure Account
for the year ended 30 September 1981

	£		£
Opening bar stocks	480	Bar receipts	4,500
Bar purchases (2,960 − 310 + 420)	3,070		
	3,550		
Less: Closing bar stocks	550		
	3,000		
Gross profit on bar sales c/d	1,500		
	4,500		4,500
Groundsman's salary	5,700	Gross profit on bar sales b/d	1,500
General expenses		Subscriptions (see working 1)	4,460
(4,750 − 170 + 210)	4,790	Miscellaneous receipts	1,450
Repairs	370	Profit on dance:	
Depreciation, equipment	500	Receipts 4,100	
Depreciation, snooker tables'		Expenditure (2,000)	2,100
surface	360	Excess of expenditure over income	2,210
	11,720		11,720

(b) *Balance Sheet as at 30 September 1981*

	£	£	£
Fixed assets			
Premises at cost			15,000
Equipment at cost		5,000	
Less: depreciation		3,500	1,500
Snooker tables (surface) at cost		1,800	
Less depreciation		360	1,440
			17,940
Current assets			
Bar stocks at cost		550	
Subscriptions owing		100	
Cash at bank		2,870	
		3,520	
Less current liabilities			
Subscriptions prepaid	80		
Bar purchases owing	420		
General expenses owing	210	710	2,810
			20,750
Represented by:			
Accumulated fund			
Opening balance, 1 October 1980 (see working 2)			22,960
Less Excess of expenditure over income			2,210
			20,750

(c) The treasurer should be advised to accept alternative B for the club, as this results in an estimated annual surplus of £760, compared with only £600 under alternative A.

	Alternative A	Alternative B
Additional membership subscriptions		
(A) 50 × £20	1,000	
(B) 100 × £20		2,000

Adjustment to bar profit

(A) Increase in takings   900

Gross profit (33⅓%)   300

(B) Increase in takings

$$\frac{140}{100} \times £4,500 = 6,300$$

Gross profit (20%) 1,260
Current gross profit 1,500

Reduction in gross profit		(240)
Reduction in miscellaneous revenue	(700)	—
Loan repayment	—	(1,000)
Annual additional estimated surplus	£ 600	£ 760

Workings:

(1)   *Subscriptions Account*

Opening subs owing b/f	20	Opening subs prepaid b/f	60
		Cash received	4,400
Income and expenditure a/c (=)	4,460		
Closing subs prepaid c/f	80	Closing subs owing c/f	100
	4,560		4,560

(=): balancing figure

(2)   *Calculation of opening accumulated fund*

	£	£
Assets at 1 October 1980:		
Premises at cost		15,000
Equipment at book value		2,000
Bar stocks at cost		480
Subscriptions owing		20
Cash at bank		6,000
		23,500
Liabilities at 1 October 1980:		
Bar purchases owing	310	
Subscriptions prepaid	60	
General expenses owing	170	540
		£22,960

COMMENTARY

All usual accounting conventions are followed in the preparation of the answers to parts (a) and (b). The income and expenditure account could be shown in a vertical style if desired. Note that the term 'net loss' is replaced by 'excess of expenditure over income'. A 'net profit' would be indicated by the expression 'surplus of income over expenditure'.

Exercises

2.1

(a) Explain the reasons for providing for depreciation in the books of account of a business.

(b) Explain briefly, giving illustrations, three methods that may be used for calculating depreciation.

2.2

(a) The following information relates to a machine:

	£
Cost, 1 January 1979	100,000
Book value, 31 December 1984	10,000

Replacement cost, 1 January 1985   240,000
Scrap (disposal) value, 1 January 1985   5,000

Assuming that the machine is replaced on 1 January 1985, show the journal entries recording the disposal of the old machine and the purchase of the new machine, including any profit or loss arising on disposal. Assume that the financial year ends on 31 December. A narrative should accompany each journal entry.

(b) The depreciation provided in (a) above was significantly less than the replacement cost of the machine.

What purposes are served by a provision for depreciation? In what ways can sufficient funds be ensured for future replacements?

(ULSEB)

2.3 W & J Wright Ltd, goods carriers of Longton, purchased three motor vans from Thomas Pepper Ltd during 1981, as follows:

Van A – purchased 1 April for £2,750
Van B – purchased 1 July for £2,800
Van C – purchased 1 October for £2,800

Subsequently the following events took place:

1982

1 June   Van A was badly damaged in an accident and taken out of use.
1 Aug.   An insurance company paid W. & J. Wright Ltd £2,000 for Van A, which had been treated as a 'write-off'.

1983

1 April   A permanent canopy was fitted to Van C at a cost of £400.
30 Sept.   In accordance with W. & J. Wright Ltd's pre-arranged maintenance programme, the four worn tyres on Van B were changed for new ones at a cost of £200.

In its accounts the company provided for depreciation at the rate of 20% per annum on original cost.

Note: Take depreciation for Van A as £420 (1981) and £230 (1982).

Required:

Prepare the following accounts in the company's ledger paying particular attention to dates and narrations:

  i   Motor vans
 ii   Provision for depreciation
iii   Disposal of vans.

Note: The accounts should be balanced each year at 31 December for three years.

(LCCI – Intermediate)

2.4 On 31 March 1985 the following balances were extracted from the books of L. Roberts and J. Davies, manufacturers and wholesalers of electrical equipment.

	DR £	CR £
Stocks 1 April 1984:		
Raw materials	40,000	
Part-finished goods	22,000	
Finished goods	26,250	
Purchases:		
Raw materials	285,695	
Finished goods	226,060	
Direct wages	116,650	
Sales		861,750
Debtors	142,350	
Creditors		81,541
Heating and lighting	17,900	
Factory general expenses	58,313	
General office expenses	30,342	

Insurances	6,280	
Selling and distribution expenses	25,500	
Provision for depreciation:		
Factory plant and machinery		57,812
Office furniture and equipment		22,240
Factory plant and machinery, at cost	212,700	
Office furniture and equipment, at cost	41,210	
Cash at bank and in hand	70,423	
Provision for bad debts		2,400
Provision for factory profit included in finished stock		920
Capital: L. Roberts		180,000
J. Davies		120,000
Current accounts: L. Roberts	5,210	
J. Davies		220
	1,326,883	1,326,883

Other matters to be taken into consideration in preparing final accounts are as follows:

(i)   The partners are entitled to interest at the rate of 10% per annum on the fixed amount of their capital accounts. J. Davies is to be credited with a partnership salary of £5,000 per annum and the balance of the profits is shared between L. Roberts and J. Davies in the proportions 3:2 respectively.

(ii) Drawings during the year were:
      L. Roberts   £25,200
      J. Davies   £23,160

(iii) Provision is to be made for depreciation as follows:
      Plant and machinery   20% per annum on cost.
      Furniture and equipment   10% per annum on cost.

(iv) Stocks at 31 March 1985 were as follows:
      Raw materials   £37,205
      Part finished goods   £20,543
      Finished goods   £30,240

(v)   Adjustments have to be made as at 31 March 1985 for £200 owing for heating and lighting and for £280 for insurance paid in advance.

(vi) Half of the cost of the heating and lighting is apportioned to the factory and half to the office. Three-quarters of the insurance is apportioned to the factory and one-quarter to the office.

(vii) Finished goods are transferred from the factory to the warehouse at factory cost plus 5%. Adjustment has to be made for overvaluation of the closing stock. Provision for factory profit included in closing stock at 31 March 1985 was £970.

(viii) Provision for bad debts has to be increased to 2% of debtors.

Required:
Manufacturing, trading and profit and loss accounts for the year ended 31 March 1985 and a balance sheet as at that date.

                                                        (WJEC)

2.5 Wentworth Ltd are manufacturers and the following balances were taken from the books of the company for the year ended 31 December 1982.

                                          £

Stocks 1 January 1982	
Raw materials	26,700
Work in progress (at prime cost)	6,900
Finished goods (at transfer price)	23,100
Raw materials purchased	297,450
Factory general expenses	8,190

Direct wages	154,050
Repairs to plant and machinery	11,850
Repairs to factory buildings	5,550
Power, light and heat	12,960
Carriage inwards	1,050
Carriage outwards	1,300
Office expenses	42,600
Sales	730,000
Rates and insurances	2,400
Returns outwards	900
Discounts allowed	1,950
Plant and machinery (cost)	365,000
Selling and distribution expenses	21,000
Leasehold factory buildings at cost	84,000
Returns inwards	1,200

Additional information is given below:

Rates and insurance prepaid amount to £600.

One-fifth of rates and insurance and one-quarter of the power, light and heat are to be charged to the offices.

The leasehold premises were acquired for 21 years on 1 January 1979.

Depreciate plant and machinery by 20% on cost.

Stocks at 31 December 1982: raw materials £18,900; work in progress at prime cost £7,950; finished goods (at transfer price) £37,950.

Finished stock is transferred from the factory at factory cost plus 10%.

Required:

For the year ended 31 December 1982:

(i) A manufacturing account showing cost of materials used, prime cost and factory cost.

(ii) A trading account.

(LCCI – Intermediate)

2.6 Swift and Metcalfe (General Stores) plc had a departmental store with departments on both sides of the High Street, Great Harwood, designated North (N) and South (S) respectively. The company commenced business on 1 January 1984. The directors required an interim statement of trading accounts for both departments for the first half-year. For this purpose, and to avoid the cost of stocktaking, they were prepared to assume a value for closing stock in trade of the difference between 'purchases' and the 'cost of sales', which latter figure was 'sales' minus 30%. The following information was ascertained relating to the first half-year:

	Dept N £	Dept S £
Purchases	96,000	58,500
Credit sales	15,000	45,000
Cash sales	105,000	30,000
Direct expenses	19,500	13,500

In addition, indirect expenses of £19,500 should be apportioned in proportion to total sales for each department.

Each department should also make provision for bad debts of 2% of credit sales.

Required:

Prepare a departmental Trading and Profit and Loss Account for the six months ended 30 June 1984: present the figures for each department in columnar form with vertical presentation and include a 'total' column.

(LCCI – Intermediate)

2.7 The treasurer of the Western Sports Club has not maintained double-entry accounting records, but analysis of the cash book for the year ended 31 March 1985 provided the following information:

Receipts	£
Bar takings (including debtors from 1983/84)	25,226
Subscriptions 1983/84	60
Subscriptions 1984/85	3,220
Subscriptions 1985/86	330
Receipts from social functions	754
Legacy from deceased member	500

Payments	£
Purchase of stocks for bar (including creditors from 1983/84)	19,290
Wages of part-time barman	3,260
Expenses of social functions	818
Purchases of new equipment	300
Rent of premises	2,000
Secretarial expenses	512
Heating and lighting	1,050

Of the receipts £29,380 was paid into the bank current account and £26,530 of the payments were made by cheque.

The balance sheet of the club at 31 March 1984 was as follows:

Balance Sheet			
	£		£
Accumulated fund	3,249	Bar stock	2,027
Creditors:			
Bar	1,480	Furniture and equipment	1,280
Secretarial expenses	162	Debtors to bar	56
Subscriptions in advance for 1984/85	118	Subscriptions owing	84
		Cash at bank	1,473
		Cash in hand	89
	5,009		5,009

At 31 March 1985 subscriptions owing amounted to £168, bar stock was valued at £1,431, bar creditors were £2,628, creditors for secretarial expenses were £266, bar debtors were £23 and £500 was still owing for the new equipment for which the total cost was £800.

It is the practice to apportion one-quarter of the secretarial expenses and one-quarter of the rent to the bar trading account. Subscriptions owing at 31 March 1984 but not received are to be written off as a bad debt. Furniture and equipment is depreciated at the rate of 20% on the balance at the end of the year. The legacy received of £500 is to be placed to a special 'prize fund' to provide small prizes for competitions.

Required:
(a) Prepare a Bar Trading Account and Income and Expenditure Account for the year ended 31 March 1985 and a Balance Sheet as at that date.
(b) The treasurer suggests that as the receipts have been much more than the payments, consideration should be given to reducing the subscription for the year 1985/86 and that as there were bad debts from the subscriptions owing from 1983/84, some allowance should be made for possible bad debts in respect of the subscriptions owing at 31 March 1985. Give your views on the treasurer's suggestions, *briefly* explaining the reasons for your views.

(WJEC)

2.8 The treasurer of the Singapore Sports & Social Club summarised his Cash Book, and prepared therefrom the following Receipts and Payments Account:

Receipts & Payments Account
for the year ended 31 December 1982

	£		£
Balance at bank	4,120	Wages of restaurant staff	8,600
Subscriptions	8,040	Wages of ground staff	4,820
Income from social events	8,920	Payments for restaurant	
Takings from restaurant	29,680	supplies	14,130
Investment income	2,000	Printing and stationery	1,680
Gift from estate of		Rates	1,920
deceased member	2,000	Electricity	340
		Telephone	215
		Purchases new equipment	
		(1 October 1982)	4,000
		Expenses of social events	3,975
		Repairs/maintenance to	
		premises	1,830
		Postage	520
		Insurance	1,240
		Purchase of investments	5,000
		Expenses of restaurant	2,460
		Balance at bank	4,030
	54,760		54,760

The gift was regarded as a capital receipt.

The following balances appeared on the accounts of the Club at:

	31 December 1981	31 December 1982
	£	£
Subscriptions in advance	110	—
Restaurant stocks	1,460	1,640
Investments at cost	6,000	11,000
Creditors for restaurant purchases	2,720	3,320
Rates prepaid	350	480
Electricity accrued due	64	88
Sports ground & club house at cost	60,000	60,000
Furniture, fixtures/fittings		
(cost £12,000)	9,600	?
Sports equipment (cost £16,400)	13,120	?
Subscriptions in arrear	—	990

It is the policy of the Club to depreciate its Fixed Assets as follows:

1. Furniture, fixtures/fittings at the rate of 10% on cost per annum.
2. Sports equipment at the rate of 20% on cost per annum.

Required:
i   Calculate the opening balance of Accumulated Fund.
    Note: Show your workings.
ii Prepare the following for the year ended 31 December 1982:
    (a)   The Club's restaurant account.
    (b)   The Club's income and expenditure account.
iii Prepare the Club's Balance Sheet as at 31 December 1982.

(LCCI – Intermediate)

CHAPTER 3

Further Accounting Procedures (2)

The financial statements should show a 'true and fair' view both of the state of the business during the financial period, and of the net asset position on the final day of that period. This will only be possible when the underlying accounting system can be relied upon to produce consistently accurate data which fully reflect all aspects of the business's financial affairs. One way of ensuring this is by means of 'controls' over certain key areas, especially the personal ledgers.

3.1 Control accounts

The personal ledgers of even a relatively small business are likely to contain many hundreds of individual accounts for customers and suppliers. For large businesses, the numbers of accounts may total tens or even hundreds of thousands, the vast majority being contained within the sales ledger.

To be able to confirm the overall accuracy of the book-keeping entries made into these ledgers, 'control accounts' (also called 'total accounts') can be drawn up. These accounts work on a simple principle: that if you can produce an account which contains summarised totals of all the thousands of individual entries posted to a ledger's accounts, then the closing balance on that one account should equal

Table 3.1

Debited entries	'Source'	Credited entries	'Source'
Opening debtors brought forward	Previous closing balance	Opening credit balances brought forward*	Previous closing balance
Sales on credit terms	Sales day book	Returns inwards	Returns in day book
Cheques dishonoured	Cash book		
Interest charged on overdue accounts†	Sales day book	Cash and cheques received	Cash book
		Discount allowed	General ledger
Cash refunded to customers	Cash book	Bad debts written off	Journal
		Contra purchases ledger‡	Journal
Closing credit balances carried forward§	—	Closing debtors carried forward	—

* These may occur owing to a debtor having mistakenly overpaid an invoice, duplicated a payment, or returned goods after having paid for them.

† A sales contract may include a clause which allows for interest to be charged if the account is not settled by a given date.

‡ If the customer also *sells* goods to the business then the balance on his sales ledger account can be 'contra'd' (i.e. set-off) against the balance due to him on his purchase ledger account. This has an advantage for both parties in that by transferring one of the two ledger balances, only one amount is then to be paid or received, thus saving unnecessary paperwork.

the total of the individual account balances within the ledger.

The check on the 'double-entry' comes about due to the fact that the 'summarised totals' mentioned in the previous paragraph do not come from the personal ledger itself, but from the appropriate 'book of prime entry'. As these totals are used within the book-keeping system to complete the double-entry transactions (e.g. by the totals of the purchase day book being debited to the purchases account in the general ledger), the satisfactory 'balancing' of the control account proves the arithmetical accuracy of that part of the accounting system.

SALES LEDGER CONTROL ACCOUNT

Table 3.1 on page 50 lists the types of entries which might appear within customers' accounts in the sales ledger, divided between debited entries and credited entries. The 'source' of the entries is also given.

The sales ledger control account will be very similar in form to the summary of entries given above. The closing balances on the account are compared with the total of the list of individual balances within the sales ledger. If they agree, then the arithmetical accuracy of the book-keeping system for this ledger is proved. If there is a disagreement, then one or more of the following errors may have occurred:

1. *Errors within the control account*
(a) Addition error within the control account.
(b) Incorrect total posted from a book of prime entry to the control account owing to arithmetical error or transposition of figures.
(c) A total which, despite appearing in a book of prime entry, was not posted to the control account.
(d) A total being understated owing to an item being posted to the ledger, but omitted from the book of prime entry.
2. *Errors within the ledger*
(a) An arithmetical error within one or more individual accounts.
(b) An item which, although shown in a book of prime entry, has been omitted from the individual ledger account.
3. *Other possible errors*
(a) The list of ledger balances being incorrectly totalled.
(b) One or more balances being excluded from the list of balances.
(c) Debit balances being listed as credit balances, or vice versa.

Example 1

The following figures relating to debtors were extracted from the books of S. Browne & Co, at 31 March 1982.

	£
Debtor balances 1 April 1981	22,093
Credit balances 1 April 1981	286
Receipts from debtors	152,686
Sales	168,212
Bad debts written off	763
Discounts allowed	1,549
Contras: Purchases ledger	274
Sales returns	3,468
Bills receivable accepted	4,782
Cash refunded to debtors	276
Bill receivable dishonoured	362
Credit balances 31 March 1982	197

A control account was prepared from the above figures but the balance of debtors at 31 March 1982 did not agree with the total of the balances extracted from the sales ledger.

Further examination revealed the following errors.

1. Cash discounts allowed for one month, of £148, had been posted to debtors' accounts but not to the discount allowed account.

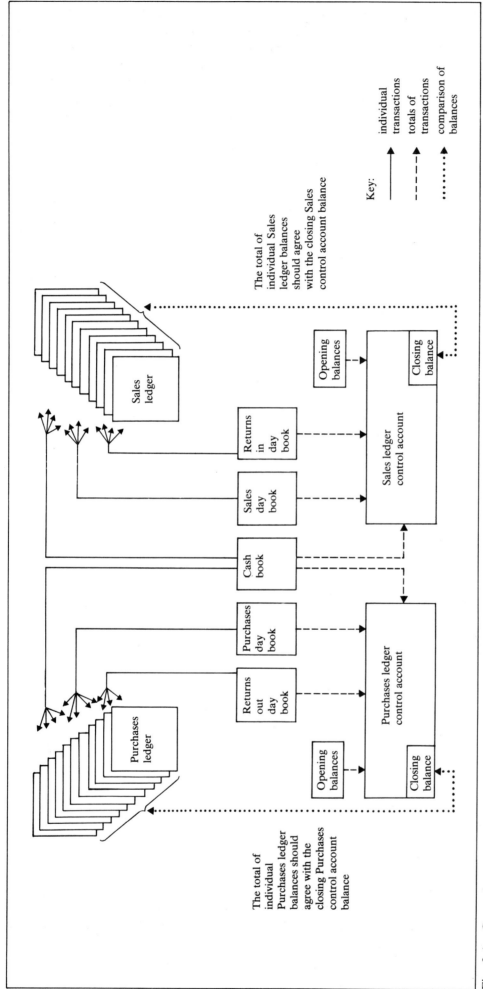

Fig. 3.1 Control accounts.

2. The debtor balance on a debtor's account had been included in the list of debtors extracted from the sales ledger as £239 instead of £329.
3. Goods returned by a customer to the value of £56 had been correctly posted to the customer's account but entered in the sales returns account as £156.
4. A sales invoice for £95 had been recorded in the customer's account but had not been entered in the sales day book.
5. A bill receivable for £120 had been posted to the credit instead of the debit of the bills receivable account.
6. The contra item transferred from the purchases ledger had been incorrectly shown in the control account, the correct figure being £247.

Required:

Draw up the sales ledger control account as at 31 March 1982, incorporating the necessary corrections to the above errors.

(WJEC)

Solution:

S. Browne & Co
Sales Ledger Control Account as at 31 March 1982

	£		£
Debtor balances 1 April 1981	22,093	Credit balances 1 April 1981	286
Sales	168,307	Receipts from debtors	152,686
Cash refunded to debtors	276	Bad debts written off	763
Bills receivable dishonoured	362	Discounts allowed	1,697
Credit balances 31 March 1982	197	Contras: Purchases ledger	247
		Sales returns	3,368
		Bills receivable accepted	5,022
		Debtor balances 31 March 1982*	27,166
	191,235		191,235

Workings:

Five of the original figures needed adjustment, as follows:

	£	re: paragraph
Sales	+ 95	(4)
Discounts allowed	+ 148	(1)
Contras: Purchases ledger	− 27	(6)
Sales returns	− 100	(3)
Bills receivable accepted	+ 240	(5)

COMMENTARY

Of the six 'errors' which were revealed, five caused adjustments to be made to the control account figures. The reasons for the adjustments are given below.

Errors (1) The total of discount allowed is obtained from the discount allowed account in the general ledger. The £148 was omitted from this account, and therefore the control account must be amended.

Error (2) Any error in compiling the list of balances has no effect on the figures in the control account. The list of debtors is only used to confirm the accuracy of the control account balance.

Error (3) As the sales returns total had been overstated by £100, a deduction of that amount must be made within the control account.

Error (4) The omitted invoice must be included in the sales total.

Error (5) When an item has been reversed, an adjustment of twice the original amount must be made to correct the error.

Error (6) The total of contra items had been overstated in the control account by £27.

The two items relating to 'bills receivable' may have caused confusion to students. Customers have given S. Browne & Co 'bills of exchange', which are legally binding documents whereby a specified sum of money will become payable

*'Balancing' figure.

by the customer at a future date. Bills of exchange are often used in export transactions where there may be several weeks between the receipt of a customer's order for goods and the date on which the customer takes possession of the goods. The advantage to the customer of arranging payment by means of a bill of exchange is that the payment will not be made until the goods have been received by him. The supplier has the benefit if he wishes of being able to 'discount' the bill of exchange at his bank as soon as he has received it, i.e. convert it into cash at face value less a discount. If a bill has been discounted, then the bank will ultimately collect the amount due from the customer.

If the customer fails to pay the amount due under the terms of the bill, then the bill becomes 'dishonoured', and the holder of the bill must then decide what action should be taken to recover the sum due.

The book-keeping entries relating to bills of exchange are as follows:

(a) *On acceptance by customer.* Debit bills receivable account (G.L.), credit customer's account (S.L.).
(b) *On discounting a bill.* Debit cash book and debit discounting charges account (G.L.), credit bills receivable account.
(c) *If bill remains undiscounted*, then on payment being received from customer: debit cash book; credit bills receivable account.
(d) *If bill was undiscounted and was subsequently dishonoured*, debit customer's account; credit bills receivable account.

PURCHASES LEDGER CONTROL ACCOUNT

This follows a similar pattern to the sales ledger control account.

The summarised entries which might be found in the purchases ledger are given in Table 3.2.

The purchases ledger control account will take a similar form to the summary given in Table 3.2. The closing balances on the account are compared with the total of the list of individual balances within the purchases ledger. If the figures agree, then the arithmetical accuracy of the book-keeping entries is proved. If there is a difference then similar errors to those relating to the sales ledger control account (see previous section) might be present.

Table 3.2

Debited entries	'Source'	Credited entries	'Source'
Opening debit balances brought f/wd*	Previous closing balance	Opening creditors brought f/wd	Previous closing balance
Returns outwards	Returns out day book	Purchases on credit terms	Purchases day book
Cash and cheques paid	Cash book	Interest charged	
Discount received	General ledger	on overdue	Purchases day
Contra sales ledger†	Journal	accounts‡	book
		Cash refunded by suppliers	Cash book
Closing creditors carried f/wd	—	Closing debit balances carried f/wd	—

*The business may have overpaid an invoice, duplicated a payment, or returned goods after having paid for them, thereby giving rise to a debit balance appearing in a supplier's account.
†This is the 'mirror image' of the contra item which is shown in the sales ledger control account. It records the transfer of a debtor's balance to offset the same person's creditor's balance.
‡The purchase contract may allow for interest to be charged if an amount is overdue for payment.

Example 2

J. Dunkley prepared a purchases ledger control account for April 1986 from the totals in his subsidiary books. The closing credit balance of the control account, which was £7,210, failed to agree with the total of the balances in the purchases ledger.

The following errors were discovered.

1. A debit balance of £367 from M. Taylor's account in the sales ledger had been transferred to M. Taylor's account in the purchases ledger, and the transfer had not been entered in the control account.
2. The total of the purchases day book for April 1986 had been undercast by £228.
3. A credit purchase of £788 from R. Sumner had been omitted from the books of account.
4. A cash payment to a supplier, F. Grant, of £870 had been correctly entered in the cash book but posted to his account as £830.

Required:

(a) Show the purchases ledger control account after the errors have been corrected.
(b) Calculate the total of the balances in the purchases ledger before the errors were discovered.

Solution:

(a)

J. Dunkley
Purchases Ledger Control Account – April 1986

	£		£
Contra item omitted	367	Closing creditors per original control account	7,210
Closing creditors after correction of errors, carried forward	7,859	Purchases day book total undercast	228
		Invoice omitted	788
	8,226		8,226

(b) Errors which affect individual balances are numbers (3) and (4).

		£
(3)	Creditors are increased by	788
(4)	Creditors are decreased by	(40)
	Net increase	748

	£
Total revised creditors per control account	7,859
Original list of balances understated by	748
Total of balances prior to discovery of errors	7,111

COMMENTARY

In part (a) the detailed control account cannot be shown, as we are only given the closing credit balance. This figure therefore becomes the starting point to enable the errors to be corrected, as follows:

(Detailed original control account)

	X		X
	X		X
	X		X
Closing creditors c/d	7,210		
	X		X
		Closing creditors b/d	7,210

In part (b), we can ignore errors (1) and (2) as they have no effect whatsoever on the total of the individual balances. Errors (3) and (4), however, require a revision to be made of the original list. The 'proof' of the figures is shown below.

Original list of balances as in (b) above	7,111	
Increase in balances due to errors	748	
	£7,859	
Balance as per control account	£7,859	

SUSPENSE ACCOUNTS

If the control accounts reveal that there are one or more errors within the ledgers, then a suspense account can be opened, pending their discovery. The suspense account, when used in this way, acts as a temporary 'holding' account whilst the work of checking is carried out. Once the mistakes have been rectified, the suspense account is dispensed with.

Example 3

After the extraction of the balances from the books of Bland, the totals of the trial balance failed to agree. In addition, the credit balance of £2,450 on the purchases ledger control account, included in the trial balance, did not agree with the total of balances extracted from the purchases ledger. The following items have subsequently been discovered.

1. The payment of £265 for office supplies has been entered correctly in the cash book but has been credited to the office expenses account in the nominal ledger as £256.
2. The payment of £290 for the maintenance of an item of machinery has been correctly entered in the cash book but has been debited to the machinery account.
3. The total of the discount received column in the cash book has been undercast by £27.
4. No entry has been made in the accounts relating to the return to a supplier of goods to the value of £175 which had been purchased on credit.
5. The purchase on credit of goods for £110 from Parks, who is a customer and a supplier, has been correctly entered in the accounts. It has now been decided to set off the amount owing against the balance on Parks' account in the sales ledger.

Required:
(a) A purchases ledger control account showing clearly the amendments to the original balance.
(b) A suspense account showing clearly the original discrepancy on the trial balance.

(AEB)

Solution:
(a)
Bland
Purchases Ledger Control Account

Discount received understated	27	Closing creditors per original	
Returns out omitted	175	control account	2,450
Contra item: Parks	110		
Closing creditors after amendments carried f/wd	2,138		
	2,450		2,450

(b) *Suspense Account*

Original trial balance discrepancy	521	Office expenses; errors in posting	521
	521		521

COMMENTARY

In part (a), the control account is affected by items (3), (4) and (5) for the following reasons:

Item (3): If the total of the discount received column in the cash book was undercast then the corresponding total in the control account must also be incorrect.

Item (4): The omitted entry has the effect of increasing the total of returns outwards in the general ledger, and of decreasing the total creditors.

Item (5): The setting off of a debtor's account against a creditor's account, whilst having no overall effect on the trial balance, does reduce the totals of both the debtors and creditors.

In part (b), the only entry to be shown in the suspense account is that relating to item (1). The amount of £521 shown in the account consists of two distinct halves; one being the amount required to cancel the original, incorrect posting (£256), the other being the corrected entry (£265). Note that there were *two* errors present in this item; not only was the incorrect amount posted but also the account had been credited instead of being debited.

The only item which had no effect on the arithmetical accuracy of either the trial balance or the control account was (2), which was an error of principle, requiring a simple transfer between accounts.

USE OF CONTROL ACCOUNTS IN A COMPUTERISED ACCOUNTING SYSTEM

Data to be input into a computerised ledger system are usually sorted into batches of items. The batch totals are ascertained and ultimately checked against the difference between the balance outstanding on the relevant control account, before and after the batch is posted.

ADVANTAGES OF MAINTAINING CONTROL ACCOUNTS

1. The closing balances on the control accounts should represent, at any date, the summarised totals of the individual sales ledger or purchases ledger balances. This ready access to debtors and creditors totals is of great importance to management when determining the current strengths or weaknesses of the business. For smaller businesses with relatively unsophisticated accounting systems, control accounts enable owners quickly to ascertain debtors and creditors figures, without the necessity of calculating individual personal ledger balances.

2. As control accounts can prove the arithmetical accuracy of individual ledgers, they can be used to locate differences occurring within the book-keeping system. For example, if a trial balance failed to balance, but the sales ledger and purchase ledger control accounts were agreed, then the difference would lie within the general ledger or the cash book.

    A further aid to the location of errors in larger companies is the division of the control accounts into several sub-sections, divided usually by letters of the alphabet, e.g. A–J, K–M, etc. This requires a similar analysis to be made within the books of prime entry, but the advantage is that if errors have been made, only small sections of the ledger need be checked.

3. If the control accounts are maintained by persons unconnected with the day-to-day book-keeping procedures, then this will provide an independent check on the quality of the accounting work being performed by the ledger clerks.

4. If the staff maintaining the control accounts are independent of the ledger clerks, then the chance of fraud is minimised, as a considerable degree of collusion would be needed for sales or purchases ledger records to be manipulated.

3.2 Incomplete records

Any method of recording the financial transactions of a business which does not use a full 'double-entry' system is described as 'incomplete'. There are varying levels of incompleteness, ranging from a total absence of written records through to the maintenance of an efficient 'single-entry' system, providing the owner of a small 'cash' business with all his day-to-day accounting needs. The following represents some of the 'incomplete' methods in use:

1. No written records; all transactions on a 'cash only' basis; invoices not issued

by the trader nor retained from suppliers. There may be a deliberate attempt to conceal true earnings in order to evade the payment of taxation.

2. A bank account is operated and copy sales invoices and purchases invoices are retained. Cheque book counterfoils and bank paying-in receipts are available.

3. 'Single-entry' records are maintained, perhaps by using a pre-printed commercially available record book (e.g. 'Simplex'). A cash book and day books are written up, but personal ledgers may not be in use.

4. Conventional accounting records are in use, but no 'final accounts' are prepared by the trader.

The necessity for most businesses in the United Kingdom to be registered for Value Added Tax (VAT) purposes has seen a decline in the number of traders who fall within categories (1) and (2) above, as businesses are regularly visited by VAT inspectors to ensure that VAT-registered traders have an accounting system capable of providing accurate records.

Although a full double-entry system might be inappropriate for very small traders owing to the time and expense involved in its maintenance, there are genuine disadvantages in having incomplete records:

(a) Control over expenses is made difficult, and comparisons between periods may not be possible.

(b) It is harder to trace errors or deal with queries from customers or suppliers on accounting matters.

(c) There is a greater risk of running foul of legislation, particularly in relation to taxation matters.

(d) No continual record is kept of assets, liabilities and capital.

(e) The owner may be unaware whether or not a profit is being made.

(f) The owner may find that the cost of employing professional accountants to unravel the records far outweighs any savings which he believes he is making by having an incomplete accounting system.

Note that limited companies are bound by legislation to keep proper books of account, and it is therefore the responsibility of company directors to ensure that an adequate book-keeping system is in operation.

PREPARATION OF ACCOUNTS FROM INCOMPLETE RECORDS

If no written records have been maintained or where records have been destroyed, then a 'statement of affairs' needs to be assembled from such information as is available.

The statement resembles a balance sheet in that it lists all assets and liabilities, with the net assets total equalling the capital balance. If it is desired to establish whether a profit or loss has been made during a period, then a closing statement of affairs is produced, and the closing capital is then compared with the opening capital. The difference when adjusted for drawings and any capital introduced or withdrawn during the period will be either a profit or a loss.

Example 4

Carl, a sole trader dealing in motor vehicles since 1982, has been trading for the past year without keeping full accounting records. The last statement of affairs which is available for the business is set out below:

Statement of Affairs as at 31 December 1987

		£	£	£
Fixed assets:	Premises at cost			31,400
	Fixtures at net book value			4,200
	Vehicles at net book value			12,700
				48,300
Current assets:	Stock in trade	29,000		
	Debtors	4,000		

Cash			1,200
			34,200
Current liabilities: Creditors		14,500	
Bank		3,400	17,900
			16,300
			64,600
Capital			64,600

The following information is available for the year to 31 December 1988:

1. Carl drew a total of £7,000 cash for his personal use during the year, but paid a legacy of £4,000 into the business bank account.
2. An extension to the premises had been built in the year, costing £12,600.
3. The fixtures and vehicles were depreciated at 20% on the reducing balance basis.
4. Stock in trade at the year-end was valued at £25,000 and creditors totalled £16,000. Debtors were valued at £6,000 of which £1,200 was thought to be doubtful.
5. The bank statement at the year-end showed a credit balance of £2,600, but a cheque for £400 in payment for a newspaper advertisement had not been presented.
6. Cash in hand at the year-end was £800.
7. Carl has refused an offer of £20,000 for the goodwill of the business, but believes that this should be shown as an asset of the business.

Required:
Carl's statement of affairs as at 31 December 1988, together with a calculation of his net profit or loss for the year ending on that date.

Solution:

Carl
Statement of Affairs as at 31 December 1988

			£
Fixed assets:	Premises		44,000
	Fixtures at net book value		3,360
	Vehicles at net book value		10,160
			57,520
Current assets:	Stock in trade	25,000	
	Debtors	4,800	
	Bank	2,200	
	Cash	800	
		32,800	
Current liabilities: Creditors		16,000	16,800
			74,320
Capital			74,320

Calculation of trading result for the year to 31 December 1988

	£
Opening capital	64,600
Add: Cash introduced	4,000
	68,600
Less: Drawings	7,000
	61,600
Closing capital per statement of affairs	74,320
Increase in net worth (i.e. net profit)	12,720

COMMENTARY

It is evident that the statement of affairs is a balance sheet by a different name. All traditional accounting conventions are followed, hence the depreciation of the fixed assets and the exclusion of doubtful debts.

The 'goodwill' in item (7) represents a value placed on the reputation of the business. It may be real or imagined, but from an accounting point of view it can only be included as an asset if the trader purchased the business at an earlier date and paid an amount for goodwill as part of the overall price paid. Even in such cases, the goodwill is usually 'written off' in as short a time as is practicable. This recognises the transitory nature of the asset, as its value depends entirely on the state of the business at *the time of its disposal*, not at the date of the capital statement (see Chapter 8).

USE OF CONTROL ACCOUNTS WHERE RECORDS ARE INCOMPLETE

The 'statement of affairs' will only be used when the trader's accounting records are very limited. However, if sufficient information is available, there is no reason why a full set of final accounts should not be prepared. The minimum required information relates to debtors and creditors, cash paid and received, accruals and prepayments, and asset valuations.

When producing the trading account, the key lies in the preparation of control accounts, where balancing figures are used to give the total sales and purchases figures.

Example 5

From the following figures relating to a sole trader, calculate the total sales and purchases for the year to 31 March 1987:

	£
Opening debtors balances 1 April 1986	13,400
Opening creditors balances 1 April 1986	20,600
Cash and cheques paid to suppliers	89,650
Cash and cheques received from customers	126,430
Total discount allowed in year	2,050
Total discount received in year	1,800
Closing debtors balances 31 March 1987	14,700
Closing creditors balances 31 March 1987	18,450

Sales = £129,780, Purchases = £89,300

Solution:

Workings:

Purchases Control Account

Cash and cheques paid	89,650	Opening creditors b/f	20,600
Discount received	1,800		
		Purchases	
Closing creditors c/f	18,450	(balancing figure)	89,300
	109,900		109,900

Sales Control Account

Opening debtors b/f	13,400	Cash and cheques received	126,430
		Discount allowed	2,050
Sales			
(balancing figure)	129,780	Closing debtors c/f	14,700
	143,180		143,180

COMMENTARY

By the simple means of preparing control accounts we are able to calculate the total sales and purchases for the year. Both of these figures will be shown in the trading account of the business. Many students fall into the trap of completely ignoring normal accounting procedures, and assume that 'sales' equals cash received and 'purchases' equals cash paid. As we shall see in the next chapter, a fundamental basis of accounting is the 'accruals concept', which states simply that accounting statements should reflect all the business's transactions of the financial period, regardless of whether or not the cash relating to those transactions has been received or paid. The following example explains the way of tackling a more comprehensive question:

Example 6

The following is a summary of the bank statements of Dakin, a trader for the year ending 31 May 1986.

Bank statements

	Paid £	Received £	Balance £
1 June 1985			500
Trade creditors	18,700		
Rent and rates	700		
Purchase of fixtures	600		
General expenses	1,600		
Drawings	4,500		
Cash sales banked		20,000	
Credit sales banked		4,000	
Proceeds on sale of fixtures (net book value £400)		300	
31 May 1986 balance overdrawn			(1,300)

The following additional information is available.

1. All takings from cash sales were banked with the exception of £4,000, out of which Dakin paid wages of £3,000 and retained the balance for his own use.
2. Discounts received and allowed from trade creditors and debtors were £1,000 and £700, respectively.
3. An examination of the cheque book and bank paying-in book revealed that a cheque for £400 was written on 31 May 1986 for the payment of suppliers and that a cheque from a customer for £500 was banked on 31 May 1986. Dakin had ignored this information and neither item appeared on the bank statement until 15 June 1986.
4. Dakin disclosed the following information.

	31 May 1985 £	31 May 1986 £
Stock	1,500	1,700
Trade creditors	1,800	1,900
Trade debtors	2,300	2,100
Rates paid in advance	200	250
General expenses creditors	100	300
Fixtures (at valuation)	1,500	1,600

Prepare trading and profit and loss accounts for Dakin for the year ending 31 May 1986 and a balance sheet as at that date.

Solution:

Dakin
Trading and Profit and Loss Account
for the year to 31 May 1986

	£	£
Sales: Cash (1)	24,000	
Credit (2)	5,000	29,000
Cost of goods sold		
Opening stock	1,500	
Purchases (3)	20,200	
	21,700	

Less: Closing stock		1,700	20,000
Gross profit			9,000
Add: Discount received			1,000
			10,000
Less: Wages		3,000	
Rent and rates (4)		650	
Discount allowed		700	
General expenses (5)		1,800	
Depreciation of fixtures (6)		100	
Underprovision of depreciation re: sale of fixtures (7)		100	6,350
Net profit			3,650

Balance Sheet as at 31 May 1986

	£	£	£
Fixed assets: Fixtures at valuation			1,600
Current assets: Stock		1,700	
Debtors		2,100	
Prepayment		250	
		4,050	
Less: Current liabilities: Creditors	1,900		
Accrued expenses	300		
Overdraft	1,200	3,400	
Net current assets			650
			2,250
Financed by:			
Dakin's capital account: Opening balance (8)		4,100	
Net profit		3,650	
		7,750	
Less: Drawings		5,500	
			2,250

Note: Figures in brackets ( ) refer to 'Workings' below.

Workings:

(1) *Cash sales*

Cash sales banked		20,000
Cash sales unbanked		4,000
		24,000

(2) *Credit sales*

Opening debtors b/f	2,300	Cheques received (4,000 + 500)	4,500
		Discount allowed	700
Sales (balancing figure)	5,000	Closing debtors c/f	2,100
	7,300		7,300

(3) *Purchases*

		Opening creditors b/f	1,800
Cheques paid (18,700 + 400)	19,100	Purchases (balancing figure)	20,200
Discount received	1,000		
Closing creditors c/f	1,900		
	22,000		22,000

(4) *Rent and rates*

Paid in advance b/f	200	Profit and loss account	650

Cheques paid	700	Paid in advance c/f	250
	900		900

(5) *General expenses*

Cheques paid	1,600	Creditors b/f	100
Creditors c/f	300	Profit and loss account	1,800
	1,900		1,900

(6) *Depreciation of fixtures*

Fixtures at valuation, 31 May 1985		1,500
Add: Fixtures purchased		600
		2,100
Less: Net book value of fixtures sold		400
		1,700
Fixtures at valuation, 31 May 1986		1,600
Depreciation for the year to 31 May 1986		100

(7) *Underprovision for depreciation re: sale of fixtures*

Net book value of fixtures at date of disposal	400
Proceeds of sale	300
Underprovision to profit and loss account	100

(8) *Calculation of opening capital*

Opening capital = Opening assets − Opening liabilities

Opening assets: Fixtures		1,500
Stock		1,500
Debtors		2,300
Prepayment		200
Bank balance		500
		6,000
Opening liabilities: Trade creditors	1,800	
Expense creditors	100	1,900
Opening capital		£4,100

COMMENTARY

Apart from a certain amount of 'detective work', this question is asking for little more than the display of basic accounting skills. Note particularly the way in which the opening capital balance is ascertained, and also the method of calculating the depreciation figure.

Exercises

3.1 From the following lists of balances, draw up four separate purchases ledger control accounts, providing the missing figures where appropriate.

	(a)	(b)	(c)	(d)
Opening creditors	87,600	12,417	22,000	58,062
Opening debit balances	520	100	—	304
Cash and cheques paid	74,200	24,300	?	79,900
Goods returned to suppliers	160	—	140	600
Discount received	1,700	600	—	1,472
Contras to sales ledger	550	—	200	480
Interest charged by suppliers	80	—	—	100
Purchases	60,410	?	38,600	74,593
Closing creditors	71,300	15,400	23,300	?
Closing debit balances	340	200	—	84

3.2 From the following lists of balances, draw up four separate sales ledger control accounts, providing the missing figures where appropriate.

	(a)	(b)	(c)	(d)
Opening debtors	31,750	81,725	8,020	29,314
Opening credit balances	240	—	100	282
Cash and cheques received	59,920	101,474	?	78,200
Goods returned by customers	1,060	2,590	240	—
Discount allowed	2,500	—	750	370
Bad debts written off	320	600	180	—
Interest charged to customers	—	—	60	100
Sales	64,650	94,330	14,040	?
Closing debtors	32,660	?	10,700	31,760
Closing credit balances	300	—	56	200

3.3 The following is a summary of the bank account of the 'New-style Boutique', for the period from 1 October 1984 to 30 November 1984:

	£ p		£ p
Capital introduced	500.00	Cash purchases	1,234.30
Cash from sales	2,467.17	Shop fittings	540.00
Balance c/f	395.05	(bought 1 October)	
		Wages	225.00
		Stationery	12.40
		Advertising	13.27
		Rent	240.00
		Pansy Fashions Ltd	610.18
		Lilly's Leotards Ltd	219.00
		Daisy's Dresses Ltd	268.07
	3,362.22		3,362.22

Notes:
  (i)   The business commenced on 1 October 1984.
 (ii)   The payment for rent relates to the 3 months to 31 December 1984.
(iii)   Invoices received during the period to 30 November 1984 were:

		£ p
1 October	Pansy Fashions Ltd	610.18
2 October	Lilly's Leotards Ltd	219.00
16 October	Daisy's Dresses Ltd	268.07
5 November	Samson Separates Ltd	438.10
8 November	The Tarzan Tights Company	596.08

 (iv)   Sales were nearly all for cash, and totalled £2,750.00. Debtors at 30 November 1984 were:

	£ p
J. Jones	31.50
A. Patel	17.30

  (v)   Only part of the cash sales was banked. The balance was used for personal expenditure by the owner, apart from £120 which was paid out for wages to staff, and £10 which was left in the till at 30 November 1984.
 (vi)   At the end of November the following cheque had not been presented for payment:

   1 November ABC Garage (motor van)   £475.20

(vii)   Closing stock valued at selling price was £1,596.48. Average mark-up on cost price is 33⅓%. There was no opening stock.
(viii) Bank interest owed at 30 November 1984 was estimated at £21.50.
 (ix)   Depreciation is to be charged at 20% per annum for each month of ownership.

You are required to:
(a) Draw up the trading and profit and loss accounts of the business for the two months ended 30 November 1984, and a balance sheet as at that date.
(b) Explain the advantages and/or disadvantages which may arise when a full double-entry book-keeping system is not maintained.

(ULSEB)

3.4 Len Jackson, a retailer who does not keep full accounting records, provided the following summarised bank account for the year ended 31 March 1984.

		£			£
1984			*1983*		
31 March	Cash receipts	86,020	1 April	Balance b/d	1,400
	Sale of fixed assets	1,500	*1984*		
	Sale of private motor		31 March	Payments to trade	
	car	5,000		creditors	76,000
				Purchase of fixed	
				assets	6,000
				Rates	2,000
				General expenses	4,500
				Balance c/d	2,620
		92,520			92,520

The following information is also available:

	31 March 1983	31 March 1984
	£	£
Premises	10,000	10,000
Stock	8,300	3,100
Trade creditors	1,610	3,610
Fixed assets	3,000	7,000
General expenses owing	130	350
Warehouse rent accrued	—	?

Before banking the receipts from cash sales Jackson withdrew £50 cash per week as drawings and paid wages of £120 per week. Although owning his own freehold shop, owing to lack of storage space Jackson rented a warehouse for £2,500 for the year. Unfortunately, the warehouse rented proved to be unsuitable and as a result Jackson had to discard some stock that was damaged by damp. The value of the stock discarded was not recorded and is not covered by insurance. However, Jackson has agreed with the owner of the warehouse that half of the stock loss can be deducted from the warehouse rent. A standard gross profit of 20% on the cost of goods sold is earned.

Required:

(a) A trading and profit and loss account for the year ended 31 March 1984.
(b) The balance sheet as at 31 March 1984.

(AEB)

3.5 J. Hill set up in business selling electrical goods, but carried on business without keeping any proper books of account. Examinations of his records shows the following position:

(a) He has kept no ledger at all.
(b) He has opened a separate banking account for business transactions, but instead of paying in all his takings to the bank he has made all sundry cash payments from them, banking only the surplus.
(c) He has maintained a cash receipts book in which is listed the total of each day's takings and a cash payments book in which all payments, whether by cash or by cheque, are entered in a single list, excepting only his personal

drawings, which have not been recorded at all. All drawings have been made through the bank account.

(d) Nearly all sales have been for cash. The few credit sales have been entered in a diary, each entry having been crossed through as payment has been made.

(e) Purchases have been mainly, though not all, on credit. Payments have been made on the basis of suppliers' statements of account. Cash discounts have been allowed by a few suppliers.

Required:
Explain how you would ascertain the following:

  i   Sales.
 ii   Purchases.
iii   Discounts received.
 iv   Any selected class of expense.
  v   J. Hill's drawings.

(WJEC)

3.6 Mr K. Ashton started a manufacturing business on 1 January 1979. He had not kept a ledger but wished to have accounts prepared for the year 1983. A preliminary statement of assets and liabilities was drawn up as at 31 December 1982 and 31 December 1983 as follows.

	31.12.82 £	31.12.83 £
Bank overdraft	5,040	3,270
Trade creditors	4,450	4,820
Accrued expenses	570	370
Prepayments	1,250	1,500
Trade debtors	12,300	14,600
Stocks:		
Finished goods	7,900	10,050
Work in progress	5,300	4,600
Raw materials	6,920	7,790
Loan from Mrs K. Ashton		500

Mr Ashton had started with a capital of £50,000 in 1979 and had introduced a further £10,000 in 1983. The machinery he bought for £20,000 on 1 January 1979 had been depreciated at the rate of 10% per annum on the straight line method. A machine which had then cost £1,500 had been sold on 1 January 1983 for its written-down value of £900. Ashton carried on his business in premises which he owned and for which he had paid £25,000. His drawings for the year 1983 were £12,000.

Required:
  i   Prepare a statement of affairs as at 31 December 1982 and 31 December 1983 respectively, in columnar form.
 ii   Prepare a statement of profit for the year 1983 after charging depreciation for that year.
iii   Prepare a statement showing the written-down value at 31.12.83 of the plant and machinery purchased for £20,000 on 1 January 1979.

(LCCI – Intermediate)

3.7 A sole trader has been in business for several years without keeping complete accounting records. The following information relates to the year ended 31 December 1984:

(a) Summarised bank account for the year ended 31 December 1984 as extracted from bank statements:

	£		£
Cash banked	24,500	Opening balance	1,200
		Rent and rates	1,450
		Telephone and electricity	600

Plant and machinery	4,500
Paid to suppliers	7,500
Drawings	4,600
Closing balance	4,650

24,500	24,500

(b) Sales during the year totalled £23,160; trade debtors at 31 December 1983 were £3,800 and a year later £4,200.

(c) Trade creditors at 31 December 1983 were £1,450 and at 31 December 1984 £1,600.

(d) The gross profit for the year was 60% of sales.

(e) Closing stock in trade at 31 December 1984 has been valued at cost £2,100.

(f) A motor vehicle which had a book value of £2,400 on 31 December 1983 was sold for £2,000 on 1 January 1984. This amount was paid into the business bank account. No replacement vehicle was purchased.

(g) All takings from customers were banked with the exception of £260 which was used to pay a supplier's invoice.

(h) £400 had been owing by the business for rent and rates on 31 December 1983, and £300 was owing on 31 December 1984.

(i) Plant and machinery at 31 December 1983 had cost £4,000, accumulated depreciation at that date being £600. Depreciation is provided at 20% on the reducing balance basis. A full year's depreciation is provided in the year of purchase, regardless of the date of purchase.

(j) The owner had paid £30 from his private funds for business stationery during the year.

i Prepare a trading and profit and loss account for the year ended 31 December 1984 and a balance sheet on that date.

ii Write a report to the owner setting out reasons why the accounting system should be improved. Give specific recommendations which are appropriate to a small trading business.

(ULSEB)

3.8 The manageress of the perfume counter of the Baytown Department Store started work on 1 December 1983. On 15 March 1984, she failed to report for work. The management of the store received a report that the manageress had unexpectedly arranged an airline flight to an unknown destination. It was decided to begin an investigation into the finances of the perfume counter.

The following facts are available:
(a) Four types of perfume are sold:

	Selling price per bottle	Cost price per bottle
'Paris Nights'	£15	£7
'London Days'	£14	£6
'Manilla Mornings'	£12	£4
'Amsterdam Afternoons'	£10	£3

(b) Details of stocks and purchases were:

	Stock at 30 Nov 1983 (bottles)	Stock at 15 March 1984 (bottles)	Stock received in period (bottles)
'Paris Nights'	40	8	100
'London Days'	20	11	300
'Manilla Mornings'	10	6	50
'Amsterdam Afternoons'	15	None	160

(c) There was a cash balance of £125 on 30 November 1983, but there was no cash in the till on 15 March 1984.

(d) The bank records for the period show total takings banked relating to the perfume counter of £1,227.

(e) Three items were paid directly from cash out of the till:

    (a) A cash refund of £20 to a customer.

    (b) Payments of £5 per week for 8 weeks to a cleaner.

    (c) Other sundry expenses of £42.

i   Prepare a statement which shows the total amount of cash which may have been stolen during the period.

ii Prepare a trading account for the period.

iii Suggest two ways in which the store could have kept greater control over the finances of the perfume counter.

(ULSEB)

CHAPTER 4

Accounting for Partnerships

4.1 Introduction

The simplest form of business organisation—that of a sole trader—is ideal for the type of person who wishes to retain absolute control over the way in which the business develops. The advantages of sole trading include:

(a) the business can be established with a minimum of legal formalities;
(b) the owner is totally in control of the fortunes of the business;
(c) personal supervision by the owner usually results in a better service to customers;
(d) the owner does not have to reveal the financial results of the business to the general public

However, there are significant disadvantages, including:

(a) the personal liability of the owner for all the debts of the business, without limitation;
(b) total control and personal supervision normally require long hours and very hard work;
(c) there is no one with whom to share the problems and anxieties associated with running the business;
(d) if the owner is absent from the business owing to sickness or other reasons, this may have a serious effect on the state of the business;
(e) exclusive reliance on the owner's ability to raise finance may hamper prospects of expansion.

Although many people prefer to remain independent and continue as sole traders with varying degrees of success, it is extremely difficult to enlarge a business without also increasing the number of people who own it. The main choice for those who wish to form or convert to a multi-owner enterprise is between a partnership or a limited liability company. Limited companies are dealt with in Chapters 6 to 8, so let us start by looking at the basic definition of a partnership as contained in the Partnership Act of 1890:

> 'The relation which subsists between persons carrying on a business in common with a view of profit.'

The qualities which a sole proprietor will look for when deciding whether or not to take a partner will include:

1. The amount of capital the prospective partner can introduce into the business.
2. The business skill and existing contacts which the potential partner may have.

In addition, and perhaps most vital of all, the sole proprietor must judge whether he will be able to work happily with the partner. Many partnerships do not survive because of clashes of personality between the partners.

4.2 The partnership agreement

Once the decision has been taken to form the partnership, the partners will agree upon various matters which affect their financial relationship, such as the way in which profits or losses are to be shared, the amount of capital to be contributed by each partner, and the amount of drawings which are to be allowed. In addition, some partnerships allow interest to be credited on capital accounts, and charge interest on drawings; the former to reward partners for allowing the partnership to use their money, the latter to deter partners from withdrawing sums from the partnership.

In order to avoid misunderstandings at some future date, it is advisable that the partners draw up a partnership agreement which covers not only the matters mentioned in the previous paragraph but also the following:

(a) basic matters concerning the business, e.g. trading name, type of business, place or places of business;
(b) the rights and duties of partners, e.g. who shall be the book-keeper, who shall be the salesman;
(c) circumstances which may cause the partnership to be dissolved, e.g. a partner setting up a rival business;
(d) the duration of the partnership, e.g. for a fixed term, for the length of a particular contract, or undefined;
(e) rules for admitting new partners to the firm.

In the perhaps unlikely event of the partners failing to reach agreement over such matters as the proportions in which profits and losses are to be shared, section 24 of the Partnership Act of 1890 helps to solve the problem. It states, *inter alia*, that subject to any agreement, express or implied, between the partners:

i   profits and losses should be shared equally
ii   no interest on capital is to be allowed
iii no partners shall be entitled to a salary
iv   interest at 5% per annum is allowed to partners on advances in excess of the agreed amount of capital to be contributed by them.

The same section further states:

'The partnership books are to be kept at the place of business of the partnership.... and every partner may, when he thinks fit, have access to and inspect and copy any of them.'

The Act does not define 'the partnership books', but there is little difference between the records required to be kept by a partnership and those needed by a sole trader. Certainly the day-to-day book-keeping will operate on identical lines; it is only the financial relationship of the partners that requires special accounts to be maintained.

During the course of the partnership's financial year, individual partners might, depending upon the partnership agreement:

(a) draw a salary;
(b) make occasional or regular cash drawings;
(c) contribute more capital or withdraw part of their existing capital.

In addition, at the year-end, they may be charged interest on the drawings that they have made, or be credited with interest on their capital account balances. Finally, they will be either credited or debited with their shares of profit or loss. In the general ledger, accounts will be opened, for convenience, in a columnar format with columns for each partner on debit and credit sides. In addition to a partners' salaries account, a drawings account, interest on drawings account and interest on capital account, the partnership has the choice of keeping either capital accounts (known as 'variable') which record all the corresponding entries from the previously mentioned accounts, or both capital accounts (known as 'fixed') which record *only* the capital contributed by each partner and subsequent additions or withdrawals of capital, and current accounts which serve to record all financial matters affecting partners, other than capital.

The latter arrangement is more common, as most partnerships wish to maintain a permanent record of the amounts of capital contributed by each partner, which is not possible with variable capital accounts.

Summary:
The general ledger of a partnership may have:

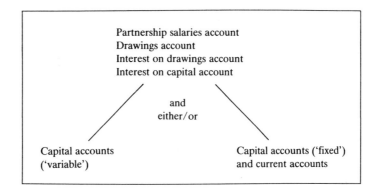

Partnership salaries account
Drawings account
Interest on drawings account
Interest on capital account

and
either/or

Capital accounts ('variable')

Capital accounts ('fixed') and current accounts

Example 1

Mills and Bloggs are in partnership, sharing profits and losses in the ratio of 3:2. Their partnership agreement provides for the following:

Bloggs to be credited with a salary of £7,000 p.a.
Interest to be charged on drawings at 8% p.a.
Interest to be allowed on capital at 6% p.a.

During the year ended 31 December 1986, the partnership made a profit of £30,000 *after* adjusting for the above items. Capital and drawings were as follows:

	Capital £	*Drawings* £
Mills	12,000	8,000
Bloggs	10,000	13,000

The capital remained unchanged throughout the year. The drawings were made in two equal instalments, on 1 March and 1 August. Current accounts are maintained, the balances on 1 January 1986 being:

	£	
Mills	1,250	DR
Bloggs	600	CR

Show the general ledger accounts in the books of the partnership recording the above information.

Solution:

Mills and Bloggs
General Ledger

Partnership salaries a/c

	Mills	Bloggs		Mills	Bloggs
1986			*1986*		
31 Dec Current a/c	—	7,000	31 Dec P&L Appropriation a/c	—	7,000
	——	——		——	——

71

Drawings a/c

	Mills	Bloggs			Mills	Bloggs
1986				**1986**		
1 Mar Cash	4,000	6,500		31 Dec Current a/c	8,000	13,000
1 Aug Cash	4,000	6,500				
	8,000	13,000			8,000	13,000

Interest on drawings a/c

	Mills	Bloggs			Mills	Bloggs
1986				**1986**		
31 Dec P&L Appropriation a/c	400	650		31 Dec Current a/c	400	650

Interest on capital a/c

	Mills	Bloggs			Mills	Bloggs
1986				**1986**		
				31 Dec P&L Appropriation a/c		
31 Dec Current a/c	720	600			720	600

Capital accounts

	Mills	Bloggs			Mills	Bloggs
1986				**1986**		
31 Dec Balances c/f	12,000	10,000		1 Jan Balances b/f	12,000	10,000

Current accounts

	Mills	Bloggs			Mills	Bloggs
1986				**1986**		
1 Jan Balance b/f	1,250	—		1 Jan Balance b/f	—	600
31 Dec Drawings	8,000	13,000		31 Dec Salary	—	7,000
Interest on drawings	400	650		Interest on capital	720	600
Balances c/f	9,070	6,550		Shares of profit	18,000	12,000
	18,720	20,200			18,720	20,200

Workings:

Interest on drawings:

		£
Mills	$8\% \times {}^{10}\!/_{12} \times £4,000 =$	267
	$8\% \times {}^{5}\!/_{12} \times £4,000 =$	133
		400
Bloggs	$8\% \times {}^{10}\!/_{12} \times £6,500 =$	433
	$8\% \times {}^{5}\!/_{12} \times £6,500 =$	217
		650

COMMENTARY

Whilst the capital accounts have remained unchanged, the current accounts have taken all the other relevant information relating to the partners. The columnar format has helped to save time and space in drawing up the accounts.

It is interesting to speculate as to why Bloggs gets a salary; perhaps it is because he is the more active partner of the two: Mills might be elderly and, although contributing both capital and expertise to the firm, plays a less demanding role than his junior partner.

4.3 The partnership appropriation account

When drawing up the final accounts of the partnership, we must be aware that they should fully reflect the financial relationship between the partners. Section 28 of the Partnership Act 1890 declares: 'Partners are bound to render true accounts and full information of all things affecting the partnership to any partner or his legal representative.'

Partners have a joint responsibility for meeting the debts of their business, and so 'full information' is vital if the partners are to be aware of the financial standing of the partnership. For this reason, an 'appropriation account' is shown following the profit and loss account in the financial statements, and a breakdown of the capital and current account position is given on the face of the balance sheet (or in a note attached to it).

Example 2

Show the profit and loss appropriation account and balance sheet extracts for the partnership of Mills and Bloggs (see Example 1).

Solution:

Mills and Bloggs

Profit and Loss Appropriation Account
for the year ended 31 December 1986

	£	£		£	£
Interest on capital:			Net profit b/d (from		
Mills	720		P&L a/c)		30,270*
Bloggs	600	1,320			
			Interest on drawings:		
			Mills	400	
Profit divisible:			Bloggs	650	1,050
Mills	18,000				
Bloggs	12,000	30,000			
		31,320			31,320

Balance Sheet as at 31 December 1986

	£	£	£
Capital accounts:	Mills	Bloggs	
	12,000	10,000	
			22,000
Current accounts:			
Opening balances	(1,250)	600	
Salary	—	7,000	
Interest on capital	720	600	
Shares of profit	18,000	12,000	
	17,470	20,200	
Drawings	8,000	13,000	
Interest on drawings	400	650	
	8,400	13,650	
Closing balances	9,070	6,550	15,620
			37,620

COMMENTARY

The remainder of the final accounts follow the same pattern as that for a sole trader.

*Balancing figure

Summary:

The 'final' accounts of a partnership are shown in Figure 4.1.

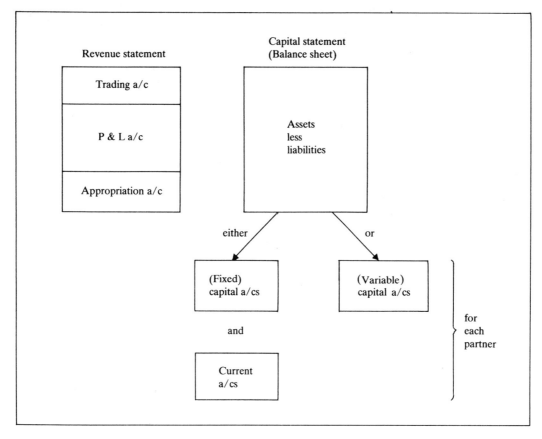

Fig. 4.1   The final accounts of a partnership.

4.4   Goodwill and changes in the structure of a partnership

Although a balance sheet has been described as 'a snapshot of the business at one moment in time' this description fails to state that the camera is fitted with a very narrow lens! Although invaluable as a record of the book value of assets and liabilities, the balance sheet is not able to show such things as:

(a)   the prospects of the business;
(b)   the reputation of the business;
(c)   the price someone might be prepared to pay for the business.

For example, the balance sheet of a practising accountant may appear as follows:

	£	£
Fixed assets (net of depreciation)		
Typewriter	300	
Office furniture (desk, etc.)	600	
		900
Current assets		
Debtors (fees owing)	2,000	
Cash	500	
	2,500	
Current liabilities		
Creditors (rent, etc.)	600	
		1,900
		2,800
Capital		2,800

The accountant might have annual fees of over £50,000 but as he rents his office and does not have any stocks, his business has a 'book value' of less than £3,000. If he wanted to sell his practice to another accountant, he would ask for rather more than £3,000; the normal method for valuing such a business is based on a multiple (e.g. one and a half times) of the annual 'recurring' fees. He would therefore seek

$$1\frac{1}{2} \times £50,000 = £75,000$$

Assuming he was able to sell the business for this sum, he is charging £72,200 (£75,000 − £2,800) for *goodwill*, i.e. the right for the purchaser to take over his profitable, well-run business. Attempts have been made for centuries to give a precise legal definition to goodwill, but, as Lord Macnaghten said in 1910:

'It is a thing very easy to describe, very difficult to define'.

However, an Australian judge (Gowans, J.) made this attempt in 1970:

'The goodwill of a business is the advantage, whatever it may be, which a person gets by continuing to carry on and being entitled to represent to the outside world that he is carrying on a business which has been carried on for some time previously.'

Goodwill might appear in the books of a sole trader, partnership or limited company: in the case of a sole trader it will only appear if it has been purchased when taking over another business (e.g. the accountant quoted previously who took over the practice would show £72,200 as goodwill). It is normal practice to write off such goodwill in the first few years after acquisition, as its continued inclusion on the balance sheet (as an intangible asset) may be misleading owing to the fact that the precise value of goodwill is only known when the business is sold.

Goodwill can be shown in the accounts of a limited company, but this is dealt with separately in Chapter 8.

In the books of a partnership, goodwill takes on a particularly important role. This is because, even though the business is not to be sold, its value must be assessed under any of the following circumstances:

i   a partner dies or retires,
ii   a new partner joins the partnership,
iii   the existing partners decide to alter their profit-sharing ratios.

The actual method of valuation will be left to the partners to decide upon, and the partnership agreement itself may lay down a precise formula for its calculation. Alternatively, especially where a new partner is to be admitted, negotiations will take place so that the value can be reached by mutual agreement. The partners may also take the opportunity to revalue other partnership assets, such as property. A 'revaluation account' will be opened in the general ledger to record the alterations being made to book values.

Once the value of goodwill has been established, the partners have the choice of either recording it in the books, or omitting it entirely. If the former alternative is taken, the balance sheet will contain a goodwill valuation, and a goodwill a/c will be opened in the general ledger. In the latter case, goodwill does not appear in the books, any adjusting entries of value between partners being made within the capital accounts.

ADVANTAGES AND DISADVANTAGES OF RECORDING GOODWILL

Advantages

Goodwill is recognised as an asset of the business, albeit an intangible one. The valuation may form the basis for any future negotiations which might arise or for an adjustment to the composition of the partnership.

Disadvantages

Goodwill valuations are notoriously unreliable, and its inclusion may seriously overstate (or understate) the true value. If goodwill has been included at a low valuation, any attempt at a future date to negotiate a higher value with a prospective purchaser may be unduly prejudiced.

THE EFFECT OF CHANGES TO THE PARTNERSHIP COMPOSITION

In the following, assume that the composition of the partnership prior to the change (the 'old' partnership), was that of three partners, A, B and C sharing profits equally.

1. A partner dies or retires

'Old' partnership

A(⅓)	B(⅓)	C(⅓)

'New' partnership
(C dies or retires)

A(½)	B(½)

Because A and B now own a greater proportion of the business than previously, they owe C or his executors an amount equivalent to his share of the old partnership (i.e. one-third of the agreed value).

2. A new partner joins the partnership

'Old' partnership

A(⅓)	B(⅓)	C(⅓)

'New' partnership
(D joins, profits to be
shared equally)

A(¼)	B(¼)	C(¼)	D(¼)

D is taking part of the value of the business from A, B and C. He must therefore compensate the three 'old' partners (i.e. by paying for one-quarter of the agreed value).

3. A change in profit-sharing ratios

'Old' partnership

A(⅓)	B(⅓)	C(⅓)

'New' partnership
(new proportions 4:3:3)

A(⅖)	B(³⁄₁₀)	C(³⁄₁₀)

As A has increased his profit-sharing entitlement, he must compensate B and C for the value that they have given up.

In each of the above cases, the book-keeping entries required to make the adjustments between the partners will depend upon whether a goodwill account exists in the partnership books.

(a) Where there is a goodwill account:
DR Goodwill   CR 'Old' partners in 'old' profit-sharing ratios — with any increase in valuation of the goodwill (vice-versa for a decrease) at the date of change
(b) Where there is no goodwill account, but an account is to be opened at the date of change:
DR Goodwill   CR 'Old' partners in 'old' profit-sharing ratios — with the full value of goodwill at the date of change
(c) Where goodwill is not to be recorded in the partnership books.
    DR 'New' partners in 'new' profit-sharing ratios   CR 'Old' partners in 'old' profit-sharing ratios — with the full value of goodwill at the date of change.

The following three examples show how to cope with questions involving the three main changes to a partnership.
    Example 3 shows a partner retiring.

Example 4 reflects the situation when a new partner is admitted.

Example 5 shows a change in a profit-sharing ratio.

Example 3 (where a partner retires)

A. Wright, B. Bloor and C. Cornes were partners in a light engineering firm and they shared profits and losses in the ratio 2:2:1. The firm's balance sheet as at 31 December 1982 was as set out below:

Capital accounts	£	£	Fixed assets	£	£
A. Wright		20,000	Freehold property		30,000
B. Bloor		15,000	Equipment		14,500
C. Cornes		10,000			
		45,000			44,500
Current accounts			Current assets		
A. Wright	2,000		Stock of goods	5,750	
B. Bloor	3,000		Debtors	4,750	
C. Cornes	1,250	6,250	Bank	3,000	
		51,250			13,500
Creditors		6,750			
		58,000			58,000

Bloor decided to retire at 31 December 1982, whereupon the partners (including Bloor) revalued the assets as follows:

Freehold property £42,500; equipment £13,250; goodwill £15,000.

Wright and Cornes decided to form a limited company to take over the partnership business and they agreed to retain the revised values for the assets except goodwill which was to be reduced to nil on an equal basis. On 31 December 1982 Wright and Cornes both paid £7,500 into the partnership cash account. The partners' current accounts were transferred to their capital accounts and £12,500 was paid to Bloor on account of the money due to him. The balance was left on loan to the company. The other two partners received from the new company £1 ordinary shares in place of their capital account balances on a £ for £ basis.

Note: The company had an authorised capital of £60,000 in ordinary shares of £1 each.

Required:

Prepare:

(a) A partnership revaluation account.
(b) The partnership capital accounts of Wright, Bloor and Cornes.
(c) The balance sheet of the new company Wright and Cornes Ltd as at 31 December 1982.

(LCCI – Intermediate)

Solution:

(a)   *Partnership Revaluation Account*

1982		£	1982		£
31 Dec Equipment		1,250	31 Dec Freehold property		12,500
			Goodwill		15,000
Surplus on revaluation:					
Wright	10,500				
Bloor	10,500				
Cornes	5,250				
		26,250			
		27,500			27,500

(b)

Partnership Capital Accounts

	Wright	Bloor	Cornes		Wright	Bloor	Cornes
1982				*1982*			
31 Dec				31 Dec			
Cash	—	12,500	—	Balance b/f	20,000	15,000	10,000
Goodwill	7,500	—	7,500	Current a/cs	2,000	3,000	1,250
Loan a/c	—	16,000	—	Cash	7,500	—	7,500
Balances to				Revaluation			
Wright and				a/c	10,500	10,500	5,250
Cornes Ltd	32,500	—	16,500				
	40,000	28,500	24,000		40,000	28,500	24,000

(c)

Wright and Cornes Ltd

Balance Sheet as at 31 December 1982

		£	£
Fixed assets:	Freehold property		42,500
	Equipment		13,250
			55,750
Current assets:	Stock of goods	5,750	
	Debtors	4,750	
	Bank	5,500	
		16,000	
Current liabilities:	Creditors	6,750	
			9,250
			65,000

Issued share capital (Authorised: 60,000 ordinary shares of £1 each)

49,000 ordinary shares of £1 each, fully paid	49,000
Loan: B. Bloor	16,000
	65,000

COMMENTARY

Because Bloor is retiring, Wright and Cornes have to compensate him for the share of the partnership which they are acquiring from him. This is achieved by the entries in the revaluation account, where the increase in the value of the 'old' partnership of £26,250 is being credited to all three partners, whilst the value of goodwill is debited only to the two remaining partners in their capital account. This automatically compensates Bloor for the value that he is passing to Wright and Cornes.

The goodwill account would appear as follows.

1982			*1982*			
31 Dec Revaluation account		15,000	31 Dec Transfer:	Wright		7,500
				Cornes		7,500
		15,000				15,000

If the partners had decided *not* to open a goodwill account in the books, then the revaluation account would have been shown as follows.

1982				*1982*	
31 Dec Equipment			1,250	31 Dec Freehold property	12,500
Surplus on					
revaluation:					
Wright	4,500				
Bloor	4,500				
Cornes	2,250	11,250			
		12,500			12,500

The changes in the distribution of goodwill between the partners is shown as an 'adjustment' in the capital account, using the journal entry:

DR 'New' partners	Wright	7,500	
	Cornes	7,500	
CR 'Old' partners	Wright		6,000
	Bloor		6,000
	Cornes		3,000

The net effect being:

DR	Wright	1,500	
	Cornes	4,500	
CR	Bloor		6,000

The capital accounts would be shown in the following way:

	Wright	Bloor	Cornes		Wright	Bloor	Cornes
1982				*1982*			
31 Dec				31 Dec			
Cash	—	12,500	—	Balance b/f	20,000	15,000	10,000
Loan a/c	—	16,000	—	Current a/c	2,000	3,000	1,250
Adjustment	1,500	—	4,500	Cash	7,500	—	7,500
Balances to				Revaluation a/c	4,500	4,500	2,250
W&C Ltd	32,500	—	16,500	Adjustment	—	6,000	
	34,000	28,500	21,000		34,000	28,500	21,000

The overall effect is identical, regardless of whether or not the goodwill account is used.

Example 4 (where a new partner joins the partnership)

X and Y are in partnership sharing profits and losses equally after allowing X a salary of £3,000 per annum. The following trial balance has been extracted from the accounts after the net profit, which accrued evenly throughout the year, has been calculated for the year ended 30 September 1981.

	DR £	CR £
Net profit		12,000
Fixed assets	11,00	
Debtors	3,700	
Stock	3,100	
Bank	11,200	
Creditors		2,400
Capital account X at 1 October 1980		4,000
Capital account Y at 1 October 1980		6,000
Prepayments and accruals	700	400
Current account X at 1 October 1980		800
Current account Y at 1 October 1980		1,200
Drawings X	3,700	
Drawings Y	3,400	
Suspense account		10,000
	36,800	36,800

It has been decided to admit C, a part-time adviser to the business, as a partner with effect from 1 January 1981, and to share profits on the following basis.

1. Interest at the rate of 12% per annum is to be paid on partners' fixed capital.
2. X is to be credited with a salary of £5,000 per annum and C with £4,000 per annum.
3. The balance of profits and losses are to be shared equally between the partners.

C paid £10,000 cash into the partnership on 1 January 1981 and the double entry made to record this transaction was to debit the bank account and credit a suspense account. The partners have agreed that C's share of goodwill should be valued at £2,000 but that no goodwill account should appear in the books of the partnership.

It has been discovered that X's salary for the year ended 30 September 1980 had not been entered in the accounts and it has been agreed to make the appropriate adjustments by entries in the partners' current accounts.

Required:
(a) The profit and loss appropriation account for the year ended 30 September 1981.
(b) The balance sheet as at 30 September 1981 after the admission of C.

(AEB)

Solution:

(a)

X, Y and C
Profit and Loss Appropriation Account
for the year to 30 September 1981

	£	£		£	£
Net profit for the year					12,000
	3 months to 31 Dec 1980			*9 months to 30 Sep 1981*	
Dividend					
Net profit		3,000			9,000
Less Salaries to partners					
X (³⁄₁₂ × 3,000)	750		(⁹⁄₁₂ × 5,000)	3,750	
C	—	750	(⁹⁄₁₂ × 4,000)	3,000	6,750
		2,250			2,250
Less Interest on partners' capital					
X	—		(12% × ⁹⁄₁₂ × 5,000)	450	
Y	—		(12% × ⁹⁄₁₂ × 7,000)	630	
C	—		(12% × ⁹⁄₁₂ × 8,000)	720	1,800
Net profit to be divided between partners		2,250			450
Divided as follows					
X (½)	1,125		(⅓)	150	
Y (½)	1,125		(⅓)	150	
C —	—	2,250	(⅓)	150	450

(b) *Balance Sheet as at 30 September 1981*

		£	£	£
Fixed assets				11,000
Current assets	Stock		3,100	
	Debtors		3,700	
	Prepayments		700	
	Bank		11,200	
			18,700	
Current liabilities	Creditors	2,400		
	Accruals	400	2,800	15,900
				26,900
Capital accounts (see workings)				
	X	5,000		
	Y	7,000		
	C	8,000		20,000
Current accounts (see workings)				
	X	4,825		
	Y	(1,795)DR		
	C	3,870		6,900
				26,900

Workings:

Capital accounts

	X	Y	C			X	Y	C
				1-10-80 b/f		4,000	6,000	—
1-1-81 Journal	—	—	2,000	1-1-81 Cash		—	—	10,000
30-9-81 c/f	5,000	7,000	8,000	Journal		1,000	1,000	—
	5,000	7,000	10,000			5,000	7,000	10,000

Current accounts

	X	Y	C			X	Y	C
30-9-81 Drawings	3,700	3,400	—	1-10-80 b/f		800	1,200	—
Omitted 1980 Salary	1,500	1,500	—	31-12-80 Salary		750	—	—
c/f	4,825	—	3,870	Net profit		1,125	1,125	—
				30-9-81 Salaries		3,750	—	3,000
				Interest on capital		450	630	720
				Net profit		150	150	150
				Omitted 1980 salary		3,000	—	—
				c/f		—	1,795	—
	10,025	4,900	3,870			10,025	4,900	3,870

Journal

1-1-81	DR	X's	Capital account	2,000	
		Y's	Capital account	2,000	Net:
		C's	Capital account	2,000	X 1,000 CR
					Y 1,000 CR
	CR	X's	Capital account		3,000	C 2,000 DR
		Y's	Capital account		3,000

– Adjustment in respect of the share of goodwill being purchased by C from the existing partners (Goodwill = £2,000 × $\frac{3}{1}$, as the three partners share profits equally).

COMMENTARY

Although this appeared to be a relatively straightforward question, there were several points of difficulty which were included. These were:

(a) the division of the appropriation account into two time periods;
(b) the calculation of salaries and interest;
(c) the treatment of goodwill.

By working through the answer, you will see a full explanation of the way in which individual figures were arrived at. It is a good examination technique to explain how figures have been calculated, and some marks are often awarded by examiners to students who have shown a reasonably correct breakdown of a calculation, even if the final total arrived at is inaccurate.

Example 5 (where partners alter their profit-sharing ratios)

James, Henry and Boot, lawyers, are partners sharing profits 3:2:1. The following summarised trial balance has been prepared at the end of 1979:

	£	£
Fixed capital accounts (1 January 1979)		
James		12,000
Henry		15,000
Boot		10,000
Current accounts: James		800
Henry		2,000
Boot	400	
Fixed assets at cost	29,060	

Accumulated depreciation on fixed assets to 31 December 1979		4,700
Fees invoiced for services rendered during the year		28,600
Business expenses for the year excluding depreciation	8,700	
Expenses owing		280
Depreciation on fixed assets for 1979	1,760	
Stocks (31 December 1979)	275	
Fees owing from clients	2,280	
Goodwill	12,000	
Bank	2,860	
Creditors		95
Drawings: James	6,060	
Henry	7,100	
Boot	2,980	
	73,475	73,475

Under the partnership agreement, interest on fixed capital balances at the commencement of each year is allowed at 8% per annum.

As from 1 January 1980, James intends to play a less active part in the business, and from that date profits will be shared 1:2:1. Goodwill is now valued at £15,000.

Required:

i Prepare the profit and loss account (including the appropriation account) of the partnership for the year ended 31 December 1979.

ii Prepare the partnership balance sheet as at 1 January 1980, effecting any adjustment(s) through the fixed capital accounts.

(LCCI – Intermediate)

Solution:

(i) **James, Henry and Boot**
Profit and Loss Account for the year to 31 December 1979

	£	£
Fees invoiced for services rendered		28,600
Business expenses for the year, excluding depreciation	8,700	
Depreciation	1,760	10,460
Net profit		18,140
Less: Interest on capital		
James	960	
Henry	1,200	
Boot	800	2,960
Net profit available for division		15,180
Divided as follows:		
James ($\frac{1}{2}$)	7,590	
Henry ($\frac{1}{3}$)	5,060	
Boot ($\frac{1}{16}$)	2,530	15,180

(ii) *Balance Sheet as at 1 January 1980*

Fixed assets:	Cost		29,060	
	Depreciation		4,700	24,360
	Goodwill			15,000
				39,360
Current assets:	Stock		275	
	Fees owing		2,280	
	Bank		2,860	
			5,415	
Current liabilities:	Creditors	95	375	5,040
	Expenses owing	280		
			—	44,400

82

Capital accounts (see Workings)

James	13,500	
Henry	16,000	
Boot	10,500	40,000

Current accounts (see Workings)

James	3,290	
Henry	1,160	
Boot	(50)DR	4,400
		44,400

Workings:

(a) Goodwill has increased by £3,000 (£15,000 − £12,000). As there is a goodwill account in the books, this will be credited to the partners in their 'old' profit-sharing ratios, as shown by the following journal entry:

DR	Goodwill	3,000	
CR	James (½)		1,500
	Henry (⅓)		1,000
	Boot (⅙)		500

∴ New capital balances are:

James	12,000 + 1,500 = 13,500
Henry	15,000 + 1,000 = 16,000
Boot	10,000 + 500 = 10,500

(b) *Current accounts*

	James	Henry	Boot		James	Henry	Boot
1-1-79 b/f	—	—	400	1-1-79 b/f	800	2,000	—
31-12-79 Drawings	6,060	7,100	2,980	31-12-79 Interest	960	1,200	800
c/f	3,290	1,160	—	Profit	7,590	5,060	2,530
				c/f	—	—	50
	9,350	8,260	3,380		9,350	8,260	3,380

COMMENTARY

The partners' shares of profits change from:

James (½)	Henry (⅓)	Boot (⅙)

to:

James (¼)	Henry (½)	Boot (¼)

It can be seen that only James' share has decreased, and therefore Henry and Boot must compensate him for the extra value that they are acquiring. This is achieved by distributing the increase in goodwill in the 'old' profit-sharing ratios, which results in James being credited with the full one-half of the updated goodwill valuation at the date of change.

4.5 The dissolution of a partnership

A partnership might be dissolved for many reasons, including:

1. The death of a partner.
2. The bankruptcy of a partner.
3. Agreement by the partners to cease trading.
4. Expiration of a fixed-term or a particular contract, if the partnership had been entered into only for a set period or to undertake a specific undertaking.

Once the decision has been taken to end the partnership, the partners must ensure that assets are realised and liabilities settled. In addition, the individual partners may have to contribute cash if there is an overall deficiency of assets compared with liabilities, or will receive cash if there is a surplus after all liabilities have been paid. Some of the partnership assets may be taken over at a valuation by one or more partners. In such a case a 'fair price' will be agreed upon by the partnership.

The book-keeping mechanism to record the closing off of the partnership's books revolves around a realisation account, which serves as a 'clearing house' for the partnership's assets. The account comprises some or all of the entries shown in Table 4.1.

Table 4.1   Realisation account

Transfer assets (other than cash) at book values	X	Transfer to capital accounts the agreed valuation of assets taken over by partners	X
Cash paid for expenses of realisation	X	Cash received from debtors	X
		Cash received from the sale of assets	X
Profit on realisation transferred to partners' capital accounts	X	(or) Loss on realisation transferred to partners' capital accounts	X
	X		X

In addition to the entries in the realisation account, the financial relationship of the partners with the partnership must also be settled. If current accounts have been maintained, their balances must be transferred to the capital accounts. Under normal circumstances the balances then remaining on the capital accounts will represent the amounts due to be paid by the partners to the partnership (debit balances) or by the partnership to the partners (credit balances). However, it sometimes happens that a partner who owes money to the partnership is unable to pay his debt owing to bankruptcy or other reasons. In such a case, the 'solvent' partners must bear the loss, *not in their normal profit/loss sharing ratios, but in proportion to their capital balances*. This is known as the 'Garner v. Murray' rule, named after a celebrated court case of 1904 which determined this principle. The court took the decision because it held that a loss caused by a partner's insolvency should be distinguished from a normal trading loss: the former thus being a 'capital' loss, to be divided in proportion to partners' capitals.

Example 6

A, B and C were in partnership sharing profits and losses equally. They decided to dissolve the partnership on 30 June 1985, when the balance sheet of the partnership was as follows:

Balance Sheet

	£			£
Capital accounts			Fixed assets	
A	7,200		Goodwill	24,000
B	4,800		Premises	24,000
C	2,400		Plant	7,200
	14,400			55,200
Current accounts			Current assets	
A	9,600		Stock	12,000
B	7,200		Debtors	2,400
C	2,400		Bank	2,400
		19,200		16,800
		33,600		
Creditors		38,400		
		72,000		72,000

Note: There is no partnership agreement.
The following additional information is available.

i   A has decided to continue in business and agrees to take over the premises and plant at an agreed valuation of £28,800 and the stock at £9,600.

ii   Debtors and creditors were realised and paid, respectively, at their book values.

iii   C has been declared a bankrupt.

Prepare the ledger accounts to record the dissolution of the partnership.

Solution:

Note: numbers in brackets, e.g. (1), show the order of entries. These are for the guidance of readers and should not be reproduced in an examination.

(a)

Goodwill a/c

Balance b/f	(1)	24,000	Transfer realisation a/c	(2)	24,000

Premises a/c

Balance b/f	(1)	24,000	Transfer realisation a/c	(2)	24,000

Plant a/c

Balance b/f	(1)	7,200	Transfer realisation a/c	(2)	7,200

Stock a/c

Balance b/f	(1)	12,000	Transfer realisation a/c	(2)	12,000

Debtors a/c

Balance b/f	(1)	2,400	Transfer realisation a/c	(2)	2,400

Creditors a/c

Cash	(19)	38,400	Balance b/f	(1)	38,400

Cash book (Bank)

Balance b/f	(1)	2,400	Cash to B	(17)	480
Debtors	(7)	2,400	Cash to creditors	(18)	38,400
Cash from A	(15)	34,080			
		38,880			38,880

Capital a/cs

	A	B	C		A	B	C
Realisation a/c:				Balances b/f (1)	7,200	4,800	2,400
assets taken over (5)	38,400	—	—	Transfer current			
Loss on realisation (9)	9,600	9,600	9,600	a/cs (11)	9,600	7,200	2,400
Transfer C's				Transfer C's			
deficiency* (13)	2,880	1,920	—	deficiency (12)	—	—	4,800
Cash (16)	—	480	—	Cash (14)	34,080	—	—
	50,880	12,000	9,600		50,880	12,000	9,600

Current a/cs

	A	B	C		A	B	C
Transfer capital							
a/cs (10)	9,600	7,200	2,400	Balances b/f (1)	9,600	7,200	2,400

Realisation a/c

Transfer assets:		A: assets taken over (4)		38,400
Goodwill (3)	24,000	Cash from debtors (6)		2,400
Premises (3)	24,000	Loss on realisation to		
Plant (3)	7,200	capital a/cs A (8) 9,600		
Stock (3)	12,000	B (8) 9,600		
Debtors (3)	2,400	C (8) 9,600		
				28,800
	69,600			69,600

COMMENTARY

C is bankrupt but owes the partnership £4,800 on his capital account. Because of the Garner *v.* Murray rule, the solvent partners have to bear the loss in proportion to their capital balances instead of their profit/loss-sharing ratios.

*Divided in proportion to A and B's capitals (7,200:4,800) as per Garner *v.* Murray rule.

Note that the *last* entry is that of £38,400 cash paid to creditors. This should be obvious when you consider that there is only £4,800 available in the bank account prior to the settlement of the partners' capital account balances.

4.6 Partnership amalgamations

Where two or more partnerships combine to form a larger enterprise, the entries required will be similar to those for a partnership dissolution with realisation accounts being opened in each firm's books. A 'new partnership' account will be opened which is debited with the agreed valuations of the assets to be taken over by the new business, the realisation account being credited. Example 7 will help to show how the amalgamation is recorded.

Example 7

A and B, and C and D are two partnerships. Profit-sharing ratios were 6:4 for A and B, and 3:1 for C and D. They have decided to combine their businesses under the trading name of 'Letters & Co' as from 1 January 1985.

The balance sheets of the two partnerships as at 31 December 1984 were as follows:

A and B

		£	£		£
Capital accounts	A	25,000		Freehold property	20,000
	B	21,000		Fixtures	10,000
			46,000	Vehicles	10,000
				Stock	9,000
Current accounts	A	1,000		Debtors	3,000
	B	500		Bank	4,000
			1,500		
Creditors			8,500		
			56,000		56,000

C and D

		£	£		£
Capital accounts	C	9,000		Fixtures	8,000
	D	4,000		Vehicles	3,000
			13,000	Stock	4,000
				Debtors	2,000
Current accounts	C	2,000		Bank	1,400
	D	(600) DR			
			1,400		
Creditors			4,000		
			18,400		18,400

For the purpose of the amalgamation, the partners agreed to the following:

1. D was to take over the vehicle appearing in the balance sheet of C and D, at a valuation of £1,000.
2. The assets of the two partnerships are to be valued as shown below:

	A and B £	C and D £
Freehold property	25,000	—
Fixtures	8,000	6,000
Vehicles	8,000	—
Stock	8,000	4,000
Debtors	Book value less 2%	Book value less 5%

3. The goodwill of the partnerships is to be valued at £10,000 for A and B, £5,000 for C and D.
4. The new profit-sharing ratio of Letters & Co is to be 4:3:2:1 for A, B, C and D respectively.
5. The total capital of Letters & Co is to be £70,000 provided by the partners in proportion

to their new profit-sharing ratios. Adjustments are to be made in cash and all partners have private funds for this purpose.

(a) Prepare the realisation accounts of the partnerships of A and B, and C and D.

(b) Show the capital accounts (in columnar form) of the partnerships of A and B, and C and D, including the entries required to close the accounts.

(c) Prepare the opening balance sheet of Letters & Co, showing clearly the working capital and the capital employed.

(ULSEB)

Solution:

(a)

A and B
Realisation Account

Transfer book values:		Assets taken over by Letters & Co:	
Freehold property	20,000	Goodwill	10,000
Fixtures	10,000	Freehold property	25,000
Vehicles	10,000	Fixtures	8,000
Stock	9,000	Vehicles	8,000
Debtors	3,000	Stock	8,500
		Debtors (3,000 − 60)	2,940
	52,000		
Profit: A 6,264			
B 4,176	10,440		
	£62,440		£62,440

C and D
Realisation Account

Transfer book values		Vehicle taken by D	1,000
Fixtures	8,000	Assets taken over by Letters & Co	
Vehicles	3,000	Goodwill	5,000
Stock	4,000	Fixtures	6,000
Debtors	2,000	Stock	4,000
		Debtors (2,000 − 100)	1,900
	17,000		
Profit: C 675			
D 225	900		
	17,900		17,900

A and B
Capital Accounts

	A	B		A	B
			b/f	25,000	21,000
New capital balances in			Current accounts trf.	1,000	500
Letters & Co	28,000	21,000	Profit from realisation		
Cash from			account	6,264	4,176
Letters & Co	4,264	4,676			
	32,264	25,676		32,264	25,676

C and D
Capital Accounts

	C	D		C	D
Current account trf.	—	600	b/f	9,000	4,000
Vehicle taken over	—	1,000	Current account trf.	2,000	—
New Capital balances in			Profit from realisation		
Letters & Co	14,000	7,000	account	675	225
			Cash to Letters & Co	2,325	4,375
	14,000	8,600		14,000	8,600

(c)

Letters & Co

Balance Sheet as at 1 January 1985

Fixed assets:	Goodwill		15,000
	Freehold property		25,000
	Fixtures		14,000
	Vehicles		8,000
			62,000
Current assets:	Stock		12,500
	Debtors	5,000	
	Less: Provision for doubtful debts	160	4,840
	Bank (see Workings)		3,160
			20,500
Less: Current liabilities:	Creditors		12,500
	Working capital		8,000
			£70,000

Capital employed A			28,000
B			21,000
C			14,000
D			7,000
			£70,000

Workings:

Bank balances transferred from A and B			4,000
from C and D			1,400
			5,400
Add: Cash from C		2,325	
Cash from D		4,375	6,700
			12,100
Less: Cash to A		4,264	
Cash to B		4,676	
			8,940
Balance as shown in balance sheet			£ 3,160

COMMENTARY

The partners have agreed on the amount of capital to be introduced into Letters & Co, and they must either 'top up' their existing capitals or have part of their excess capital refunded.

Note that the creditors' totals in the two partnerships are simply combined on the balance sheet of the new business.

4.7 Conversion of a partnership into a limited company

At the beginning of this chapter it was seen how a sole trader might take the decision to share the ownership of his business with one or more persons by establishing a partnership. For reasons discussed in Chapter 6, there may come a time when the partnership decides to change its form of business organisation into that of a limited company. The partners will receive shares in the company in return for transferring their portion of the partnership value.

A simple illustration of such a conversion was given in Example 3 above. Although not required in that question, a realisation account would be opened, with asset values being debited in the normal way, and the 'purchase consideration' (shares in the new company and possibly cash or debentures) being credited ('new company' account debited). The profit/loss on realisation is then transferred to the partners' capital accounts. The capital accounts are closed by firstly transferring each partner's portion of the value of shares, etc. to the debit of his account, with the 'new company' account being credited. Secondly, each partner pays in or withdraws cash to clear the capital account balance remaining.

Example 8

Thomas Ward and Edward Grant are in partnership, and at 1 January 1980 they agreed to sell their business to Laws Ltd. The partnership balance sheet was as follows:

Balance Sheet as at 31 December 1979

Capital accounts	£	£	Fixed assets	£	£
Thomas Ward	12,000		Freehold premises		6,000
Edward Grant	8,000		Plant and machinery		4,500
		20,000	Fixtures and fittings		1,200
					11,700
Current accounts			*Current assets*		
Thomas Ward	200		Stock	5,000	
Edward Grant	350		Sundry debtors	6,000	
		550	Balance at bank	1,250	12,250
Current liabilities					
Sundry creditors		3,400			
		£23,950			£23,950

Laws Ltd was a new company formed to purchase the above partnership business. Its authorised share capital was £150,000 made up of 50,000 8% preference shares of £1 each, and 100,000 ordinary shares of £1 each.

The company agreed to take over all the assets except the bank account, and also agreed to take over the responsibility for payment of the creditors. The company valued the acquired assets as follows:

	£
Freehold premises	10,000
Plant and machinery	3,500
Fixtures and fittings	600
Stock	4,600

The company also agreed to pay £5,850, included in the purchase price, for the total debtors taken over. The purchase price was to be £25,000, and the company proposed to settle this amount by the issue at par of 18,000 £1 ordinary shares, issued as fully paid to the partners, the balance of the purchase price to be settled in cash on 15 January 1980.

Required:

In the books of the partnership, show the entries necessary, in the following accounts, to close the business:

1. Realisation account.
2. Bank account.
3. Partners' capital accounts.
4. Business purchase account (Laws Ltd account).

Note: Assume that the share distribution was made in the capital ratio of the partners at 31 December 1979.

(LCCI – Intermediate)

Solution:

Realisation Account (T. Ward and E. Grant)

(1)

1980		£	1980		£
1.1	Freehold premises	6,000	1.1	Creditors	3,400
	Plant and machinery	4,500		Laws Ltd (business	
	Fixtures and fittings	1,200		purchases a/c)	25,000
	Stock	5,000			
	Debtors	6,000			
	Profit on realisation				
	to				
	Capital a/cs:				
	T. Ward 2,850				

	E. Grant	2,850		
			5,700	
			28,400	28,400

(2)

Bank Account

1980		£	1980		£
1.1	Balance b/d	1,250	15.1	Capital a/cs: T. Ward	4,250
15.1	Laws Ltd (business			E. Grant	4,000
	purchase a/c)	7,000			
		8,250			8,250

(3)

Capital Accounts

1980		Ward £	Grant £	1980		Ward £	Grant £
1.1	Laws Ltd	10,800	7,200	1.1	Balances b/d	12,000	8,000
	(shares)			1.1	Current a/cs	200	350
15.1	Bank	4,250	4,000	1.1	Realisation a/c	2,850	2,850
		15,050	11,200			15,050	11,200

(4)

Business Purchase Account (Laws Ltd)

1980		£	1980		£
1.1	Realisation account	25,000	15.1	Capital a/cs (shares)	
				T. Ward 10,800	
				E. Grant 7,200	18,000
			15.1	Bank	7,000
		25,000			25,000

Workings:
Division of shares between the partners:

$$18,000 \times \frac{12,000}{20,000} = 10,800 \text{ for T. Ward}$$

$$18,000 \times \frac{8,000}{20,000} = 7,200 \text{ for E. Grant}$$

COMMENTARY

As the company is taking over responsibility for the payment of creditors, the realisation account is credited with £3,600. Often the partnership itself will pay creditors, as in the previous example.

Exercises

4.1 Explain the importance of a partnership agreement.

4.2 R.S. and L.P. were in partnership as merchants. An inexperienced book-keeper prepared the following statement in respect of their trading for the year 1985.

Profit and Loss Account as at 31 December 1985

	£	£		£
Stock 1-1-85		9,600	Sales	44,800
Purchases			Sales returns	1,040
Goods for resale	30,000		Discount allowed	240
Furniture and fixtures	1,200		Stock 31-12-85	8,000
		31,200	Carriage outwards	140

Purchases returns		600	Amount received from		
		41,400	sale of old delivery van		
			(book value £2,400)		2,000
Discount received		200	Bad debts written off		100
Wages		2,800	Bank overdraft		4,860
Sundry expenses		800			
Drawings					
R.S.	2,500				
L.P.	3,300	5,800			
Insurance (including					
£60 prepaid)		500			
Rent and rates		1,720			
Carriage inwards		160			
Purchase of new					
delivery van (28-12-85)		4,800			
Partner's salaries:					
R.S.	1,500				
L.P.	1,500	3,000			
		61,180			61,180

Assume that the figures are arithmetically correct and the descriptions mean what they say.

Required:
Prepare a trading, profit and loss and appropriation account in proper form for the year 1985.

(LCCI – Intermediate)

4.3 Ray Dyo, Harry Ull and Val Vez are in partnership, trading under the name of Radtel Services, as radio and television suppliers and repairers, sharing profits and losses in the ratio one-half, one-third and one-sixth, respectively. Val Vez works full-time in the business with responsibility for general administration for which she receives a partnership salary of £4,000 per annum.

All partners receive interest on capital at 5% per annum and interest on any loans made to the firm, also at 5% per annum.

It has also been agreed that Val Vez should receive not less than £4,000 per annum in addition to her salary. Any deficiency between this guaranteed figure and her actual aggregate of interest on capital, plus residual profit (or less residual loss) less interest on drawings, is to be borne by Dyo and Ull in the ratio in which they share profits and losses; such deficiency can be recouped by Dyo and Ull at the earliest opportunity during the next two consecutive years provided that Val Vez does not receive less than the guaranteed minimum described above. During the year ended 30 September 1983, Dyo and Ull had jointly contributed a deficiency of £1,500.

Radtel Services rents two sets of premises—one, a workshop where repairs are carried out, the other, a shop from which radio and television sets are sold. The offices are situated above the shop and are accounted for as part of the shop.

The workshop and shop are regarded as separate departments and managed, respectively, by Phughes and Sokkitt who are each remunerated by a basic salary plus a commission of one-ninth of their departments' profits after charging their commission.

On 30 September 1984, the trial balance of the firm was:

	£	£
Stocks at 1 October 1983:		
shop (radio and television sets)	19,750	
workshop (spares, components, etc.)	8,470	

Purchases:	£	£
radio and television sets	155,430	
spares, components, etc.	72,100	
Turnover:		
sales of radio and television sets		232,600
repair charges		127,000
Wages and salaries (employees):		
shop and offices	54,640	
workshop	18,210	
Prepaid expenses (at 30 September 1984)	640	
Accrued expenses (at 30 September 1984)		3,160
Provision for doubtful debts at 1 October 1983		920
Rent and rates:		
shop and offices	7,710	
workshop	8,450	
Stationery, telephones, insurance:		
shop and offices	2,980	
workshop	1,020	
Heating and lighting:		
shop and offices	4,640	
workshop	3,950	
Debtors	4,460	
Creditors		15,260
Bank	48,540	
Cash	960	
Other general expenses:		
shop and offices	3,030	
workshop	2,830	
Depreciation:		
shop and offices (including vehicles)	2,400	
workshop	2,580	
Shop fittings (cost)	17,060	
Workshop tools and equipment (cost)	55,340	
Vehicles (cost)	27,210	
Discount received:		
shop		420
workshop		390
Bank loan (repayable in 1988)		15,000
Loan from Harry Ull		10,000
Capital accounts:		
R. Dyo		40,000
H. Ull		40,000
V. Vez		20,000
Current accounts (after drawings have been debited):		
R. Dyo	290	
H. Ull		1,040
V. Vez		920
Loan interest:		
bank loan	2,400	
loan from H. Ull	500	
Provision for depreciation:		
shop fittings		3,190
workshop tools and equipment		10,020
vehicles		5,670
	£525,590	£525,590

The following matters are to be taken into account:

Manager's commissions.
Partnership salary (Vez).
Interest on partners' capital accounts (these have not altered during the year).
Interest on partners' drawings: Dyo £70; Ull £30; Vez £20.
Closing stocks: shop £31,080; worksop £10,220.
Provision for doubtful debts at 30 September 1984, £540.
Residual profits/losses.

Note: Loan interest and the movement in the provision for bad debts are regarded as 'shop' items.

Required:
(a) Prepare columnar departmental trading and profit and loss accounts and a partnership appropriation account for the year ended 30 September 1984 and the partnership balance sheet at that date.
(b) Complete the posting of the partners' current accounts for the year.

(ACCA – Level 1)

4.4 (a) Explain what is meant by goodwill in the accounting context, and give an illustration of how it arises in the books of a business.
(b) Give the different reasons why a purchaser of an established business may be willing to pay more for the business than the net value of the tangible assets.
(c) Explain briefly the different circumstances under which goodwill may arise in the books of a partnership.

(WJEC)

4.5 What are the arguments for and against the inclusion of goodwill in the books of a partnership?

4.6 Aye, Bee and Cee are in partnership, sharing profits and losses in the ratio 3:2:1. On 1 January 1984 Dee is admitted into the partnership and it is agreed that profits and losses will be shared equally.

On 31 December 1983 the balance sheet of the partnership stood as follows:

Capital accounts	£	Fixed assets	£
Aye	22,000	Freehold Premises	20,000
Bee	18,000	Plant	15,000
Cee	6,000	Motor vehicles	10,000
Current liabilities		*Current assets*	
Creditors	23,000	Stock	6,000
		Debtors	12,000
		Bank	6,000
	69,000		69,000

The four partners agree on the following adjustments.

Goodwill is valued at £18,000; revised values were placed on the freehold premises (£25,000) and the plant (£12,000). It was also agreed to reduce the debtors total by £2,000 because a customer, A. Jackson, may not pay his account.

These adjustments were decided upon for the sole purpose of ascertaining the current valuation of the business and only the partners' capital accounts are affected by the revaluations. Dee is not able to introduce cash or assets into the partnership and so the other partners agree to let him pay for his share of the business out of future profits.

On 1 April 1984, Aye decides to retire, on the following terms:

(a) He will receive £8,000 payable by cheque immediately.
(b) The balance on Aye's capital account is to be left on loan with the partnership.

93

(c)   Goodwill is to be valued at the greater of either
   i   £18,000
or   ii   Twice the average profits of the partnership over the previous three years.
         The profits of those years were:

         Year to 31 December 1983   £13,000
         Year to 31 December 1982   £ 6,000
         Year to 31 December 1981   £12,500

No goodwill account is to be opened in the books of the partnership.

(d)   The remaining partners will continue to share profits and losses equally.

   On 31 March 1984 the balance sheet of the partnership stood as follows:

	£		£
Capital accounts	46,000	Fixed assets	
Current liabilities:		Freehold premises	20,000
Creditors	22,000	Plant	15,000
		Motor vehicles	10,000
		Current assets:	
		Stock	8,000
		Debtors	10,000
		Bank	5,000
	68,000		68,000

Note:

(a)   Balance sheet valuations of fixed assets remain as at 31 December 1983.

(b)   Any profit or loss which may have arisen during the period from 1 January 1984 to 31 March 1984 is to be ignored.

(c)   A. Jackson, who still owed £2,000 at 31 March 1984, was declared bankrupt on 3 May 1984. By a majority vote of the partners, it had been decided not to provide for this debt in the balance sheet as at 31 March 1984.

(a)   You are required to prepare:
   i   The partnership balance sheet immediately after Dee's admission on 1 January 1984, clearly showing the capital account balances for each of the four partners.
   ii   The partnership balance sheet immediately after Aye's retirement on 1 April, clearly showing the capital account balances for the three remaining partners and the balance of Aye's loan account.

(b)   What is meant by the 'goodwill' of a partnership?

(c)   The partners had been aware that A. Jackson's account was doubtful in January 1984, but no adjustment was made in the balance sheet at 31 March 1984.
   i   If provision had been made, how would that have affected the balance on Aye's loan account immediately after his retirement?
   ii   Which fundamental accounting principle should have influenced the partnership when deciding whether or not to provide for the doubtful debt?

(ULSEB)

4.7   Chan, Ten and Hiew were in partnership sharing profits and/or losses in the ratio 3:1:1. At 31 December 1982 their balance sheet was as follows:

Balance Sheet as at 31 December 1982

Capital accounts	£	Fixed assets	£
Chan	80,000	Freehold premises	84,000
Ten	36,000	Motor vehicles	16,600
Hiew	12,000	Fixtures and fittings	8,400
	128,000		109,000
		Goodwill	4,000

Current liabilities		*Current assets*		
Creditors	4,350	Stocks	4,980	
		Debtors	8,240	
		Balance at bank	6,130	19,350
	132,350			132,350

On 1 January 1983 the partners agreed to sell their business to Singapore Stores Co, who agreed to take over the following assets at the following valuations:

	£
Freehold premises	90,000
Motor vehicles	10,000
Fixtures and fittings	5,000
Stocks	3,000

The Singapore Stores Co also agreed to pay £6,000 for the goodwill of the partnership, and settled the amount due by a cash payment on 5 January 1983. The expenses of the dissolution of the partnership were paid by the partners from the business bank account on 3 January 1983, amounting to £440.

The partners collected their own debts from their customers, realising £7,960. The partners also paid the debts due to their suppliers, by paying £4,100, which was accepted as full settlement.

Required:
Prepare the following accounts in the books of the partnership, to show the closing of the partnership:

Realisation account.
Partner's capital accounts.
Singapore Stores Co. account
Partnership's bank account.

(LCCI – Intermediate)

CHAPTER 5

Accounting Standards: procedures to be followed and concepts to be observed

5.1 Introduction

If you buy a map to enable you to find your way to a certain destination, or to explore a particular locality, you naturally assume that the map-maker has followed the usual conventions relating to his profession: that the top edge of the map represents 'north'; that the scale of the map has been applied consistently over the entire area covered; and that the symbols used accurately reflect the physical nature of the landscape which is represented.

The accountant, as with the map-maker, must also follow 'usual conventions' when drawing up a set of accounts. The reason for this is simply so that the user of the accounting information can be assured that the statements have been drawn up according to best practice as recognised by the accountancy profession as a whole, and not merely according to the whim of the individual accountant. The interpretation of 'best practice' has been evolving since the early days of accounting, although it is only in comparatively recent times that Statements of Standard Accounting Practice (SSAPs) have been issued by the major professional accountancy bodies to describe the recommended procedures and practices to be adopted by their members when faced with particular accounting problems or circumstances.

Although some SSAPs cover relatively routine matters such as how to account for value added tax, or the treatment of government grants, there are many SSAPs which are very complex. In this chapter, the reader will find a summary of only those SSAPs which are relevant to examination syllabuses at this level, and students are recommended to refer to an up-to-date syllabus, to confirm which of the SSAPs may be examinable. A copy of all current SSAPs may be obtained by writing to The Institute of Chartered Accountants in England and Wales, Moorgate Place, London EC2P 2BJ, enclosing the appropriate fee.

5.2 Background to accounting standards

The late 1960s saw a growing public awareness of the divergencies in accounting practice between companies, often resulting in misleading information being given, and a lack of comparability in published financial statements. In addition, companies were able to indulge in 'creative accounting' in order to present their figures in the best possible light to facilitate takeover bids or to raise additional share capital.

As a result of widespread criticism of existing standards of reporting, an Accounting Standards Steering Committee (subsequently renamed the Accounting Standards Committee) was set up in 1970 by the six major British accountancy bodies. The terms of reference of the committee were to:

(a) review the standards of financial accounting and reporting;
(b) publish consultative documents (known as 'exposure drafts') with a view to developing accounting standards;
(c) propose accounting standards to the councils of the six accountancy bodies comprising the committee;

(d) consult with representatives of industry, commerce, government, finance, etc. about such standards.

The first SSAP was issued in January 1971, and since that date the number has risen to the mid-twenties. A number of standards have been revised and reissued during the period, and two have been withdrawn. It is likely that the process of standard-setting will continue for the foreseeable future. Critics of SSAPs argue that, *inter alia*, certain standards may be appropriate for some companies but not for others and that the Accounting Standards Committee may be influenced by lobbying or governmental pressure when arriving at their decisions. However, the advocates of SSAPs would argue that they reduce the risks of 'creative accounting' distorting financial results and also that they enable the accountancy profession to discuss major topics and decide upon the best ways of treating them within the financial statements of the business concerned.

If individual members of the major accountancy bodies decide to ignore SSAPs when preparing accounting statements* then they run the risk, in extreme cases, of being fined or excluded from membership.

5.3 The accounting standards

As stated earlier in the chapter, the depth of knowledge required by students regarding SSAPs will depend upon the syllabus of the examination for which they are entering. It is advisable therefore to determine the specific syllabus require-ments prior to embarking on a detailed study of this topic.

SSAP 1   ACCOUNTING FOR THE RESULTS OF ASSOCIATED COMPANIES

This topic is covered in Chapter 8.

SSAP 2   DISCLOSURE OF ACCOUNTING POLICIES

The standard identifies and defines three terms which are used when attempting to describe the assumptions upon which financial statements are based: *fundamental accounting concepts*, *accounting bases* and *accounting policies*.

1. Fundamental accounting concepts (sometimes referred to as conventions or postulates) are defined as 'broad basic assumptions which underlie the periodic financial accounts of business enterprises'. It goes on to mention four specific concepts: the 'going concern' concept, the 'accruals' concept, the 'consistency' concept and the 'prudence' concept. These are dealt with in detail below.
2. Accounting bases are defined as 'the methods which have been developed for expressing or applying fundamental accounting concepts to financial trans-actions and items.' Examples of accounting bases include the procedure of charging depreciation on the fixed assets of the business, and the valuation methods for stocks and work-in-progress.
3. Accounting policies are defined as 'the specific accounting bases judged by business enterprises to be most appropriate to their circumstances and adopted by them for the purpose of preparing their financial accounts'. Examples of accounting policies include the choice of the 'straight line' basis for charging depreciation, and the 'first in, first out' method of valuing stocks.

The standard requires that, if accounts are prepared on the basis of assumptions which differ in material respects from any of the four fundamental accounting concepts stated in paragraph (1) above, the facts should be explained. It further states 'In the absence of a clear statement to the contrary, there is a presumption that the four fundamental concepts have been observed.'

Finally, it states that 'The accounting policies followed for dealing with items. . . should be disclosed by way of note to the accounts.'

*SSAPs apply to all financial accounts which are 'intended to give a true and fair view of financial position and profit and loss'.

Hanson Trust plc and subsidiaries

Accounting policies

(a) Accounting convention

The accounts have been prepared using the historical cost convention adjusted for revaluations of certain fixed assets.

(b) Basis of consolidation

The consolidated accounts incorporate audited accounts for the company and its subsidiaries.

(c) Related companies

The results include the relevant proportion of the profit of related companies based on their latest audited accounts. In the consolidated balance sheet the investments in related companies are shown at the group's share of underlying net assets.

(d) Sales turnover

Sales turnover represents the net amounts charged to customers in respect of services rendered and goods supplied.

(e) Tangible fixed assets

The cost of fixed assets is shown, where applicable, after deduction of government grants. Assets acquired under finance leases are capitalised and outstanding instalments are shown in creditors. No depreciation is provided on freehold land except where mineral reserves are being depleted when amortisation is provided on the basis of tonnage extracted. Depreciation of other fixed assets is calculated to write off their cost or valuation over expected useful lives.

(f) Deferred taxation

Deferred taxation is provided in respect of timing differences except where the liability is not expected to arise in the foreseeable future.

(g) Stocks

Stocks are valued at the lower of cost and net realisable value. Cost includes an addition for overheads where appropriate.

(h) Research and development

Expenditure on research and development is written off in the year in which it is incurred.

(i) Pensions

The company and its major subsidiaries operate pension schemes covering the majority of employees. The schemes are funded by contributions partly from the employees and partly from the companies at rates determined by independent actuaries in the light of regular valuations. Such contributions are held in trustee administered funds completely independent of the group's finances.

(j) Foreign currencies

Balance sheets and profit and loss accounts of overseas companies are translated at rates ruling at the balance sheet date. Differences on translation arising from changes in the sterling value of overseas net assets at the beginning of the accounting year, or at the date of any later capital injection, due to subsequent variations in exchange rates are shown as a movement on the statement of retained reserves. Other exchange differences are dealt with in the profit and loss account.

Fig. 5.1 Hanson Trust plc – disclosure of accounting policies.

THE CONCEPTS IN DETAIL

(a) The 'going concern' concept

Under this concept it is assumed, unless stated otherwise, that the business enterprise will continue in operational existence for the foreseeable future.

The significance of the concept is perhaps best understood by looking at the situation if a business can *not* be regarded as a 'going concern'. In such a case the balance sheet is likely to contain several totally unrealistic valuations, particularly for fixed assets and stock. This is because the forced termination of a company's business almost invariably leads to the disposal of fixed assets and stock at minimal prices, often by way of auction. Estimates of these lower valuations must be made and incorporated within the balance sheet of a company which is no longer a 'going concern'.

(b) The 'accruals' concept

This is also known as the 'matching' concept, whereby revenue and costs are accounted for as they are earned or incurred, *not* as money is received or paid, and they should be matched with one another so that, for example, the cost of goods should not be charged against profit until those goods have been sold. Other implications of this concept include the following:

  (i)   The cost of fixed assets should be matched with the period of their usage, by apportioning the diminution in value over the asset's life by means of depreciation.
  (ii) An adjustment will be made in the accounts for expenses incurred within the accounting period but not paid for until after the end of the period (e.g. an accrual for electricity).
  (iii) An adjustment will be made in the accounts for payments made within the accounting period for expenses which have not been fully utilised within the period (e.g. a prepayment of insurance).

(c) The 'consistency' concept

This concept is that the same accounting treatment of items should be adopted from one period to the next.

Note that this is not a rigid requirement, for if a better way of treating an item becomes apparent then this revised treatment should be adopted. The company's accounts will contain a note explaining the nature of, and the reasons for, the revised treatment.

(d) The 'prudence' concept

Also known as 'conservatism', this concept states that revenue and profits should not be anticipated but should only be included in the profit and loss account when *realised* in the form of cash or other asset (e.g. as a debtor). In addition, provision is made for all known liabilities (expenses and losses) either where the amount is known with certainty, or a reasonable estimate can be made.

The prudence concept is of paramount importance to the users of accounting information, as it ensures that the accounting statements have not been drawn up on the basis of over-optimistic or speculative forecasts, and that due consideration has been taken of the likely impact of all foreseeable expenses and losses. If there is a conflict between any of the concepts when determining the treatment of a particular item, the prudence concept takes precedence.

The concept is not without its critics, however, who argue that an over-cautious approach may result in a company being undervalued and an easy prey for takeover bids at unrealistically low levels.

SSSAP 2 AND THE COMPANIES ACT

The four accounting concepts listed in SSAP 2 have statutory backing, being included in the 1985 Companies Act. The Act refers to these concepts as 'fundamental principles', and adds two other principles of its own:

i   It is not permissible to *set off* amounts representing assets or income against amounts representing liabilities or expenditure, or vice-versa.

ii   In determining the *aggregate amount* of any item in the accounts, the amount of each component item must be determined separately.

Whilst (i) above is self explanatory, item (ii) requires some explanation.

Example 1

A company has stocks of five separate products, A, B, C, D and E. At its year-end, the value of the stocks was recorded as follows.

	Cost	*Net realisable value**
	£	£
A	18,000	24,000
B	15,000	9,000
C	34,000	37,000
D	10,000	15,000
E	4,000	5,000
	81,000	90,000

At what value should stock be shown in the balance sheet?

Solution:
Due to the principle that the value of assets should be determined separately, the value of each stock item must be calculated.

The basic rule for stock valuation (see SSAP9) is that stock should be valued at the *lower of cost and net realisable value*. Consequently, the valuations must be:

	£
A	18,000
B	9,000
C	34,000
D	10,000
E	4,000
Total valuation	75,000

This contrasts with the 'combined' lower figure of £81,000, which cannot be used.

Finally, there is one important provision contained within the Companies Act which has a direct influence over the way in which the concepts are applied. Known colloquially as the 'true and fair view override', the Act states that the requirement for the financial statements to show a 'true and fair view' shall over-ride *all other requirements of the Act*. Thus, if by slavishly following a fundamental concept, the accounts fail to show a 'true and fair view' then there is no alternative but to *abandon the use of that concept*, with an explanatory note being given in the accounts giving full particulars of the circumstances.

'NON-STATUTORY CONCEPTS'

Whilst SSAP 2 (and the Companies Act) contains four fundamental concepts, there are a number of other concepts which, although not given the status of inclusion in either a Standard or Companies Act, are nevertheless of great importance in providing a full conceptual framework to the accounts. Some of these other concepts are listed below.

The business entity concept

The financial affairs of the owner or owners of the business should be kept separate from those of the business itself.

The cost concept

The assets of the business should normally be recorded at the price paid for them,

*the value, net of expenses, which the stock would realise on disposal.

except where a diminution in value has occurred, in which case prudence dictates that a lower value be incorporated. This concept is, however, modified to the extent that it is normal practice for freehold land and buildings to be revalued at periodic intervals, provided that the revaluation is made objectively. It is worth noting at this point that we shall look at an alternative accounting system in Chapter 10, 'Current Cost Accounting', which does not abide by the 'cost concept'.

The duality concept

The financial transactions of the business are capable of interpretation between value received and value given, and that the basis of double-entry book-keeping is that the sum total of the business's assets at any date will exactly equal the sum total of the business's liabilities.

The materiality concept

'Insignificant items do not deserve over-complicated treatment in the accounts.' For example, pencils purchased by a business should not be classified as fixed assets even though they may last several years. They should be 'written off' to the stationery account.

The money measurement concept

It is assumed that the assets and liabilities of a company are capable of being measured in a common currency, regardless of the nature of those assets and liabilities. However, there are a number of beneficial (or adverse) influences on a company's prosperity which are not capable of being so measured, including: a dynamic managing director; a contented and productive work force; a poor record of dealing with customer's complaints.

The 'time intervals' concept

The financial statements will be drawn up to cover a specific time period, e.g. a year. This is done for various reasons, including the need for annual accounts to be submitted for taxation purposes or to comply with company legislation, and also as an aid to comparability of figures between periods. The time period is, however, artificial in the sense that the trading activities of the business are geared to the calendar year rather than the financial year, the latter being created by accountants for the reason given previously.

SSAP 3   EARNINGS PER SHARE

This standard only applies to listed companies (i.e. those public companies whose shares are traded on the stock market). The earnings per share (eps) is calculated, in simple terms, by the following formula:

$$\text{eps} - \frac{\underline{\text{Net profit before extraordinary items}^* - (\text{tax} + \text{preference dividends})}}{\text{Number of ordinary shares in issue}}$$

The reason for the inclusion of an eps figure in published accounts is to provide a simple measure of comparison between the results of companies. It is of particular importance to potential investors in companies, as one of the most commonly used indicators of a company's standing in the eyes of the stock market is the *price/earnings* (p/e) *ratio* which is calculated in the following way:

$$\text{p/e} = \frac{\underline{\text{stock market price}}}{\text{eps}}$$

The higher the p/e ratio (e.g. over 15) then the higher the market expectations of future profits. A low p/e ratio (e.g. under 10) indicates a depressed share price due (usually) to continually poor company performance.

*See SSAP 6 for definition of extraordinary items

Consolidated profit and loss account (extract)

	1985 (£000)
Profit for the financial year	6,599
Dividends paid and proposed	2,654
Profit transferred to reserves	3,945
Earnings per ordinary share	8.2p

Notes to the financial statements

Earnings per share

The calculation of earnings per share is based on the profit of £6,599,000, less the cost of preference dividends and on 80,004,000 ordinary shares being the number of shares in issue throughout the financial year.

Fig. 5.2   Bryant Holdings plc – earnings per share.

DRAPERY & STORES

1985/86 High	Low	Stock	Price	+ or −	Div Net	C'vr	Y'ld Gr's	P/E
110	72½	Stead. & Sim 'A'	76	......	t3.4	1.6	6.4	14.6
113	58	Steinberg 10p	106	−1	†2.2	3.5	3.0	10.5
106	65	Stirling Group 20p	93	−1	†1.05	8.0	1.6	10.8
*36½	14½	Stormgard 10p	17	......	—	—	—	27.0
82	28	Sumrie 20p	40	......	—	—	—	—
503	375	Superdrug Strs. 10p	435	−3	†4.2	4.2	1.4	21.8
170	119	T & S Stores 5p	160	......	L2.63	3.9	2.3	26.3
54	23	Telefusion 5p	51	......	♦1.3	—	3.6	—
60	39	Tern Group	39	−1	B2.0	0.2	7.3	—
61½	27½	Time Prods. 10p	61	......	†1.5	2.7	3.5	12.7
82	46	Top Value Inds 10p	60	......	—	—	—	—
212	181	Underwoods 10p	183	......	R1.65	3.0	1.3	38.3
38	19	Upton (E) 'A'	34	......	—	—	—	—
460	266	Vantona Viyella 20p	428	−10	12.0	q2.7	4.1	10.1
230	140	WW Group	200	......	d7.94	3.2	5.7	7.9
328	197	Ward White	288	......	†5.69	2.8	2.8	15.2
73	45	Wassall (J. W.)	52	......	1.0	5.8	2.7	6.6
143	97	Wigfalls	97	−1	u2.5	0.6	3.8	41.7
610	277½	Woolworth Hldgs 50p	488	−5	†h7.75	3.5	2.3	13.8
£154	£106	Do. 8½pc Ln 2000	£129	−1	8½%	—	f6.7	—
187	148	World of Leather 10p	177	+2	R2.5	3.0	2.0	23.6

Fig. 5.3   Share information from the *Financial Times* (25 September 1985) including p/e ratios.

SSAP 4   THE ACCOUNTING TREATMENT OF GOVERNMENT GRANTS

If a company receives a government grant towards meeting an expense, e.g. rent or rates, then the grant is simply credited against that expense in the same period.

If the grant relates to capital expenditure (i.e. fixed assets) then two treatments are permissible:

1.   Reduce the cost of the fixed asset by the amount of the grant, e.g. a machine costs £10,000 and the grant received is £2,000. The asset will appear at a cost of £8,000, which is then depreciated in the normal way.

2.   Treat the grant as a 'deferred credit' which is written back to profit and loss account over the life of the asset, e.g. facts as in (1) above. The asset will appear at a cost of £10,000 in the balance sheet which is then depreciated in the normal way. The grant is credited to a separate account (disclosed as 'deferred income' on the balance sheet) and then transferred to profit and loss account over the depreciation period.

Tangible fixed assets
Depreciation of tangible fixed assets, other than land and buildings, is calculated on the cost, after deduction of government grants, at a fixed annual rate expected to write off the cost within the useful life of the assets.

Fig. 5.4(a)   The 600 group plc – treatment of Government grants.

Government grants
Grants receivable are taken to a deferred income account and credited to profit over the estimated useful lives of the relevant assets.

Fig. 5.4(b)   Bass plc – treatment of Government grants.

SSAP 5   ACCOUNTING FOR VALUE ADDED TAX

Value Added Tax (VAT) is a system of taxation in the United Kingdom whereby businesses with an annual turnover in excess of a certain prescribed limit must be 'registered' with HM Customs and Excise. The tax is payable whenever goods or services pass from one registered business to another or to a private consumer. In the case of registered businesses, a VAT return (usually covering a three-month period) will be prepared, showing whether the business paid more VAT than it received, or vice-versa. The business will then either have to pay 'excess collections' to the Customs and Excise, or will have 'excess payments' refunded by the Customs and Excise. Those who bear the tax are the private consumer and unregistered businesses, who have no means of recouping the VAT paid.

The technical name for VAT charged on sales is 'Output' tax, whilst VAT paid on purchases and expenses is known as 'Input' tax.

When a business becomes 'registered' it must maintain an accounting system which can identify both output and input tax, as well as provide the other information required in the VAT return. The major components of such a system are illustrated in Figure 5.5.

The Standard does not refer to the ways in which VAT should be recorded in the book-keeping system, but states how VAT information should be disclosed in the financial statements of a registered business, as follows: turnover as shown in the revenue statement should *exclude* VAT; on certain assets, e.g. motor cars, VAT input tax cannot be offset against output VAT. In such cases, the 'irrecoverable' VAT should be included as part of the cost of the asset.

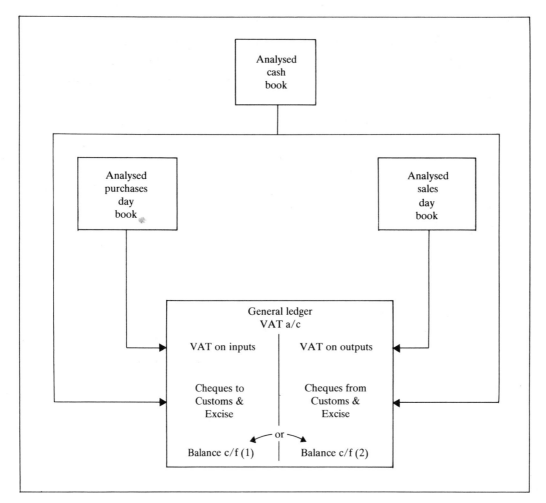

Fig. 5.5 VAT analysis system. (1) Would indicate an amount owing *to* Customs and Excise. (2) Would indicate an amount owing *by* Customs and Excise.

In the case of an unregistered business, VAT is included as part of the cost of goods, services and fixed assets.

SSAP 6 EXTRAORDINARY ITEMS AND PRIOR YEAR ADJUSTMENTS

Although the vast majority of a company's transactions will be related to its normal trading operations, there are occasions when significant transactions take place which, due both to their materiality and their unusual nature, require separate disclosure in the accounting statements. These 'extraordinary items' are defined in the standard as 'those items which derive from events or transactions outside the ordinary activities of the business and which are both material and expected not to recur frequently or regularly'. They do not include items which, though exceptional on account of size and incidence (and may therefore require separate disclosure), derive from the ordinary activities of the business. Neither do they include prior year items merely because they relate to a prior year.

Extraordinary items, as defined above, should be shown separately in the profit and loss account *after* the net profit from 'ordinary' activities has been disclosed.

The definition of 'extraordinary items' includes a reference to items which are 'exceptional'. This is the only point within the standard where the term is used, but it is obvious that any such items should be separately disclosed, but *within* the part of the profit and loss account leading to the profit on ordinary activities. An explanatory note should be given for each item so classified.

Another definition given in the standard is that of 'prior year adjustments', as follows: '. . . . are those material adjustments applicable to prior years arising from changes in accounting policies and from the correction of fundamental errors. They do not include the normal recurring corrections and adjustments of accounting estimates made in prior years.'

Fitch Lovell plc

Group profit and loss account (extract)
(for the 52 weeks ended 27 April 1985)

	Notes	£000
Profit on ordinary activities after tax		12,066
Extraordinary items	6	458
Profit for the financial year		12,524

Notes to the financial statements

6 Extraordinary items

	£000
Surplus arising from the disposals of subsidiaries (net of tax, £435,000)	1,502
Costs of restructuring and closure (net of tax, £158,000)	(1,079)
Surplus on sale of related company (net of tax, £34,000)	35
	458

Fig. 5.6   Fitch Lovell plc treatment of extraordinary items.

Notes to the accounts (extract)

1 Accounting policies

Comparative figures
Prior year's results have been restated to reflect the changed accounting policy in respect of foreign exchange translation. In addition, certain other comparative figures in the accounts and the notes thereto have been revised in minor respects onto a basis consistent with that applied in the current year.

Fig 5.7   United Biscuits (Holdings) plc – treatment of prior year adjustments.

The standard requires prior year adjustments, as defined, to be accounted for by restating prior years, with the result that, for a limited company, the opening balance of the profit and loss account (i.e. the 'retained profits' at the end of the previous year) will be adjusted accordingly. Full explanatory notes must be given.

Summary:

1. Extraordinary items are shown separately in the profit and loss account after 'profit for the year on ordinary activities'.
2. Exceptional items are shown separately in the profit and loss account, prior to arriving at the 'profit for the year on ordinary activities'.
3. Prior year adjustments, arising either from a change in accounting policy or a fundamental error, are accounted for by adjusting the opening balance on the profit and loss account.

Note: In all three cases, explanatory notes must be given.

SSAP 7   (WITHDRAWN)

SSAP 8   THE TREATMENT OF TAXATION UNDER THE IMPUTATION SYSTEM IN THE ACCOUNTS OF COMPANIES

Although a detailed discussion of this standard is outside the scope of this book, students should be aware of the way that the corporation tax charge is shown in the accounts (see Figure 5.8).

Companies are subject to corporation tax on their taxable profits. The taxable profit is unlikely to be the same as the profit as recorded in the profit and loss account, owing to a number of factors, including: (a) certain expenses deducted in arriving at the net profit are 'not allowable' when determining the taxable profit (e.g. depreciation, entertainment of suppliers); (b) the company may receive capital allowances on fixed asset expenditure, which serve to reduce the amount of profit upon which corporation tax is levied.

(*Note:* The corporation tax liability is also shown as a creditor on the balance sheet.)

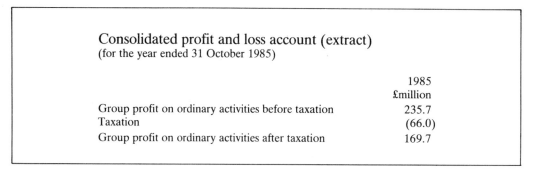

Consolidated profit and loss account (extract)
(for the year ended 31 October 1985)

	1985 £million
Group profit on ordinary activities before taxation	235.7
Taxation	(66.0)
Group profit on ordinary activities after taxation	169.7

Fig. 5.8 Imperial Group plc – taxation.

SSAP 9 STOCKS AND WORK-IN-PROGRESS

The subject of the valuation of stocks and work-in-progress is dealt with in detail in Chapter 2 of *Cost and Management Accounting* by Trevor Daff. It is sufficient at this stage to be aware of the main principles of valuation as contained in the standard.

1. Stocks and work-in-progress, other than long-term contract work in progress, should be valued at the lower cost and net realisable value of the separate items of stock and work-in-progress or of groups of similar items.

2. Long-term contracts (exceeding one year's duration work-in-progress) should be valued at cost plus any attributable profit, less any foreseeable losses and progress payments received and receivable. If, however, anticipated losses on individual contracts exceed cost incurred to date less progress payments received and receivable, such excesses should be shown separately as provisions. Note that the accounting policies used in the calculation of the value of stocks and work-in-progress must be disclosed in the financial statements.

One of the main problems relating to valuation is the exact meaning of *cost*, and the standard defines it in the following way:

'Cost is defined in relation to the different categories of stocks and work-in-progress as being that expenditure which has been incurred in the normal course of business in bringing the product or service to its present location and condition. This expenditure should include, in addition to cost of purchase, such costs of conversion as are appropriate to that location or condition.'

The terms 'cost of purchase' and 'cost of conversion' are further defined:

'Cost of purchase comprises purchase price including import duties, transport and handling costs and any other directly attributable costs, less trade discounts, rebates and subsidies.'

'Cost of conversion comprises:

(a) costs which are specifically attributable to units of production, i.e. direct labour, direct expenses and sub-contracted work;

(b) production overheads (materials, labour or services relating to the production for the year);

(c)   other overheads, if any, attributable in the particular circumstances of the business to bringing the product or services to its present location and condition.'

Where stock comprises a number of identical items purchased at different times and at different prices, various methods have been devised to relate prices to stock units. Three such methods are LIFO (last in, first out), FIFO (first in, first out) and AVCO (average cost). Each of these is a *theoretical* basis of valuation and does not necessarily reflect the way in which the stock physically moves through the business. Once a particular valuation method is chosen, it should be used in future years owing to the *consistency* concept.

In periods of rising prices the LIFO method will result in a lower stock valuation and consequently a lower profit figure than either of the other two methods, as the following illustration shows. (Note that SSAP 9 does not regard LIFO as an acceptable method of stock valuation.)

Example 2

A businessman started trading with a capital in cash of £6,000 which he placed in the business bank account at the outset.

His transactions, none of which were on credit, were as follows (in date sequence) for the first accounting period. All takings were banked immediately and all suppliers were paid by cheque. He traded in only one line of merchandise.

	Purchases		Sales	
Transaction	Quantity	Price per unit	Quantity	Price per unit
	No.	£	No.	£
1	1,200	1.00		
2	1,000	1.05		
3			800	1.70
4	600	1.10		
5			600	1.90
6	900	1.20		
7			1,100	2.00
8	800	1.25		
9			1,300	2.00
10	700	1.30		
11			400	2.05

In addition he incurred expenses amounting to £1,740, of which he still owed £570 at the end of the period.

Required:
Prepare separately using both the FIFO (first in, first out) and the LIFO (last in, first out) methods of stock valuation:
(a)   trading and profit and loss account for the period, and
(b)   a balance sheet at the end of the period.

(ACCA – slightly amended)

Solution:
(a)   *Trading and Profit & Loss Accounts*

	FIFO basis		LIFO basis	
	£	£	£	£
Sales		8,120		8,120
Less: Cost of sales (no opening stock)				
Purchases	5,900		5,900	
Less: Closing stock	1,285	4,615	1,090	4,810
Gross profit		3,505		3,310
Less: Expenses		1,740		1,740
Net profit		1,765		1,570

(b)

Balance Sheets

	FIFO basis £		LIFO basis £
Current assets			
Stock	1,285		1,090
Bank	7,050		7,050
	8,335		8,140
Less: Creditors	570		570
	7,765		7,570
Capital	6,000		6,000
Add: Net profit	1,765		1,570
	7,765		7,570

Workings:

Note: there is an alternative way of showing calculations (i) and (ii) below by using an 'account' format. Refer to the companion volume for examples of calculations presented in that way. The following presentation has been chosen by virtue of its simplicity.

(i) Calculation of closing stock, assuming 'last in, first out' (LIFO)

Cost prices:	£1	£1.05	£1.10	£1.20	£1.25	£1.30
Transaction						
1 Purchase (P)	1,200					
2 P		1,000				
3 Sales (S)		(800)				
		200				
4 P			600			
5 S			(600)			
			—			
6 P				900		
7 S		(200)		(900)		
		—		—		
8 P					800	
9 S	(500)				(800)	
	700				—	
10 P						700
11 S	____					(400)
Closing stock						
(units) =	700					300
Price	£1					£1.30
Value =	£700					£390

(Total value £700 + £390 = £1,090)

(ii) Calculation of closing stock, assuming 'first in, first out' (FIFO)

Cost prices:	£1	£1.05	£1.10	£1.20	£1.25	£1.30
Transaction						
1 P	1,200					
2 P		1,000				
3 S	(800)					
	400					
4 P			600			
5 S	(400)	(200)				
	—	800				

6	P			900	
7	S	(800)	(300)		
		—	600		
8	P		800		
9	S	(600)	(600)	(100)	
		—	—	700	
10	P			700	
11	S		(400)		

Closing stock
(units) = 300 700
Price £1.25 £1.30
Value = £375 £910

(Total value = £375 + £910 = £1,285)

(iii) Sales total obtained by multiplying units sold by sales price per unit, i.e:

$$800 \times £1.70$$
$$600 \times £1.90 \qquad \text{etc.}$$

(iv) Purchases total obtained by multiplying units purchased by purchase price per unit, i.e:

$$1,200 \times £1.00$$
$$1,000 \times £1.05 \qquad \text{etc.}$$

(v)

Bank Account

Cash introduced	6,000	Purchases	5,900
Cash from sales	8,120	Expenses	1,170
		Balance c/f	7,050
	14,120		14,120

COMMENTARY

In times of rising prices, LIFO results in stock values which reflect the earliest and lowest prices. FIFO assumes that the earliest stock purchased is used before newer stock, with the consequence that stock values are based on the most recent, and higher prices.

The AVCO method of valuation results in a stock valuation lying between the other two, as the following calculations show:

Transaction			Price	£
1	P	1,200 units	£1	1,200
2	P	1,000 units	£1.05	1,050
		2,200	(£1.02 av.)	2,250
3	S	(800)	(£1.02 av.)	(816)
		1,400		1,434
4	P	600	£1.10	660
		2,000	(£1.05 av.)	2,094
5	S	(600)	(£1.05 av.)	(630)
		1,400		1,464
6	P	900	£1.20	1,080
		2,300	(£1.11 av.)	2,544
7	S	(1,100)	(£1.11 av.)	(1,221)
		1,200		1,323

8	P	800		£1.25	1,000
		2,000		(£1.16 av.)	2,323
9	S	(1,300)		(£1.16 av.)	(1,508)
		700			815
10	P	700		£1.30	910
		1,400		(£1.23 av.)	1,725
11	S	(400)		(£1.23 av.)	(492)
Closing stock		1,000			1,233

Using this stock figure in the trading and profit and loss account, the profit would be:

		AVCO basis	
	£		£
Sales			8,120
Less: Cost of sales			
Purchases	5,900		
Less: Closing stock	1,233		4,667
Gross profit			3,453
Less: Expenses			1,740
Net profit			1,713

Summary:	FIFO	LIFO	AVCO
Net profit	1,765	1,570	1,713

SSAP 10   STATEMENTS OF SOURCE AND APPLICATION OF FUNDS

This standard is covered in detail in Chapter 9.

SSAP 11   (WITHDRAWN)

SSAP 12   ACCOUNTING FOR DEPRECIATION

Specific methods for depreciating assets have been explained in Chapters 1 and 2, but it is useful to note the definition of depreciation as given in the standard: 'Depreciation is the measure of the wearing out, consumption or other loss of value of a fixed asset whether arising from use, effluxion of time or obsolescence through technology and market changes.'

The accounting treatment should already be clear to you, but the following summary of the standard's recommendations may be found useful.

1.   Provision for depreciation of fixed assets having a finite useful life should be made by allocating their cost less residual values over the periods expected to benefit from their use.
2.   Where there is a change in the method of depreciation, the cost of the asset should be written off over the remaining useful life on the new basis commencing with the period in which the change is made.
3.   Where assets are revalued, depreciation should be based on the revalued amount, and current estimate of remaining useful life.
4.   The following information should be given in the financial statements.

   (a)   the depreciation methods used;
   (b)   the useful lives or the depreciation rates used;
   (c)   total depreciation allocated for the period;
   (d)   the gross amount of depreciable assets and the related accumulated depreciation.

> **Depreciation**
>
> Depreciation is calculated to write off the cost of plant, land and buildings over their expected lives by equal annual instalments; depreciation is not provided on freehold land or assets under construction.
>
> In general, asset lives are determined in accordance with local commercial practice. The assumed life of buildings is 50 years (or the term of the lease if shorter), whilst most plant is written off over 10 to 20 years.

Fig. 5.9 Bowater Corporation plc – depreciation policy.

SSAP 13 ACCOUNTING FOR RESEARCH AND DEVELOPMENT

Many companies can only maintain their profitability and market leadership by investing large sums in researching and developing new products, techniques and designs.

Prior to the inception of this standard, companies were able to decide for themselves how such expenditure should be disclosed in the accounts. Some took the prudent view of 'writing off' all such expenditure as it was incurred, whilst others 'capitalised' the expenditure by including it on the balance sheet as an asset.

This divergence of treatment led to some companies overstating their profits (or understating their losses) as well as overstating balance sheet values, by virtue of capitalising massive sums spent on futile or non-commercial ventures.

The standard distinguishes between 'research' and 'development' costs as follows:

1. *Research* can be either 'pure' or 'applied'; both are undertaken in order to gain new scientific or technical knowledge and understanding, but the former is not primarily directed towards any practical aim or application, whereas the latter is.
2. *Development* is the use of scientific or technical knowledge in order to produce new or substantially improved materials, devices, products, processes, systems or services prior to the commencement of commercial production.

The accounting treatment is as follows.

(a) Fixed assets bought for research and development activities (e.g. laboratory equipment) should be capitalised and written off over their useful lives.
(b) Expenditure on research (pure and applied) should be *written off* in the year of expenditure.
(c) Development expenditure should also be *written off* in the year of expenditure, *except in the following circumstances*, when it may be shown as a 'deferred asset' on the balance sheet that:

  i   there is a clearly defined project;
  ii the related expenditure is separately identifiable;
  iii the project is technically feasible and commercially viable;
  iv further development costs (if any) are expected to be more than covered by related future revenue:
  v   adequate resources exist or are reasonably expected to be available, to enable the project to be completed and to provide any consequential increases in working capital.

It is hardly surprising, therefore, that the vast majority* of companies will write off all research and development expenditure as it is incurred, with the exception of that spent on related fixed assets, which can be capitalised.

If development costs are deferred to future periods, amortisation should begin

*97% of companies surveyed in 'Financial Reporting 1983–4', published by the ICAEW, section contributor R.H. Gray

---

Research and development

Expenditure incurred in product research and development is charged to profit and loss account in the year in which it is incurred. Research laboratories' equipment is written off over its expected life.

Fig. 5.10 Foseco Minsep plc – treatment of research and development expenditure.

when the commercial production of the process or product commences, and should then be written off over the period which the product or process is expected to be sold or used.

Example 3

Celltech Ltd is involved in the development and manufacture of high-technology electrical and electronic products. You are involved in the production of the financial accounts of the year ended 31 March 1985, and have ascertained the following facts and estimates.

1. The company has incurred expenditure of £230,000 during the year on a project which is concerned with developing new forms of energy storage. The project is continuing, but no conclusive results have been obtained.
2. £180,000 has been spent on updating an existing product which is selling well. The management have high expectations for the sales of the updated product. It is expected to have a life of five years. Sales are also expected to grow over the next five years.
3. £120,000 has been spent during the year on developing a new electronic device. Manufacture is due to commence in August 1986. The managers are confident that the product will sell as long as a number of persistent technical problems can be overcome.

You are required to advise the directors of the company how these items should be treated in the accounts. Make reference, where appropriate, to any relevant Statements of Standard Accounting Practice.

(JMB)

Solution:

The criteria relating to the accounting treatment are set out in the section on SSAP 13 above, but the specific items referred to in the question should be treated as follows:

1. Does not meet the criteria, as no conclusive results have been obtained, and must, therefore, be written off to the profit and loss account.
2. This does meet the criteria and can, if the company wishes, be capitalised and amortised over the five-year period.
3. As there is an uncertainty over the technical feasibility of the device, the prudent treatment is to write off the expenditure against profits.

COMMENTARY

The company will, if the advice given in the solution is accepted by the directors, write off £350,000 against profits whilst capitalising £180,000. This complies with the concept of prudence, whereby neither profits nor assets should be over-stated when uncertainties exist.

SSAP 14   GROUP ACCOUNTS

This topic is covered in Chapter 8.

SSAP 15   (WITHDRAWN)

SSAP 16   CURRENT COST ACCOUNTING

This topic is covered in Chapter 10.

SSAP 17   ACCOUNTING FOR POST BALANCE SHEET EVENTS

Although the financial statements are dated 'for the year ended . . .' and 'as at . . .', it is wrong to assume that events taking place after the date quoted have no bearing on their contents. It should be recognised that several months may elapse between the end of the accounting year and the date on which the directors are expected to approve those accounts for publication to the shareholders, and many things might happen in that period which could cause either a revision to be made to the figures, or the necessity for an explanatory note to be given.

The standard defines a 'post balance sheet event' as an event which occurs between the balance sheet date and the date on which the financial statements are approved by the board of directors, and classifies them into *'adjusting' events* and *'non-adjusting events'*, as follows.

1. *Adjusting events*, if material, *require changes to be made* in the financial statements. Such events provide additional evidence relating to conditions existing at the balance sheet date, examples being;
    (a) The determination of the purchase price or sales proceeds of fixed assets bought or sold before the year-end (e.g. where a sale contract had been signed before the year-end, but the price agreed after the year-end).
    (b) Evidence that the valuation of stocks was inaccurate (e.g. where the sale proceeds of the stock were substantially lower than the year-end value placed on that stock).
    (c) A valuation of property which provides evidence of a permanent diminution of value.
    (d) The insolvency of a debtor in the post-balance sheet period, causing the provision for bad debts to be revised as at the balance sheet date.

    It is important to appreciate that the occurrence of some post-balance sheet events, such as a critical deterioration in operating results and in the financial position, may indicate a need to reconsider the appropriateness of the going concern for the preparation of the financial statements.

2. *Non-adjusting events* are events which arise after the balance sheet date and concern conditions which did not exist at the time. *They do not require changes to be made to amounts in the financial statements*, but must, if material, be disclosed by way of notes. Examples include: (a) issues of shares; (b) purchases and sales of fixed assets; (c) opening new trading activities; (d) strikes and other labour disputes.

Post balance sheet events

Rights issue

Following the rights issue on 16 April 1984, the issued share capital is £1,350,000, represented by 13,500,000 allotted, called-up and fully paid ordinary shares of 10p each.

A pro-forma group balance sheet prepared on the basis of the accounts at 31 March 1984 and reflecting the effects of the rights issue is shown on page X.

Fig. 5.11   Immediate Business Systems plc – post-balance sheet events (non-adjusting).

SSAP 18   ACCOUNTING FOR CONTINGENCIES

A contingency is a condition which exists at the balance sheet date, where the outcome will be confirmed only on the occurrence or non-occurrence of one or more uncertain future events. This definition is not intended to apply to the routine estimates which have to be made regarding such matters as the anticipated lives of fixed assets, the likely amount of bad debts or the net realisable values of stocks.

Thus, a contingency is something which *may* happen, and it can be either good or bad for the company if it does! For example, a company may have been the subject of a legal action by a customer relating to faulty goods, and has in turn sued the customer for a breach of the contract relating to payment for those goods. The legal cases might be won or lost: in the former case the company may have to pay legal costs, but may be awarded damages. In the latter case, the company may have to pay both costs and damages.

The standard reminds us of the prudence concept in SSAP 2 when it says that:

1. A material contingent loss should be accrued in the financial statements where it is *probable* that a future event will confirm a loss which can be estimated with reasonable accuracy at the date on which the financial statements are approved by the board of directors. Any material contingent loss not accrued, should be disclosed by way of note, except where the possibility of loss is remote.
2. Contingent gains should *not* be accrued in financial statements, and should only be noted in the financial statements if it is probable that the gain will be realised.

So what about the court cases? It depends entirely upon their progress in the courts in the post-balance sheet period: if it is apparent that the cases are likely to be lost, then full provision for costs and damages should be made in the accounts. If the outcome is uncertain, the prudence concept would indicate that provision be made for the likely legal costs involved, and that the contingent loss regarding damages be noted in the accounts.

If the cases have gone well, but the court ruling is still awaited, prudence dictates that legal costs should still be provided for. A note regarding a contingent gain should not be made under those circumstances, not least for the risk that if the judge happens to read it he may well regard the company as both arrogant and presumptive!

Contingent liabilities

The company has guaranteed certain borrowings of subsidiary companies, related companies and third parties. At 30 September 1984 these amounted to £644m, £2m and £92m respectively (1983 – £546m, £5 and £88m respectively). The group has guaranteed borrowings of related companies and third parties which at 30 September 1984 amounted to £7m and £158m respectively (1983 – £12m and £160 respectively).

In addition, there are a number of legal claims or potential claims against the group, the outcome of which cannot be foreseen. Full provision is made in these financial statements for all liabilities which are expected to materialise.

Fig. 5.12(a)   Grand Metropolitan plc – contingent liabilities.

Contingencies

The company has agreed to purchase stock at a cost of approximately £700,000 in connection with the sub-contract entered into with Plessey Microsystems Limited to produce equipment for delivery to the South of Scotland Electricity Board. At 31 March 1984, £201,433 was still outstanding in respect of this agreement.

Fig. 5.12(b)   Immediate Business Systems plc – contingent liabilities.

SSAP 19   ACCOUNTING FOR INVESTMENT PROPERTIES

Investment properties are fixed assets held not for use by a business for the purposes of manufacturing or trading, but purely for their investment potential. Examples are buildings owned by a property company to be let to tenants.

The standard exempts such properties from the depreciation requirements of SSAP 12, except for properties held on leases of less than twenty years' duration, which would be amortised in the usual way. In addition, investment properties should be included in the balance sheet at their open market value rather than the price originally paid for them. Details of the value and the basis of the valuation must be given.

SSAP 20   FOREIGN CURRENCY TRANSLATION

This topic is outside the scope of this textbook.

SSAP 21   ACCOUNTING FOR LEASES AND HIRE PURCHASE CONTRACTS

Leases and hire purchase contracts are means by which companies obtain the right to use or purchase assets. In the United Kingdom there is normally no provision in a lease contract for ownership of the asset to pass to the lessee (i.e. the company using the asset). A hire purchase contract has similar features to a lease except that the hirer can acquire legal title by exercising an option to purchase the asset upon fulfilment of certain conditions (normally the payment of an agreed number of instalments).

From the point of view of the hirer or lessee, such contracts give the major advantage of improving cash flow, as the company has only to meet the (relatively modest) contract instalments, and does not have to find the much greater sums needed to purchase the asset outright.

The accounting treatment depends on whether the contract is categorised as a 'finance lease' or an 'operating lease'. As the treatment of both hire purchase and lease contracts is virtually identical, the term 'lease' is used to cover both types of transaction.

An *operating lease* involves the lessee paying a rental for the hire of an asset for a period of time which is normally substantially less than its useful economic life (e.g. a builder hiring a concrete mixer for a period of two months).

A *finance lease* usually involves payment by a lessee to a lessor of the full cost of the asset together with a return on the finance provided by the lessor (i.e. the company which initially purchases the asset). Finance leases are likely to be relatively long term, covering the full useful economic life of the asset (e.g. a company leasing a computer for a five-year period).

The standard recognises that many companies regularly use assets which they do not (and may never) own. It is felt to be misleading to exclude from the balance sheet those assets where the lessee has both rights and responsibilities extending over virtually their entire useful lives. The standard 'turns a blind eye' to the fact that the company does not have legal ownership, but instead recognises that 'substance over form' demands that the assets be included in the balance sheet total.

A simple summary of the accounting treatment recommended by SSAP 21 is as follows:

		Finance lease	*Operating lease*
(a)	*Lessor's books*		
	P + L a/c	Earnings from leases allocated to relevant accounting periods	Rentals treated as income, using a straight line basis over the lease term
	Balance sheet	(Assets subject to finance leases are excluded from 'fixed assets')	Assets subject to operating leases are *included* in 'fixed assets'
		Debtors include the appropriate amount due from the lessee	Debtors include the appropriate amount due from the lessee
(b)	*Lessee's books*		
	P + L a/c	Expenditure includes a proportion of the total finance charge payable under the lease	Expenditure includes rental payments, using a straight line basis over the lease term.

Balance sheet	Assets subject to finance leases are *included* in 'fixed assets'	(Assets subject to operating leases are excluded from 'fixed assets')
	Creditors include the appropriate amount due to the lessor for future rentals	Creditors include the appropriate amount due to the lessor for future rentals.

SSAP 22   ACCOUNTING FOR GOODWILL

This topic is dealt with in Chapter 8.

SSAP 23   ACQUISITIONS AND MERGERS

This topic is outside the scope of this textbook.

Exercises

5.1 The financial director of Portland Ltd has prepared the following information with a view to drawing up the company's profit and loss account for the year to 30 June, 1983:

	£000
Retained profit at 1 July, 1982	7,200
Turnover	17,500
Cost of sales (Note 1)	10,800
Loss on closure of factory in Scotland	760
Administration expenses (Note 2)	3,660
Distribution costs	1,200
Taxation (Note 3)	635
Dividends paid and proposed	100

Notes:
1. The calculation of cost of sales includes opening stock of £1,000,000 and closing stock of £1,200,000, each valued on the marginal cost basis. The directors have since decided that the total cost basis gives a fairer presentation of the company's results and financial position, and the auditors agree with this assessment. Using the total cost basis, opening stock should be valued at £1,425,000 and closing stock at £1,840,000. You may ignore the effect on tax payable of this change in the method of stock valuation.
2. Administration expenses include bad debts of £850,000. Bad debts are normally in the region of £100,000 per annum, whereas the figure for the current year includes a loss of £750,000 incurred when a major customer went into liquidation.
3. The figure for taxation is made up of the following items:

	£000	*£000*
Tax payable on 'normal' trading profit		1,180
Less: Tax relief on bad debt arising from liquidation of a major customer	375	
Tax relief arising from loss on closure of factory in Scotland	170	545
		635

Required:
(a) Define exceptional items and extraordinary items in accordance with the provisions of Statement of Standard Accounting Practice 6. Give two examples of each.
(b) Prepare the profit and loss account and statement of retained earnings of Portland Ltd, not necessarily in a form suitable for publication but in accordance with good accounting practice and complying with the provisions of Statement of Standard Accounting Practice 6.

(IOB)

5.2 (a) Certain fundamental accounting concepts should be observed in the preparation of financial statements. Explain the meaning of:

  i the accruals concept,
  ii the consistency concept.

(b) A company which manufactures cardboard boxes has the following fixed assets:

	Cost £000	Deprecia- tion £000	Book value £000	Market value £000
Factory buildings	600	125	475	300
Plant and machinery	250	100	150	30
	850	225	625	330

(a) Explain how the book value of the fixed assets could be greater than the current market value.

(b) Assume the business is in severe financial difficulties. What might be the effect on the value at which the fixed assets appear in the balance sheet?

(ULSEB)

5.3 Explain what is meant by 'accounting policies' in relation to the published accounts of companies and the main matters that you would expect to find dealt with under this heading.

5.4 Name four fundamental accounting concepts and explain what is meant by them.

5.5 'The preparation of financial statements is based upon what are generally referred to as accepted concepts, conventions or postulates of accountancy.'

Describe these concepts and explain their importance in the preparation of trading and profit and loss accounts and balance sheets.

5.6 Explain the following accounting terms:

(a) Prior year adjustments.
(b) Exceptional items.
(c) Extraordinary items.
(d) Contingent liabilities.

5.7 The Companies Act 1985 uses the terms 'extraordinary charges' and 'extraordinary profit or loss' in the format for profit and loss accounts. What do you understand these terms to mean?

5.8 Explain the treatment in the financial statements of the following items of research and development expenditure:

(a) £200,000 spent on laboratory equipment.
(b) £90,000 paid to research workers engaged in 'pure' research.
(c) £170,000 spent on developing a product which has proved to be non-viable.
(d) £100,000 spent on developing a viable and commercial process which will be marketed in three years' time. The company has adequate resources to see the project through to its completion.

5.9 What action should be taken in respect of the financial statements of a company for the year ended 31 March 1986 in respect of the following events which took place after that date? The directors have not yet approved the statements for publication.

(a) A customer has sued the company, but the court case has not commenced. Legal costs are estimated at £70,000.
(b) A valuation of a property reveals that the balance sheet value was overstated

by £100,000 (there is no effect on the company's 'going concern' status, however).

(c) The company issued 4 million ordinary shares.

(d) Although the amount has not been finalised, the company expects to gain substantial compensation from a road-widening scheme near its factory.

5.10 You are interested in acquiring some shares in Varac plc and have acquired the most recent set of the company's accounts for appraisal purposes.

The accounts are supported by explanatory notes, extracts of which are reproduced below:

'Turnover

The figure includes only the cash actually received for cash and credit sales less actual and estimated amounts of bad debts.'

'Cost of sales

Stocks

Opening stock is at FIFO cost. Following a policy review the directors have decided that a more accurate valuation would be obtained by a percentage addition for overheads; accordingly closing stock has been valued on this new basis. (See also Purchases below.)

Purchases

Purchases have been accounted for at their gross (catalogue) prices. Trade discounts received on purchases have been included in discounts received and have been credited to profit and loss account.

It is the company's policy to account only for those goods for which it has paid. Goods which the company has received before the year-end, but for which it has not paid, are excluded from purchases, from closing stocks and from creditors.'

'Depreciation

During the current year the level of business activity has been much lower than had been anticipated resulting in a greatly reduced amount of net profit. It has been decided, therefore, that it would be inadvisable to charge any depreciation to profit and loss account as to do so would convert the small net profit into a net loss.

Should this situation recur in the next financial year, the directors propose to transfer a suitable amount from the accumulated provision for depreciation to the credit of profit and loss account in order to maintain the ordinary dividend.'

Required:

Comment on the extent to which Varac plc's accounts adhere to, or conflict with, recognised accounting principles and practices, so far as can be elicited from the above extracts.

(ACCA)

CHAPTER 6

Accounting for Limited Liability Companies (1)

6.1 Introduction

Although sole traders and partnerships are the most common form of business organisation in the United Kingdom,* their advantages of simplicity and informality are often heavily outweighed by the fact that the owner or partners have personal responsibility for all the debts of their business. Whilst this may be of little concern to the proprietors of a healthy and profitable business, it can have a devastating effect on the fortunes of owners of failing and loss-making enterprises, as it means that they must meet the claims of their creditors from their personal assets (possibly by selling their house and its contents) if the assets of the business are insufficient. Another major disadvantage of operating as a sole trader or partnership is the restricted opportunity to raise money in order to expand and develop the business.

These disadvantages have long been recognised and consequently a third type of business organisation, that of the limited liability company, has become well established. The main feature of limited companies is that they are treated as a separate legal entity, able to own assets and owe money in their own right. The owners (the shareholders or 'members') of the company have the satisfaction of knowing that, even if the company amassed considerable debts, their own loss is limited to the amount of share capital (and possibly any loans) which they have subscribed. In small companies, the shareholders are often the managers of the business with one or more of them taking an official capacity as a director. In larger companies, the directors may own only a minute proportion of the shares in issue†.

It must not be thought, however, that limited liability status is totally without obligations. They can be summarised as follows.

1. The annual accounts must be audited

An audit is an examination of the final accounts by a professionally qualified accountant to see whether or not they show a 'true and fair view' of the state of affairs of the business and of its profit or loss. There is no equivalent requirement for sole traders and partnerships, although at the time of writing there is considerable discussion as to whether 'small' limited companies should be exempt from the audit requirements.

2. Companies must publish their audited annual accounts

This is done by sending a copy of the accounts to the Registrar of Companies, where they are made available for public inspection on the payment of a small fee. This lack of privacy is justified by the legitimate interest of creditors and lenders, who should satisfy themselves that the business is financially sound before entering into a credit or loan agreement with the company. The fact that the name of every limited company must contain the word 'limited' or 'public limited company' or their abbreviations is a warning to potential creditors and others that they have no recourse to the personal assets of the owners if the business fails. Consequently,

*In 1983, there were 2.5 million sole traders and 910,000 registered limited companies.
†For example, the directors of Marks and Spencer plc owned less than 0.14% of the company's issued ordinary share capital at 31 December 1984.

any research on the Company's financial stability should be done *prior to* entering into the transaction.

3. A copy of the audited annual accounts must be sent to shareholders and debenture holders

Whilst this may not appear to be too onerous for a small limited company with perhaps a handful of shareholders, the cost of production and distribution may be significant in the case of larger companies (e.g. British Telecom plc has over a million individual shareholders). Again, the cost must be seen as essential to satisfy the legitimate interests of the owners of the business.

4. There are greater legal complexities and bureaucratic requirements

The 1985 Companies Act imposes a mass of statutory regulations concerning the running of a limited liability company, and the company's directors frequently have to consult professional advisers to ensure correct compliance with the Act. Such matters as the appointment or resignation of directors or auditors must be notified to the Registrar of Companies and an annual return giving particulars of share capital and shareholders must also be completed.

Although the cost of forming a limited company may be as little as £100, the costs of complying with the various rules and regulations are far greater.

6.2 Types of limited company

In the previous section, one disadvantage of the lack of limited liability status was seen to be the restricted ability to raise funds for business development. Not every limited company can, however, raise funds from the general public, as this is restricted to those companies which are designated public limited companies (plcs) as defined by the Companies Act.

The definition of a plc is a company:

(a) limited by shares;
(b) whose memorandum of association (i.e. 'rule book') states that the company is to be a public company;
(c) which is registered under the Companies Act as a plc.

In addition, it must have a minimum value of allotted (i.e. distributed to shareholders) share capital – currently £50,000.

Any limited company which is not a plc is referred to as a *private* limited company. Both plcs and private limited companies must have a minimum of two shareholders, with no maximum being specified.

The only advantage for a plc over a private company is the former's right to offer shares or debentures (see below) to the public. In return for this benefit, plcs are subject to far more stringent controls than private companies. On 1 January 1984 there were only 6,231 plcs out of the total of 910,000 registered companies. In terms of size and influence, however, they far outweigh all the private companies. Readers wishing to study this topic in greater detail are advised to consult one of the many textbooks devoted to the topic of company law.

6.3 Types of share capital

The two major types of share capital are those of ordinary shares and preference shares.

ORDINARY SHARES

Every company has ordinary shares. They give the holder the right to vote at general meetings of the company (e.g. to vote in an election of directors), rights to share in any dividends which are declared, and, if the company ceases to exist by being put into liquidation, the right to share in any surplus which remains after the claims of creditors and preference shareholders have been met. Each share has a nominal or 'par' value, e.g. 25p or £1, on which dividends are based as a percentage.

Although they carry the risk of loss in the event of the company failing, their attraction is the potential dividend which can be earned if the company is profitable, and also the increase in their intrinsic value.

PREFERENCE SHARES

These are shares which confer a preference to the holder as to income or capital, or both, over the ordinary share capital of the company. The dividend paid to preference shareholders is expressed as a fixed percentage of the nominal value and is presumed to be cumulative (a dividend not paid in one year being carried forward to be paid in a future year) unless stated to be non-cumulative. Preference shareholders do *not* normally have the right to vote at company general meetings.

Preference shares are a safer form of investment than ordinary shares owing to their prior claims to dividend and capital repayment in the event of a liquidation. The drawback is that the dividend will remain static, regardless of any growth in company profits.

Both ordinary and preference shares can be classified as 'redeemable', a topic which is covered in detail in Chapter 7.

The only other type of share worth noting is that of deferred or founders' shares which are occasionally issued to the initial promoters of a company. They may carry disproportionately high voting rights, whilst leaving the bulk of the capital to be subscribed by the ordinary shareholders.

A company's balance sheet will contain details of both its *authorised* share capital and its *issued* share capital. The former is simply the maximum amount of share capital which the company is allowed to issue, as stated in its memorandum of association, whereas the latter is the actual amount issued to shareholders at the balance sheet date.

6.4 Other means of funding

Nearly all limited companies have the implied power to borrow money for the purposes of their business. Many businesses use this power to raise overdrafts or loans from banks, whilst others, being plcs, seek to raise finance from the general public by means of issuing loan capital as distinct from share capital.

Whichever form the borrowing takes, the company will be committed to paying interest on the amount advanced, and may well have to offer some or all of its assets to provide security to the lender by means either of a 'fixed' charge over specific assets, or a 'floating' charge over all the company's assets. The most common form of contract which the company enters into in relation to the borrowing is known as a *debenture* deed, and the loan capital is usually referred to either as debenture stock (if secured) or loan stock (if unsecured), preceded by the interest percentage which the stock carries. If the stock is repayable at a certain date then the year of repayment, or earliest and latest years for repayment, will also be stated, e.g. 8% debenture stock 1995–1998.

If the debenture deed has been entered into with one or only a small number of persons, then the word 'stock' is usually omitted from the title.

It must be emphasised that debenture or loan stock is *not* part of the company's share capital, and payments made to the stockholders represent interest and not dividends. Interest is an overhead of the company (shown in the profit and loss account) and is treated as an 'allowable' expense which serves to reduce the company's taxation charge. A dividend is an appropriation of the company's profits (shown in the company's appropriation account) and is not allowable for taxation purposes. In the event of the company's liquidation, the debenture holders will be able to utilise their security to gain repayment of their loans.

6.5 Reserves and dividend policy

If a sole trader's business makes a profit it is simply transferred to his capital account, and treated as his private income which may be subject to income tax. A company which makes a profit will find that there is a certain amount of choice available to the directors regarding the amount of profit which finds its way back to the owners in the form of dividends.

There are four stages to this process, which can best be explained by showing a simplified profit and loss appropriation account of a company (Table 6.1). (The figures in brackets represent deductions.)

Table 6.1

	Net profit for year		X
1.	*Less:* Corporation tax		(X)
	Net profit after tax		X
2.	Transfer to or from reserves		(X) or X
			X
3.	Dividends:		
	on preference shares	(X)	
	on ordinary shares	(X)	(X)
	Retained profit for the year		X
4.	Retained profit brought forward		X
	Retained profit carried forward		X

A detailed explanation of these stages is as follows.

1. As the company is a separate legal entity, it is liable to pay corporation tax on its profits.
2. The company can transfer part of its profit into general or specific *reserves*, which can be brought back into the appropriation account at some future date as the need arises. These reserves are not necessarily matched by equivalent amounts of cash, but are represented by value in various assets, including fixed assets, debtors or stock. They are known as 'distributable' or 'revenue' reserves (i.e. available for dividend payments if required) if they have been built up out of 'earned' profits.
3. After providing for its corporation tax liability and deciding whether or not to transfer profits to or from reserves, the company will then turn its corporate mind to the question of dividends. Unfortunately, profit does not equal cash, as much of the profit may be 'tied up' in the form of stocks, debtors, machinery, etc. Consequently, the company must perform a balancing act between the needs of the shareholders for an income from their investment, and the necessity for the company to retain a reasonable cash balance (or to limit the size of its overdraft). Assuming that the company has both profit and cash available, then it will firstly propose the payment of the fixed dividend on its preference shares, and then decide upon the amount to be proposed for the ordinary dividend.
4. Any profit which remains is known as 'retained profit' and is added to the balance of retained profits which was brought forward at the start of the year. The combined total is another 'distributable reserve'.

A company may have other types of reserves, known as 'non-distributable' or 'capital' reserve. These have been built up, not out of 'earned' profits, but from various adjustments to the capital structure of the company or from the revaluation of fixed assets. As their name suggests, they are *not* available for the payment of dividends.

The three main non-distributable reserves are as follows.

I. SHARE PREMIUM ACCOUNT

When a company sells its shares, it may ask a price in excess of the nominal value of those shares (e.g. £2 for a share with a 25p nominal value). The excess over the nominal value (£1.75) is known as the share premium, and must be transferred to a separate account. Whilst the balance on the share premium account cannot be used for the payment of dividends, it can be used, *inter alia*, for the purpose of issuing bonus shares to existing shareholders. (Bonus shares are shares issued free of charge to existing shareholders—see next chapter.)

2. CAPITAL REDEMPTION RESERVE

The topic of redemption of share capital is dealt with in detail in the next chapter, but at this stage it is sufficient to appreciate that if shares are redeemed otherwise than out of the proceeds of a new issue of shares (i.e. part or all of the redemption money comes from 'profits') a sum equal to the shares so redeemed must be transferred to a non-attributable capital redemption reserve. This reserve can be used for the issue of bonus shares.

3. REVALUATION RESERVE

Many companies decide to revalue fixed assets at periodic intervals to ensure that balance sheet values reflect material and permanent changes. Any increase arising on a revaluation is not available for the payment of dividends, which is a prudent policy considering that the mere fact of revaluing assets has no beneficial effect whatsoever on the company's bank balance! On the contrary, the expenses of employing a professional valuer and subsequent increases in insurance premiums related to the property values may substantially decrease the company's cash resources.

Why then do companies revalue assets? Apart from the need to update balance sheet values as mentioned above, a company with significantly undervalued assets

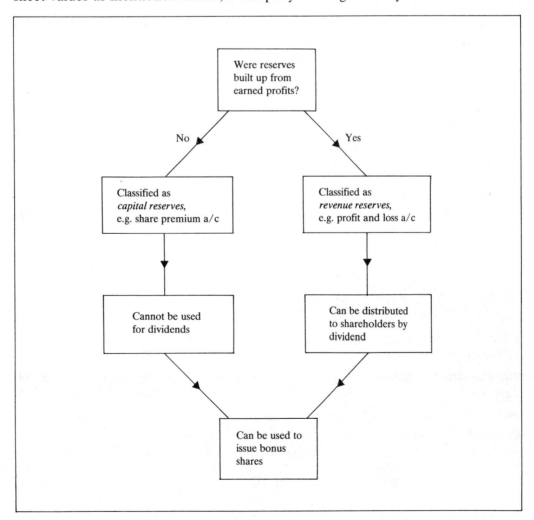

may become the target for a takeover bid, with the price offered being based on the historic values rather than current ones. This tactic is known as 'asset stripping' and was prevalent in the late 1960s and early 1970s, before companies became wise to its dangers.

As with the other capital reserves, the revaluation reserves can be used for the issue of bonus shares.

SUMMARY: (see foot of p. 123)

6.6 Gearing

It has already been stated that every company will have ordinary shares, and in many cases they will be the business's only form of capital. Whether or not a company seeks 'fixed return' funding in the form, primarily, of preference shares and debentures is a decision which may have far-reaching consequences for both the company and its existing and future shareholders.

The relationship between 'risk' capital (i.e. ordinary shares) and fixed return funding is known as the company's *gearing*, and is of major importance because of the varying priorities of interest and dividend payments, as follows:

First priority: Debenture interest—must be paid.

Second priority: Preference dividend—only paid if profits are available after paying debenture interest.

Third priority: Ordinary dividend—only paid if profits are available after both debenture interest and preference dividend have been paid.

It can be seen that the ordinary shareholders will do well in a profitable year when there is 'plenty for everybody', but a poor year may result in no dividend being paid to the providers of the risk capital after the fixed charges have been paid. This danger increases in direct proportion to the level of the company's gearing.

Gearing can be either high or low, and is calculated by using either of the following formulae:

$$\frac{\text{Fixed return funding}}{\text{Total long-term capital} + \text{Reserves}^*} \quad or \quad \frac{\text{Fixed return funding}}{\text{Equity capital} + \text{Reserves}^*}$$

These formulae will produce a gearing *ratio*, but a gearing *percentage* can be obtained simply by multiplying by 100/1. 'High' gearing is said to exist where the proportion of fixed return funding is relatively high (over 50%) in relation to total funding. 'Low' gearing is where the risk capital is dominant.

The effect that different gearing levels have on a company's ability to pay dividends can be seen in the following illustration.

Example 1

Two companies, H and L, each have total long-term capital and reserves of £150,000, divided as follows:

	H £	L £
Fixed return funding (8% preference shares)	100,000	10,000
Equity capital (£1 shares)	30,000	120,000
Reserves	20,000	20,000

The net profit before appropriations of each company for the three years ended 31 December 1983 were:

	£
1981	8,000
1982	25,000
1983	50,000

*In both cases the value of goodwill, if any, is deducted from this total owing to the intangible nature of the asset and the basic unreliability of its valuation.

Calculate: (a) the gearing ratio of each company; (b) the maximum percentage dividend which each company could pay to its ordinary shareholders in each of the three years ended 31 December 1983.

Solution:

(a) Using the formula

$$\frac{\text{Fixed return funding}}{\text{Total long-term capital} + \text{Reserves}}$$

The ratio for H is $\dfrac{£100,000}{£150,000}$ or 0.67:1 (67%)

The ratio for L is $\dfrac{£10,000}{£150,000}$ or 0.07:1 (7%)

Company H is said to be high geared; company L is low geared.

(b)

	H			L		
	1981	*1982*	*1983*	*1981*	*1982*	*1983*
Profits before appropriations	8,000	25,000	50,000	8,000	25,000	50,000
Preference dividend	8,000	8,000	8,000	800	800	800
Available for ordinary dividend	NIL	17,000	42,000	7,200	24,200	49,200
Maximum percentage dividend*	NIL	56.7	140	6	20.2	41

$*\ \dfrac{\text{Profits available}}{\text{Equity capital}} \times \dfrac{100}{1}$

COMMENTARY

Shareholders in L are able to receive a dividend in each of the three years due to the low gearing ratio of their company. Only a relatively small proportion of profits is committed to paying the fixed percentage dividend, and consequently the holders of the 120,000 ordinary shares can expect a 6% dividend even in 1981 when profits are at their lowest point.

H's ordinary shareholders will not receive a penny in 1981, as the prior commitment to the holders of the 100,000 preference shares has meant that there are no surplus profits available.

Once the profit level goes beyond the level of the fixed dividend, the holders of the 30,000 ordinary shares enjoy significantly greater dividends than their counterparts in the low-geared company. This is best illustrated by means of a graph as shown in Figure 6.1.

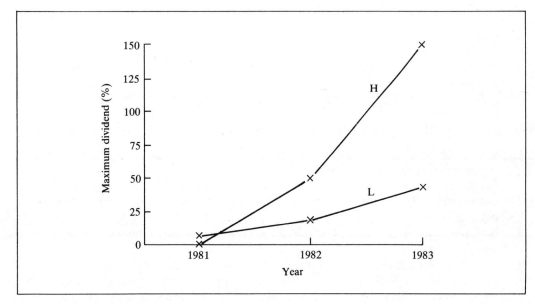

Fig. 6.1　The effect of gearing on dividend levels.

The importance of gearing

A company may decide to increase its gearing ratio for a number of reasons, as follows:

(a) Debenture interest (but not preference dividends) is an allowable charge against profits for the purposes of taxation assessment, and so the real rate of interest payable is reduced.

(b) If the company can earn a greater return on its capital than the cost of that capital, then the company will benefit by using borrowed money to expand its business.

(c) A high gearing ratio will attract 'risk' investors in a period of high profits as they are likely to receive much higher dividends than would be the case in a low-geared company.

(d) In periods of inflation, companies which borrowed money at fixed percentage rates are at a distinct advantage over companies whose cost of capital is directly linked to prevailing interest rates.

The major disadvantages which gearing carries for a company are:

i The loss of flexibility enjoyed by directors concerning the way in which the profit might be appropriated, as a large proportion is already committed for the fixed interest payments.

ii The possibility that potential investors would prefer low geared companies at a time when an economy is depressed and profits are stagnant, as only a small amount of such profits are attributed to fixed rate borrowing.

Example 2

Albert Contango was considering the purchase of ordinary shares in one of two limited companies. The following information was extracted from the balance sheets of the companies concerned as at 31 March 1984.

Acton Ltd	£000	*Becom Ltd*	£000
Issued capital		*Issued capital*	
50p ordinary shares, fully paid	700	£1 ordinary shares, fully paid	200
10% preference shares, fully paid	300	9% £1 preference shares, fully paid	400
	1,000		600
Share premium	200	Revaluation of freehold property reserve	200
General reserve	250	Profit and loss account	200
Profit and loss account	150	12% debentures (1998)	600
	1,600		1,600

For the year ended 31 March 1985 the companies had made the following reports.

1. Both companies had reported a net profit of £250,000 after charging interest, but before any appropriations had been made.

2. The directors of Acton Ltd had recommended a dividend of 5p for each ordinary share issued, whilst those of Becom Ltd had recommended an ordinary share dividend of 10%.

3. Both companies had recommended that the preference share dividends for the year be paid.

4. Each company had decided to transfer £100,000 to the company's general reserve.

5. The chairmen of both companies reported that profits (after charging interest, but before appropriations) for the next year would be £100,000 and were likely to remain at that level in the foreseeable future.

Required:

(a) Profit and loss appropriation accounts for the year ended 31 March 1985, preferably in columnar from.

(b) Suitable comparative diagrams showing:
  (i) the dividends paid as a proportion of the distributable reserves of each company as at 31 March 1985 before any appropriations are made;
  (ii) the issued and loan capital of each company identifying the gearing ratio.

(c) On the information available, advise Contango which company appears to offer the better prospects as an investment.

(d) List three other relevant factors which would assist Contango in making a decision.

(AEB)

Solution:

(a) *Profit and Loss Appropriation Accounts
for the year ended 31 March 1985*

	Acton Ltd		Becom Ltd	
	£000		£000	
Net profit		250		250
Less: Appropriations				
Transfer to general reserve	100		100	
Preference share dividend	30		36	
Ordinary share dividend	70		20	
		200		156
Retained profit for year		50		94
Retained profit b/f		150		200
Retained profit c/f		200		294

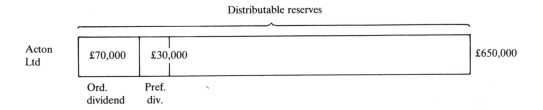

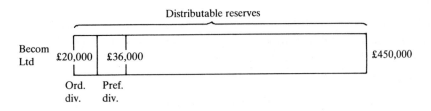

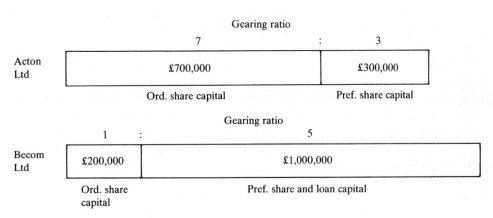

(b) *Distributable Reserves as at 31 March 1985 before any appropriations are made:*

	Acton Ltd £000		Becom Ltd £000
General reserve	250		—
Profit and loss account			
(150 + 250)	400	(200 + 250)	450
	650		450

(c) Acton Ltd is a low-geared company whilst Becom Ltd is high geared. In future years, when profits are at the £100,000 level, the equity sharolders of Becom Ltd are likely to receive a higher percentage dividend than the Acton Ltd shareholders, as can be seen from the following predicted P + L appropriation account for the year to 31 March 1986.

	Acton Ltd £000	Becom Ltd £000
Net profit	100	100
Less: Preference dividend	30	36
Available for ordinary dividend	70	64

Maximum possible % dividend

$$\frac{70}{700} \times 100 \qquad 10\%* \qquad \frac{64}{200} \times 100 \, 32\%$$

However, Acton Ltd had £550,000 of distributable reserves at 31 March 1985 compared with Becom's £394,000, and this could be drawn on to boost the proposed dividend.

Becom's *pre-interest* profit is £72,000 greater than Acton's, and this may be another indicator of the relative strengths of the two companies. If Contango intends the investment to be a long-term one, then the repayment of debentures in 1998 will have a dramatic effect on the profit available for ordinary dividends.

(d) Three other factors are

i The reliability of the profit forecasts.

ii The efficiency of the two companies as measured by, for example, the sales : fixed assets ratio.†

iii The relative solvency of the two companies as measured by the current ratio and the acid test ratio.†

COMMENTARY

Although straightforward on a first reading, this question was deceptive, an example being the calculations required in order to prepare the 'suitable comparative diagrams' required in part (b). Other forms of diagram would have been acceptable, e.g. pie charts.

6.7 The conversion of an unincorporated business into a limited company

When a sole trader or a partnership takes the decision to become a limited company, one form of business organisation ends its life whilst another is born. This 'death and birth' is reflected in the accounting records by closing off the sole trader's or partnership's books and the making of opening entries in the books of the company.

The closing entries are made via a *realisation account*, which contains the following transfers from asset and liability accounts, as well as the purchase consideration for the business.

Debit	*Credit*
Transfer asset balances	Transfer liability balances
	Purchase consideration (e.g. shares, cash, debentures)

*Equivalent to 5p per share of 50p nominal value.
†See Chapter 10.

Occasionally certain balances, notably trade creditors, are not to be transferred to the new company, but are to be paid off prior to the transfer. In such cases, there is no necessity to post the creditors' balances to realisation account, as they will be paid out of the business's bank account.

A number of assets and/or liabilities might be revalued prior to the transfer, and the purchase price of the business might be greater or less than the book value of its net assets.

Where the purchase price is greater than the agreed value of the net assets, the company is paying for goodwill. This represents a profit for the owners of the business being taken over, and is transferred from the realisation account to the capital account(s) of the owner or owners. If the purchase consideration is less than the agreed value of the business's net assets, then this represents *negative* goodwill, and is a loss to the owners which is debited to their capital accounts.

Note that the capital account balances are not posted to the realisation account, but are closed by transferring the appropriate amount of cash, shares, etc.

Example 3 illustrates the various techniques involved when a sole trader converts into a limited company.

Example 3

The balance sheet of a trader at 31 May 1985 stood as follows,

	£		£
Capital	19,000	Plant and machinery	13,000
		Fixtures and fittings	2,300
		Stock in trade	4,500
Trade creditors	4,500	Trade debtors	3,100
		Bank	600
	23,500		23,500

As from 1 June 1985 the business is to be converted into a limited company. The new company is to have an authorised share capital of £40,000 divided into 30,000 ordinary shares of £1 each and 10,000 5% preference shares of £1 each.

The company is to take over the assets and liabilities of the trader at book value, with the exception of the following:

	Agreed valuation £
Plant and machinery	9,000
Fixtures and fittings	2,000
Stock in trade	4,700
Trade creditors	4,400

The purchase price of the business, £22,200, is to be satisfied by the issue of:

£6,000 4% Debenture stock issued at par.
£5,000 5% Preference shares of £1 each, issued at par and credited as fully paid.
7,000 Ordinary shares of £1 each, issued at a premium and credited as fully paid.

On 1 June 1985 a further 20,000 ordinary shares of £1 each were issued at a premium of 60p per share to relatives of the trader. The issue was immediately fully subscribed, with the full price being paid on application.

You are required to:

(a) Prepare the journal entries, including narratives, to close the books of the trader.
(b) Draft the balance sheet of the limited company as at 2 June 1985. (Assume that no other transactions have taken place other than those mentioned above.)
(c) Calculate the gearing ratio of the limited company, and briefly explain its significance.

(ULSEB)

Solution:

(a)

(i)

		DR	CR
DR Realisation		19,000	
Trade creditors		4,500	
CR Plant and machinery			13,000
Fixtures and fittings			2,300
Stock in trade			4,500
Trade debtors			3,100
Bank balance			600

Transfer of net asset values on cessation of business entity.

(ii) DR Limited company's a/c   22,200

    CR Realisation   22,200

    Agreed purchase price of business

(iii) DR Realisation   3,200

    CR Capital   3,200

    Profit on realisation

(iv) DR Capital   22,200

    CR Limited company's a/c   22,200

    Agreed value of securities transferred in settlement

(b)

Limited Company

Balance Sheet as at 2 June 1985

Authorised share capital			Goodwill (1)	7,200
30,000 Ordinary £1 shares	30,000		Plant and machinery	9,000
10,000 5% Pref. shares of £1	10,000		Fixtures and fittings	2,000
				18,200
	£40,000			
Issued share capital				
27,000 ordinary £1				
shares (fully paid)	27,000			
5000 5% pref. shares of £1	5,000			
	32,000			
Share premium account (2)	16,200	Stock		4,700
4% debenture stock	6,000	Debtors		3,100
Creditors	4,400	Bank		32,600
	58,600			58,600

Workings:

(1)	Purchase price		22,200
	Book value of net assets		15,000
	Goodwill		£ 7,200
(2)	Purchase price		22,200
	Nominal value of securities		18,000
	Premium (7,000 × 60p)		4,200
	Additional 20,000 × 60p		12,000
	Total share premium		£16,200

(c) *Gearing ratio*

This can be calculated in a number of ways, but in this case the following formula has been used:

$$\frac{(\text{Preference shares} + \text{debentures})}{(\text{Total capital employed} - \text{goodwill})}$$

$$= \frac{(5,000 + 6,000)}{(54,200 - 7,200)} = \frac{11,000}{47,000} = 0.23$$

The company is low geared, with the company having to find only £490 out of profits to cover the debenture interest and preference dividend. Remaining profits are then available for distribution to ordinary shareholders.

COMMENTARY

The realisation account is the medium whereby the remaining accounts of the trader are closed off. The profit of £3,200 transferred to Capital Account is the difference betwen the purchase consideration of £22,200 and the book value of the net assets, £19,000. In the company's books the revised values of the net assets are brought in to the books (net value £15,000), with the difference of £7,200 as compared to the purchase price being debited to goodwill.

6.8 The unpublished financial statements of limited companies

It has already been stated that all limited companies must *publish* their annual financial statements. These published 'accounts' must be in a format prescribed by the 1985 Companies Act, as described later in this chapter. Prior to preparing accounts for publication, the company will prepare 'unpublished' accounts which are more detailed than those required by statute. In addition to being the basis for the published accounts, they will be used by the Inland Revenue for the purposes of taxation assessment and, in all probability, a copy will also be sent to the company's bank manager in order to give him a detailed insight into the company's performance.

The preparation of a limited company's final accounts in their unpublished form follows the usual book-keeping conventions, but there are a number of items which are unique to companies when contrasted with the final accounts of sole traders and partnerships, as can be seen in Figure 6.2.

Example 4

The following balances were extracted from the accounts of W. D. Jones & Co Ltd at 31 March 1983 after the manufacturing account had been drawn up.

	£	£
Capital		
500,000 ordinary shares of 50p each, 40p paid		200,000
100,000 10% preference shares of £1 each, fully paid		100,000
Share premium account		40,000
General reserve		59,300
Profit and loss account		56,600
9% debentures (secured)		80,000
Debtors and creditors	121,000	93,200
Cash at bank and in hand	65,800	
Freehold premises, at cost	320,000	
Plant and machinery, at cost	285,000	
Office equipment, at cost	61,200	
Stock	112,030	
Provision for bad debts		4,150
Provision for depreciation:		
Freehold premises		90,000
Plant and machinery		80,300
Office equipment		25,000
Gross profit		246,000
Cash discounts	2,126	3,636
Debenture interest	3,600	
Salaries	49,100	
Insurances	1,870	
General expenses	17,220	
Selling expenses	23,530	
Delivery expenses	15,710	
	1,078,186	1,078,186

Revenue statement	Sole trader	Partnership	Limited company
Manufacturing account (if applicable)	✓	✓	✓
Trading account (if applicable)	✓	✓	✓
Profit and loss account	✓	✓	✓ includes directors' salaries, auditors' fees and possibly debenture interest
Appropriation account	No	✓ showing financial implications of partnership agreement (see 4.3)	✓ showing the ways in which profit is appropriated (see 6.5)
Capital statement			
Fixed assets	✓	✓	✓
Current assets	✓	✓	✓
Current liabilities	✓	✓	✓ may include liabilities for corporation tax, dividends and debenture interest
Capital account	✓	✓ for each partner	No
Current account	No	✓ for each partner if 'fixed capital method' used	No
Share capital	No	No	✓ separate headings for 'Authorised' and 'Issued'
Reserves	No	No	✓
Debentures	No	No	✓ (if any)

Fig. 6.2 Comparison between the financial statements (unpublished) of limited companies and those of sole traders and partnerships.

Notes (to account on page 131):

(a) Depreciation has to be provided as follows:
Freehold property 2½% per annum on cost.
Office equipment 10% per annum on cost.
(b) Included in the cost of office equipment is an item purchased on 1 October 1982 for £1,800; there were no disposals and there have been no additions to, nor disposals from, plant and machinery during the year.
(c) The bad debts provision is to be adjusted to 2½% of debtors.
(d) Provision has to be made for the half year's debenture interest outstanding.
(e) Insurance amounting to £350 has been paid in advance.
(f) Provision has to be made for the 10% dividend on the preference shares and a recommended dividend of 20% on the paid-up amount of the ordinary shares.
(g) £50,000 is to be transferred to the general reserve.

(h) Authorised capital consists of 600,000 ordinary shares of 50p each and 100,000 preference shares of £1 each.

Required:
Profit and loss account for the year ended 31 March 1983 and a balance sheet as at that date taking the above matters into consideration. Ignore taxation.   (WJEC)

Solution:

W. D. Jones & Co Ltd
Profit and Loss Account for the year ended 31 March 1983

	£	£	£
Gross profit			246,000
Add: Cash discounts received			3,636
Provision for bad debts, written back			1,125
			250,761
Less: Expenses			
Salaries		49,100	
Insurances		1,520	
General expenses		17,220	
Selling expenses		23,530	
Cash discounts allowed		2,126	
Delivery expenses		15,710	
Depreciation: Freehold property	8,000		
Office equipment	6,840*	14,840	
Debenture interest		7,200	131,246
Net profit			119,515
Appropriation:			
Transfer to general reserve		50,000	
Proposed dividends:			
preference	10,000		
ordinary	40,000	50,000	
			100,000
Retained profit for the year			19,515
Retained profit b/f			56,600
Retained profit c/f			£76,115

Balance Sheet as at 31 March 1983

Fixed assets	£	£	£
Freehold premises, at cost		320,000	
Less: Provision for depreciation		98,000	222,000
Plant and machinery, at cost		285,000	
Less: Provision for depreciation		80,300	204,700
Office equipment, at cost		61,200	
Less: Provision for depreciation		31,840	29,360
			456,060
Current assets			
Stock		112,030	
Debtors	121,000		
Less: Provision for bad debts	3,025	117,975	
Prepayment		350	
Cash at bank and in hand		65,800	
		296,155	

*Working: [10% × (61,200 − 1,800)] + [10% × (6/12 × 1,800)]
=   5,940   +   900   = £6,840

Less: Current liabilities			
Trade creditors		93,200	
Accrual: Debenture interest		3,600	
Proposed dividends		50,000	146,800
			149,355
			£605,415

Share capital			
Authorised: 600,000 ordinary shares of 50p each			300,000
100,000 preference shares of £1 each			100,000
			£400,000
Issued:	500,000 ordinary shares of 50p each, 40p paid		200,000
	100,000 10% preference shares of £1 each, fully paid		100,000
			300,000
Reserves:	Share premium account	40,000	
	General reserve	109,300	
	Profit and loss account	76,115	225,415
			525,415
Long-term liability: 9% Debentures			80,000
			£605,415

COMMENTARY

There are only two items which require further explanation, both relating to the share capital. The authorised share capital, which is the maximum amount of capital which the company is allowed to issue, is shown as a *note* on the balance sheet for information only. The issued share capital, in this question, included ordinary shares of 50p each of which only 40p was paid. This simply means that shareholders had not yet paid the full amount due on their shares, the company having 'called' for only 40p. The company is likely, at some future date, to request the remaining instalment from its shareholders.

6.9 The published accounts of limited companies

With over 900,000 registered companies in the United Kingdom, it is of obvious benefit to have a degree of uniformity in the form of presentation adopted for the published accounts. Prior to 1981, individual companies were given relative freedom as to the way in which information was given, provided that the disclosure requirements of company law were observed. The 1981 Companies Act (later consolidated in the 1985 Act) brought an end to such individuality by requiring companies to use the formats given in the Act when presenting profit and loss accounts and balance sheets for publication.

The formats (four for the profit and loss account and two for the balance sheet) are shown in Appendix 2. The choice of format is even more restricted than appears at first sight, as the balance sheet format 2 is merely the 'horizontal' version of format 1, whilst profit and loss account formats 3 and 4 are the 'horizontal' versions of formats 1 and 2 respectively.

Once a company has chosen between the various formats, the same format must be used each year unless, in the opinion of the directors, there are special reasons for a change. Items may be shown in *greater* detail than required by the formats, and headings or subheadings in the formats may be deleted if there is no amount to be shown in respect of the financial year in question and the previous year.

WHICH FORMAT TO CHOOSE?

1. Balance sheet – there is no real choice, as format 2 contains the same information as format 1, but in a horizontal as opposed to a vertical layout. In practice most companies use the vertical style of format 1.

Stoddard Holdings PLC and subsidiary companies

Balance Sheets

as at 31 March, 1985

Holding Company 1984 £'000	1985 £'000		Notes	Group 1985 £'000	1984 £'000
		Fixed assets:			
—	—	Tangible assets	10	3,719	3,998
—	—	Properties held for disposal	11	690	824
1,541	261	Investments in subsidiaries	12	—	—
1,541	261			4,409	4,822
		Current assets:			
—	—	Stocks	13	7,882	7,767
9,528	5,269	Debtors	14	5,572	5,876
—	1,734	Cash at bank and in hand		153	108
9,528	7,003			13,607	13,751
3,041	720	**Creditors: amounts falling due within one year**	15	11,130	10,156
6,487	6,283	**Net current assets**		2,477	3,595
8,028	6,544	**Total assets less current liabilities**		6,886	8,417
		Creditors: amounts falling due after more than one year:			
—	—	Loans	16	52	93
8,028	6,544			6,834	8,324
		Accruals and deferred income:			
—	—	Deferred government grants		290	296
8,028	6,544			6,544	8,028
		Capital and reserves:			
5,766	5,766	Called up share capital	17	5,766	5,766
(1,443)	(2,801)	Revaluation reserve	18	1,461	1,603
2,007	2,007	Other reserves	18	3,916	3,916
1,698	1,572	Profit and loss account	18	(4,599)	(3,257)

G. D. J. Hay ⎫ *Directors*
C. A. B. MacLean ⎭

18 July, 1985.

| 8,028 | 6,544 | | | 6,544 | 8,028 |

Fig. 6.3 Balance sheet (Format 1) – Stoddard Holdings plc.

2. Profit and loss account – ignoring the horizontal options of formats 3 and 4, the choice is between:

(a) Format 1, which discloses gross profit, and presents the information in a way which should be reasonably familiar to students. Most companies use this format.

(b) Format 2, which is more suited to a manufacturing business, does not disclose the company's gross profit, but requires more detail than format 1 concerning such matters as 'own work capitalised' (e.g. wages paid to the company's own workers for the construction of fixed assets) and staff costs.

Note that items 7–20 in format 1 are identical to items 9–22 in format 2. Students are unlikely, at this stage of their studies, to require a comprehensive knowledge of this topic, but should be aware of the main features of the formats.

In addition to the information to be shown within the specified format, the Companies Act also requires disclosure of numerous other aspects of the company's financial picture, which are given in a series of notes to the accounts.

The principal disclosure requirements are as follows:

Group Profit and Loss Account

for the 52 weeks ended 27th April 1985

	Notes	1985 £000	1984 £000
Turnover		463,240	471,387
Cost of sales		401,164	403,681
Gross profit		62,076	67,706
Distribution costs		32,807	37,730
Administrative expenses		16,400	17,250
		12,869	12,726
Other operating income		1,518	769
Share of profits of related companies		—	260
		14,387	13,755
Interest (net)	1	1,925	2,383
Profit on ordinary activities before tax	2	16,312	16,138

Fig. 6.4   Profit and loss account (Format 1) – Fitch Lovell plc.

Group Profit and Loss Account

for the fifty-two weeks ended 28 April 1985

	Notes	£000	1985 £000	£000	1984 £000
Turnover	1		80,229		74,221
Change in stocks of finished goods and in work in progress			1,163		855
			81,392		75,076
Other operating income			861		969
			82,253		76,045
Raw materials and consumables		53,998		50,367	
Other external charges		1,479		1,435	
			55,477		51,802
			26,776		24,243
Staff costs	2	13,315		12,058	
Depreciation of tangible assets	3	1,639		1,622	
Other operating charges	4	2,822		2,486	
			17,776		16,166
			9,000		8,077
Share of profits of associated companies		446		600	
Income from trade investments	5	24		18	
Interest receivable	6	304		202	
			774		820
			9,774		8,897
Interest payable	7		120		141
Profit on ordinary activities before taxation			9,654		8,756

Fig. 6.5   Profit and loss account (Format 2) – Greene, King & Sons plc.

Turnover

Analyses of turnover are required in respect of:

(a) classes of business; and
(b) geographical markets supplied.

Staff costs

(a) Wages, salaries, etc. Formats 2 and 4 provide for the profit and loss account to show an analysis under this heading as between (i) wages and salaries; (ii) social security costs; and (iii) other pension costs. Where format 1 or 3 is adopted, aggregate costs so analysed are to be disclosed in the notes.
(b) Average number of employees. Information is to be given as to the average number of persons employed in the year (including part-time employees).
(c) Directors' emoluments are to be stated separately in a note to the accounts showing:
  i   aggregate emoluments,
  ii aggregate of directors' pensions,
  iii aggregate of compensation paid for loss of office,
  iv the number of directors whose emoluments fall in each bracket of a scale in multiples of £5,000,
  v   the emoluments of the highest-paid director(s) if in excess of those of the chairman.

(Items (iv) and (v) above do not apply to directors whose duties were wholly or mainly outside the United Kingdom or to a company where the aggregate directors' emoluments do not exceed £60,000.)

(d) Chairman's emoluments.
(e) Emoluments of employees receiving more than £30,000 per annum.

Depreciation and other amounts written off tangible and intangible fixed assets

Amounts written off investments. Provision for diminution in value of investments included in either fixed or current assets and (separately) any provisions written back are to be shown.

Interest payable and similar charges

Separate disclosure is required of interest, etc. on:

(a) bank loans and overdrafts or other loans to the company which are repayable within five years; and
(b) loans of any other kind to the company.

Profit or loss on ordinary activities before taxation. This is a required heading, though not listed in the prescribed formats.

Tax on profit or loss on ordinary activities

Extraordinary income and extraordinary charges. Particulars are to be given of any extraordinary income or charges arising in the financial year.

Further disclosures required are:
Transfers to or from reserves (shown in the profit and loss account).
Dividends paid and proposed (shown in the profit and loss account).
Rents from land (if they form a substantial part of the revenue for the year).
Hire of plant and machinery.
Remuneration of the auditors.
Amounts relating to preceding years.
Exceptional transactions.

Example 5

Redwood plc is a retailing company. The following trial balance has been extracted from the books of account as at 30 June 1984:

	£000 DR	£000 CR
Accrued expenses		26
Accumulated depreciation on furniture and fittings (at 1 July 1983)		100
Administration expenses	150	
Auditors remuneration	20	
Cash at bank and in hand	56	
Debenture interest	5	
Debenture loan stock (10%)		50
Distribution costs	100	
Dividends received (on 1 June 1984)		14
Fixed assets: listed investments	70	
Furniture and fittings at cost	200	
Hire charges (distribution plant, machinery, equipment and vehicles)	340	
Interim dividend (paid on 1 January 1984)	10	
Issued share capital		280
Prepaid expenses	29	
Profit and loss account (balance at 1 July 1983)		
Purchases	500	90
Sales (exclusive of VAT)		1,200
Share premium account		70
Stock (at 1 July 1983)	200	
Trade creditors		100
Trade debtors	250	
	£1,930	£1,930

Additional information:

After compiling the trial balance, it was realised that some transactions had not been entered in the books of account, and the following additional information should be allowed for in the preparation of the published accounts:

1. Stock at 30 June 1984 was valued at £300,000.
2. Depreciation of £40,000 (classed as an administration expense) is to be charged on the furniture and fittings for the year to 30 June 1984. There were no purchases or sales of furniture during the year.
3. Administration expenses include directors' emoluments of £55,000.
4. The corporation tax payable (based on the profits for the year to 30 June 1984 at a rate of 50%) is estimated to amount to £50,000.
5. Redundancy costs of £30,000 (not expected to recur) had accrued on 30 June 1984, but upon which there will be corporation tax relief of £15,000.
6. The company proposes to pay a final ordinary dividend of 10%.
7. The market value of the fixed assets listed investments at 30 June 1984 was £85,000.
8. The authorised share capital of the company was 350,000 ordinary shares of £1 each.

Required:

Prepare the company's profit and loss account for the year to 30 June 1984 and a balance sheet as at that date in accordance with the Companies Act and with best practice (in so far as the information permits).

Relevant notes to the accounts along with your workings should be submitted with your answer.

(AAT – slightly amended)

Solution:

Redwood plc
Profit and Loss Account for the year to 30 June 1984

	Notes	£000
Turnover	1	1,200
Cost of sales (Workings 1)		(400)
Gross profit		800
Distribution costs (£100 + 340)		(440)
Administration expenses (£150 + 40 + 20)		(210)

	Notes	£000
Operating profit	2	150
Other income	3	14
Interest payable and similar charges	4	(5)
Profit on ordinary activities before taxation		159
Tax on profit on ordinary activities	5	(50)
Profit on ordinary activities after taxation		109
Extraordinary item	6	(15)
Profit for the financial year		94
Dividends paid and proposed	7	(38)
Retained profit for the year		56
Earnings per ordinary share	8	39p

Statement of retained profit

	£000
Balance at 1 July 1983	90
Retained profit for the year	56
Balance at 30 June 1984	146

Redwood plc
Balance Sheet at 30 June 1984

	Notes	£000
Fixed assets:		
Tangible assets	9	60
Investments	10	70
		130
Current assets:		
Stocks	11	300
Debtors	12	279
Cash at bank and in hand		56
		635
Creditors:		
Amounts falling due within one year	13	(219)
Net current assets		416
Total assets less current liabilities		546
Creditors:		
Amounts falling due after more than one year	14	(50)
		496
Capital and reserves:		
Called-up share capital	15	280
Share premium account		70
Profit and loss account		146
		496

The accounts were approved by the Board on ....

_____

Directors

_____

Redwood plc

Redwood plc

Notes:

		£000
1	Turnover	

Turnover represents the amount receivable for goods sold exclusive of Value Added Tax

2 Operating profit

Operating profit has been arrived at after charging:

	£000
Director's emoluments	55
Depreciation	40
Hire of plant, machinery and equipment	340
Auditors' remuneration	20

3 Other income

Other income arises from listed fixed asset investments 14

4 Interest

Interest payable on debenture loan stock 5

5 Taxation

Taxation on the profit for the year:

UK corporation tax at 50% 50

6 Extraordinary item

	£000
Redundancy costs	30
Less: UK corporation tax	15
	15

7 Dividends

		£000
Ordinary – interim	3.5p per share	10
– proposed final	10p per share	28
		38

8 Earnings per ordinary share

The calculation of earnings per ordinary share is based on the profit before the extraordinary item and on 280,000 ordinary shares of £1 each in issue during the year.

9 Tangible fixed assets

Furniture and fittings

Cost

	£000
At 1 July 1983 and at 30 June 1984	200

Accumulated depreciation

	£000
At 1 July 1983	100
Charge for the year	40
At 30 June 1984	140

Net book value

	£000
At 30 June 1984	60
At 1 July 1983	100

10 Fixed asset investments

Shares at cost in respect of investments listed on a recognised stock exchange (market value £85,000)

11 Stocks

Stocks represent goods for resale

12 Debtors

Amounts falling due within one year

	£000
Trade debtors	250
Prepayments and accrued income	29
	279

13 Creditors: Amounts falling due within one year

Trade creditors	100
Taxation and social security (Workings 2)	35
Accruals and deferred income (£26 + 30)	56
Proposed dividend	28
	219

14 Creditors: Amounts falling due after more than one year

Debenture loans	50

15 Called up share capital
    Allotted and fully paid

Ordinary shares of £1 each	280
Authorised	350

Workings: £'000

1. Cost of sales

Opening stock	200
Purchases	500
	700
Less: Closing stock	300
	400

2. Creditors: amounts falling due within one year
    Taxation and social security

Corporation tax based on the profits for the year	50
Less: Tax relief on extraordinary item	15
	35

COMMENTARY

Students who are able to obtain a copy of an actual set of a company's published accounts will appreciate the complex requirements imposed, not only by the Companies Act, but also by the various statements of standard accounting practice. The above example gives a good introduction to the subject of published company financial statements, and readers would be well advised to work through the question carefully in order to gain a reasonable knowledge of the topic.

6.10 Small and medium-sized companies

The Companies Act allows certain companies to file *modified* accounts with the Registrar of Companies, although unmodified accounts must still be presented to the shareholders. The companies which are eligible for these accounting exemptions are those which the Act defines as being either 'small' or 'medium-sized', as follows:

	Small company	*Medium-sized company*
Turnover not exceeding	£1,400,000	£5,750,000
Balance sheet total not exceeding	£ 700,000	£2,800,000
Average number of persons employed (on a weekly basis) not exceeding	50	250

In order to be classified as either 'small' or 'medium-sized', the company must:

(a) satisfy at least two of the three criteria listed above;
(b) not be a public company;
(c) not be a banking, shipping or insurance company.

Assuming that a company does qualify, what exemptions are available? For a 'small' company, only a summarised balance sheet and certain important notes to the accounts (e.g. those relating to accounting policies, share capital and creditors falling due after more than five years) need be published. Neither the profit and loss account nor the directors' report is delivered for publication.

In the case of a 'medium-sized' company, the exemptions are less generous, as a profit and loss account, balance sheet and directors' report must be filed. However, the profit and loss account may commence with the 'gross profit or loss', without the need for the company's turnover to be disclosed, and the notes to the accounts are only those required by statute (other than that relating to turnover). Those required by accounting standards need not be given.

The decision whether or not to prepare modified accounts will depend upon the directors' assessment of the sensitivity or confidentiality of the information which is being withheld from public record. As full statutory information must be prepared for shareholders, the directors may feel that the additional costs to be incurred in the preparation of modified accounts may well outweigh any benefit to be gained.

Exercises

6.1 The owner of a small manufacturing business is considering converting the business to a limited company. Explain the main changes in connection with his personal liability for the debts of the business and with the preparation and keeping of accounts that would arise from converting the business from a sole trader to a limited company.

6.2 Explain the difference between a private limited company and a public limited company.

6.3 Explain the significance of a *provision* in the accounts of a company, and contrast it with the creation of a *reserve*.

6.4 The basic data from the accounts for the last financial year are summarised below.

	£
Share capital and reserves	45,667
Creditors due after one year (fixed interest loans)	22,984
Creditors due within one year	16,892
	£85,543
Tangible fixed assets	34,287
Current assets	51,256
	£85,543
Sales	105,684
Variable costs	49,221
Contribution margin	56,463
Fixed costs (excluding interest)	24,308
Profit before interest	32,155
Interest	2,298
Profit after interest	£29,857

You are required to:

(a) state two definitions of financial gearing;
(b) calculate them using the data provided;
(c) explain the importance of gearing to shareholders with numerical illustrations where appropriate;
(d) explain the importance of gearing to management with numerical illustrations where appropriate.

(CDAF)

6.5 The following information was extracted from the balance sheets of two limited companies, X Ltd and Y Ltd, for the financial year ended 30 April 1984:

	X Ltd £000	Y Ltd £000
Authorised share capital		
50p ordinary shares	250	400
10% £1 preference shares	150	—
Issued share capital		
50p ordinary shares	200	300
10% £1 preference shares	150	—
Reserves		
Share premium	70	100
Other capital reserves	130	50
Retained earnings	150	200
Loan Capital		
8% debentures (1992)	300	—
10% loan stock	—	150

Required:

(a) Explain what is meant by the term 'gearing', when examining a limited company's capital structure.

(b) Using an appropriate formula, determine the gearing factor for each of the companies X Ltd and Y Ltd.
Interpret your results.

(c) What possible advantages arise to a limited company when using a high gearing factor?

(d) Explain why an ordinary shareholder of X Ltd would be concerned during a period of falling profits.

(AEB)

6.6 Ferrous Manufacturing Ltd, of Silverdale, had an authorised capital of 600,000 ordinary shares of £0.50 each and 150,000 8% preference shares of £1 each. The following balances were taken from the company's books as at 31 December 1983.

	£
Ordinary share capital	200,000
8% preference share capital	80,000
Trade creditors	80,800
Work-in-progress 1-1-83	68,000
Stock of finished goods 1-1-83	63,200
Raw materials stocks 1-1-83	46,000
Fixtures and fittings at cost	6,000
Discounts received	2,200
Bank overdraft	30,000
Accumulated provision for depreciation of fixtures and fittings	3,000
Bank interest (debit balance)	6,400
Office salaries	64,600
Sales	956,000
Advertising	14,000
Salesmen's commissions	10,600
Unappropriated profit b/f	8,000
Debtors	59,200
Directors' fees	20,600
Carriage outwards	24,000
Returns inwards	4,000
Preference dividend paid 30-6-83	3,200
Interim ordinary dividend	15,000

Notes:

1. Stocks at 31 December 1983, valued at cost, were raw materials £52,000, work-in-progress £72,000, finished goods £58,000.
2. Depreciate fixtures and fittings for one year at 10% on cost.
3. The factory production was charged to the finished goods warehouse at a cost of £760,000 and the manufacturing account for the year 1983 showed a profit of £23,200.
4. £16,000 is to be transferred to a reserve for increased replacement costs of fixed assets.
5. A final dividend of 12½% on the ordinary share capital is proposed.

Required:

Using only those figures from the above list of balances that are required for the purpose, prepare a trading and profit and loss account and an appropriation account for the calendar year 1983.

(LCCI – Intermediate)

6.7 The following balances were extracted from the books of account of the Hampden Trading Co Ltd at 31 March 1984.

	DR £	CR £
Issued Share Capital, 400,000 shares of £1 each, 80p paid		320,000
General reserve		50,000
Profit and loss account balance		27,233
Share premium account		30,000
Lease of premises, at cost	200,000	
Provision for amortisation of lease		60,000
Fixtures and fittings, at cost	46,000	
Provision for depreciation of fixtures and fittings		25,000
Motor vans, at cost	27,000	
Provision for depreciation of motor vans		13,000
Stock, 1 April 1983	115,672	
Purchases	698,526	
Sales		929,647
Purchases returns		5,721
Sales returns	6,819	
Creditors		58,618
Debtors	167,543	
Salaries	32,108	
Directors' fees	6,200	
Provision for bad debts		6,810
Cash discounts allowed	17,512	
Cash discounts received		12,208
Bad debts	5,268	
General administrative expenses	76,818	
Cash at bank and in hand	120,150	
Provision for costs of legal action		10,200
Selling expenses	28,821	
	1,548,437	1,548,437

The following information is also available:

(a) The authorised capital is £500,000 in ordinary shares of £1 each.
(b) The provision for costs of legal action is no longer required.
(c) Provision is to be made for depreciation as follows:
    i   motor vans at the rate of 20% per annum on cost.
    ii fixtures and fittings at the rate of 10% per annum on cost.
(d) The term of the lease is 40 years and amortisation is provided in equal annual instalments.

(e) Provision for bad debts is to be provided as to £503 for a specific debt, plus 2½% of the remainder of the debtors.

(f) Stock at 31 March 1984 was valued at £107,561.

(g) Commission of £210 is owing to representatives and the general administrative expenses include £1,200 for insurance paid in advance.

(h) A dividend of 10% on the nominal value of the shares has been authorised.

Required:

Trading and profit and loss accounts for the year ended 31 March 1984 and a balance sheet as at that date. Ignore taxation

(WJEC)

6.8 The following balances have been extracted from the books of Malham Ltd, a trading company, as at 31 March 1984:

	£000
Issued share capital: 800,000 ordinary shares of £1 each	800
Bank loan	140
Retained profit at 1 April 1983	573
Net profit for the year to 31 March 1984	229
Freehold properties at cost	780
Fixtures and fittings at cost	217
Accumulated depreciation on fixtures and fittings at 31 March 1984	76
Creditors	206
Trade debtors	391
Prepaid expenses	13
Stocks at cost	464
Balance of cash at bank	75
Cash in hand	24
Goodwill at cost	60

The following additional information is provided:

(a) The freehold properties purchased in 1965 were revalued at £1,050,000 on 31 March 1984. The valuation was made by Collins and Co, a firm of chartered surveyors, and the directors have decided to use this figure for the purpose of the accounts.

(b) The company purchased fixtures and fittings costing £67,000 during the year to 31 March 1984. The depreciation charge for the year amounted to £22,000. There were no sales of fixed assets.

(c) The figure for creditors includes advance payments of £15,000 from a customer who was not supplied with the goods ordered until 5 April 1984.

(d) The following information is provided in respect of groups of similar items of stocks:

Group	Cost	Net realisable value
	£000	£000
W	127	186
X	35	7
Y	209	352
Z	93	184

(e) The goodwill arose on the purchase of the business assets of Tarn Ltd, a small private company, on 1 April 1983. The goodwill is believed to have a useful economic life of five years.

(f) A bank loan of £160,000 was raised to help to finance the acquisition of Tarn's business assets. The loan carries interest at a fixed rate of 12% and is repayable by eight equal annual instalments. The first instalment was paid on 31 March 1984 together with interest accrued to that date.

(g) The directors propose to recommend to the annual general meeting the payment of a dividend of 8p per ordinary share.

Required:

The balance sheet of Malham Ltd at 31 March 1984 together with relevant notes complying with the minimum requirements of the Companies Act so far as the information permits.

Notes:

1. Ignore depreciation of freehold properties and taxation.
2. Show your calculation of the profit and loss account balance for inclusion in the balance sheet.

(IOB)

Required:

The balance sheet of Malham Ltd at 31 March 1984 together with relevant notes complying with the minimum requirements of the Companies Act so far as the information permits.

CHAPTER 7

Accounting for Limited Liability Companies (2)

7.1 Issues of shares

The issued share capital of a limited company can increase in three ways:

1. By a sale of shares, usually for cash: only plcs are allowed to sell their shares *to the general public*, by means of a prospectus issue or an offer for sale. Private limited companies are not allowed to offer their shares to the public.
2. By a rights issue, whereby shares are sold to existing shareholders, usually at a discounted price.
3. By a bonus issue, whereby shares are given to existing shareholders without any cash being payable to the company.

7.2 Sale of shares

As mentioned in the previous chapter, the overwhelming majority of companies in

This advertisement is not an invitation to subscribe for or to purchase any Securities.

TOWERBELL RECORDS plc

(Incorporated in England under the Companies Acts 1948 to 1976 — Number 1504633)

OFFER FOR SALE
by

CLEVELAND SECURITIES plc and **HARVARD SECURITIES PLC**

(Licensed Dealer in Securities)   (Licensed Dealer in Securities)

of

3,182,286 Ordinary shares of 1p each at 35p per share
payable in full on application
The subscription lists will close at
3.00pm on Thursday 11th July 1985.

TOWERBELL RECORDS plc is a successful British independent record company with a number of major international stars, such as Shirley Bassey, Nils Lofgren, Cilla Black and Justin Hayward of the Moody Blues already signed to the label and Chas and Dave to the affiliated label "Rockney". Further important signings are expected during the year as well as the development of its associations with television companies through the establishment of a new label which exclusively handles theme music. The company is prominent in the promotion of records via television advertising which coupled with an aggressive marketing stance places it well on the way to becoming a major force in the UK record business.

To: Harvard Securities PLC, Harvard House,
42/44 Dolben Street, London SE1 0UQ   Tel: 01-928 2661
Please send a copy of the prospectus for TOWERBELL RECORDS plc

Name...

Address...

....

....

1% commission will be paid to professional intermediaries through whom successful applications are submitted.

Fig. 7.1 Reproduced from *Financial Weekly*, 5–11 July 1985.

the United Kingdom are private ones and as such are not allowed to offer their shares or debentures to the general public. However, they *are* able to sell their shares, but the persons buying are likely to be friends, relatives or business acquaintances of existing shareholders.

A plc wishing to raise capital by means of a share issue will usually do so by means of an *offer for sale*, whereby the shares are sold by the company to a merchant bank, which in turn offers the shares for sale to the general public by placing advertisements (known as prospectuses) in national newspapers. The prospectus contains very detailed information concerning the background of the company, its past financial performance and profit forecasts. Persons wishing to buy shares simply return an application form to the merchant bank, together with a cheque for the appropriate amount.

The price at which shares are offered will be set at the point which, in the opinion of the company, demand for the shares will match the supply. In practice, however, share issues are either *oversubscribed* or *undersubscribed*, the former resulting from a high demand for shares due to such factors as a favourable price and good press comment, the latter resulting from weak demand caused perhaps by adverse newspaper reports or over-pricing. The share price, whether considered high or low, will invariably be set at a premium to the nominal value, and the company may require the purchase price to be paid at intervals, rather than in one lump sum. Example 1 shows how the company accounts for a share issue where part of the purchase price is paid when the shares are applied for, part when the shares are allotted (i.e. issued to shareholders) and the final part (known as a 'call') four months after the application date.

Example 1

Corker plc (which has issued share capital of £4 million) wishes to raise additional capital by the issue of shares.

On 1 April 1986, 400,000 ordinary shares of £1 each were issued at £2.25 per share, payable as to £1.50 on application, including the premium, 30p on allotment due by 30 June 1986 and 45p on the first and only call to be made on 1 August 1986. By the closing date, applications for 450,000 shares were received, and all applications were scaled down on a pro rata basis. All surplus cash received on applications was used as part payment of the amount due on allotment.

Write up the ledger accounts necessary to record the above transactions and prepare an extract from the company's balance sheet at 1 August 1986. Assume that all sums due were paid in full by the appropriate dates.

Solution:

Corker plc

Bank account

1986			£
1 April	Application monies	(2)	675,000
30 June	Allotment monies	(8)	45,000
1 Aug	Call money	(14)	180,000

Application and allotment account

1986			£	1986			£
1 April	Share capital (400,000 × £0.25)	(4)	100,000	1 April	Cash on application (450,000 × £1.50)	(3)	675,000
	Share premium (400,000 × £1.25)	(6)	500,000	30 June	Cash on allotment (400,000 × £0.30 less £75,000)	(9)	45,000
30 June	Share capital (400,000 × £0.30)	(10)	120,000				
			720,000				720,000

Call account

1986			£	1986			£
1 Aug	Share capital	(12)	180,000	1 Aug	Cash (400,000 × £0.45)	(15)	180,000

Share capital account

1986			£
1 Apr	b/f	(1)	4,000,000
	Application and allotment a/c	(5)	100,000
30 Jun	Application and allotment a/c	(11)	120,000
1 Aug	Call account	(13)	180,000
			4,400,000

Share premium account

1986			£
1 Apr	Application and allotment a/c	(7)	500,000

Balance Sheet as at 1 August 1986 (extract)

Share capital		£
Authorised:	? ordinary shares of £1 each	?
Issued:	4,400,000 ordinary shares of £1 each, fully paid	4,400,000
Reserves:	Share premium account	500,000

COMMENTARY

The sequence of entries is very straightforward, and can best be followed by referring to the entry order shown in brackets. (These numbers would *not* be included in the actual ledger.) The net effect of the entries is to increase the bank account by £900,000, the share capital account by £400,000 and the share premium account by £500,000. It has been assumed that there was no opening balance on the share premium account.

Forfeited shares

Most share issues are paid for in full at the time of application, but the offer for sale particulars will make it quite clear whether calls are to be made at intervals after the shares have been allotted. Occasionally, shareholders may have difficulty paying these calls, in which case they run the risk of having their shares forfeited, and the loss of the monies paid on application and allotment. The company may, if it wishes, re-issue these shares at some future date.

7.3 Rights issues

If a plc decides to sell shares by means of an offer for sale, it will have to pay a considerable sum by way of advertising costs and fees to professional advisers. An alternative method of raising money by an established company is to make a *rights issue* whereby existing shareholders are given the right to buy more shares from the company at a price which is lower than the current market value. The company will, at the time it announces the rights issue, send a document to the shareholders explaining why it has decided to raise more capital. Reasons most often cited include the expansion of the business by takeovers, the reduction in the level of borrowings, and the need to fund research and development. Shareholders have the following choices when the company makes a rights issue:

(a) Take up the rights issue by buying the additional shares.
(b) Sell the rights to another person, who will then take up the rights in place of the original shareholder. This course of action is taken by shareholders who either do not have the money available to pay for the rights, or do not wish to invest further sums in the company owing to there being better investment opportunities elsewhere.

7.4 Bonus issues

Also called a capitalisation issue or scrip issue, a bonus issue is an issue of shares to existing shareholders without any cash being required by the company. The shares

Hazlewood Foods in £20.5m cash call

By Stefan Wagstyl

Hazlewood Foods, the fast-expanding food manufacturer with a range of products from pickles to pizzas, is raising £20.5m with a deeply-discounted one-for-one rights issue.

The Derby-based company, which earlier this month announced a 98 per cent increase in pre-tax profits to £6.09m for the year to the end of March, wants the money to reduce its £21m borrowings and have the means to fund further expansion.

Since April last year, the company has spent £22m on acquisitions exanding from its original business in bottling pickles and sauces. The biggest purchases were F. H. Lee, a maker of kitchen tissues, and Knight European Food Group, which supplies salads and delicatessen foods.

Mr Dennis Jones, finance director, said that the company was concentrating its expansion on chilled foods but it would not overlook opportunities in other parts of the food and groceries market.

Hazlewood was considering a number of further acquisitions, all privately-owned companies, he said.

Fig. 7.2 Reproduced from the *Financial Times*, 21 June 1985.

are 'paid up' by utilising the reserves (both capital and revenue) of the company. This distribution of the reserves is an effective way of transferring value to shareholders without the need for cash to be paid to them. There are many reasons why the reserves increase in value over a period, including the upward revision of fixed asset values, particularly land and buildings, and the accumulation of retained earnings from profit and loss account over several years. Capital reserves can, of course, also increase by virtue of a share issue at a premium over nominal value, or the transfer of profits into a capital redemption reserve when shares are redeemed other than from the proceeds of a new share issue.

A bonus issue has the following effects on the company:

1. The company's balance sheet becomes more realistic following the issue, as the shareholders are then likely to be shown as holding the major part of the company's value, rather than such value being left within the company as reserves.

2. As value is being distributed, but not cash, there is no drain on the company's liquid resources, as would be the case if a dividend were to be paid.

3. The increase in share capital might spur the company to make higher profits if the dividend per share is to be maintained.

4. Although companies often regard bonus issues as worthwhile in terms of good 'public relations' *vis-à-vis* its shareholders, the administration costs of the issue might be high when contrasted with the benefits to be gained.

From the shareholder's viewpoint:

(a) The bonus issue will result in each shareholder owning proportionately more shares in the company. The overall value of the shares does not change as a direct result of the issue, however, as the market price of each share will be reduced in consequence of the issue. The possession of a greater number of shares does lead to an increase in their marketability as it becomes easier for shareholders to dispose of part-holdings.

(b) If the company is able to maintain its dividend per share, then shareholders will receive a greater total dividend than enjoyed prior to the bonus issue.

Note that a bonus issue should be distinguished from a *share split*, whereby the marketability of shares with a very high market value (e.g. £20) is improved by splitting the nominal value (e.g. by a '10 for 1' share split). All that results is a share with a lower nominal value (10p if previously £1) and a corresponding reduction in its market value (£2).

Example 2 includes a bonus issue, a share split and also a redemption of debentures.

Example 2

After the trading and profit and loss accounts had been drawn up for Goring plc for the year ended 31 March 1986, the following balances remained in the accounts:

	DR £	CR £
Issued share capital (£1 shares)		200,000
General reserve		160,000
Profit and loss account balance		70,000
Debentures		87,500
Debtors and creditors	87,500	61,250
Goodwill	5,000	
Plant and machinery	231,250	
Stock	115,000	
Cash at bank	140,000	
	578,750	578,750

It was decided:

i   To capitalise £100,000 of the general reserve by issuing 25p bonus shares in proportion to the number of shares already held by shareholders.

ii To convert the existing £1 ordinary shares to ordinary shares of 25p each.

iii To pay a dividend of 20% on the existing ordinary shares. No dividend was to be paid on the bonus shares.

iv To write £3,000 off goodwill by a transfer from profit and loss account.

v   To redeem £35,000 of the debentures.

Required:

Give the ledger entries necessary to record the above transactions and show the (unpublished) balance sheet as it would appear after the transactions were completed.

Solution:

Goring plc
General Ledger

Issued share capital a/c

			31-3-86	b/f	200,000
31-3-86	c/f	300,000		Transfer general reserve	100,000
		300,000			300,000

General reserve a/c

			31-3-86	b/f	160,000
31-3-86	Transfer share capital	100,000			
	c/f	60,000			
		160,000			160,000

Profit and loss a/c

			31-3-86	b/f	70,000
31-3-86	Goodwill written off	3,000			
	Proposed dividend (20% × £200,000)	40,000			
	c/f	27,000			
		70,000			70,000

Debentures a/c

31-3-86	Redemption of debentures c/f	35,000 52,500	31-3-86	b/f	87,500
		87,500			87,500

Redemption of debentures a/c

31-3-86	Cash	35,000	31-3-86	Debentures	35,000

Goodwill a/c

31-3-86	b/f	5,000	31-3-86	Profit and loss c/f	3,000 2,000
		5,000			5,000

Cash a/c

31-3-86	b/f	140,000	31-3-86	Redemption of debentures c/f	35,000 105,000
		140,000			140,000

Proposed dividend a/c

31-3-86	c/f	40,000	31-3-86	Profit and loss a/c	40,000

Balance Sheet as at 31 March 1986

		£	£
Fixed assets:	Plant and machinery		231,250
Intangible asset:	Goodwill		2,000
Current assets:	Stock	115,000	
	Debtors	87,500	
	Cash at bank	105,000	
		307,500	
Current liabilities:	Creditors	61,250	
	Proposed dividend	40,000	
		101,250	
			206,250
			439,500
Share capital:			
Authorised and issued			
1,200,000 ordinary shares of 25p each, fully paid			300,000
Reserves:	General	60,000	
	Profit and loss account	27,000	
			87,000
			387,000
Long-term liabilities: Debentures			52,500
			439,500

COMMENTARY

There are no book-keeping entries for a share split, the only effect being a revision of the number of shares and their nominal value as shown on the balance sheet. The bonus (capitalisation) issue is accounted for by simple transfer from the general reserve account to the share capital account. Note that some questions state it is the policy of the directors to maintain the *utmost flexibility* regarding the company's reserves. This is merely another way of saying that if there is a choice of using reserves which are available for dividend distribution (i.e. revenue reserves) and those which may not be distributed (i.e. capital reserves), then the latter should be used for the purpose of the bonus issue in preference to the former.

In some cases the redemption of debentures is accompanied by a transfer from profits into a debenture redemption reserve of a sum equal to the amount redeemed. Although not a statutory requirement (cf. capital redemption reserve) it is considered prudent to reduce profit and loss account by the cash repaid to debenture holders, since the liquid funds available for future dividend payments have been depleted. By making the transfer, the balance of distributable reserves will not be overstated to the detriment of the company.

If the question had required such a transfer, the journal entry would have been:

DR	Profit and loss account	35,000	
CR	Debenture redemption reserve		35,000
–	Transfer of an amount equal to the cost		
of debentures redeemed.			

7.5 Redemption and purchase of a company's own shares and debentures

In Example 2 it was seen how debentures could be cancelled by repayment of the loan to the debenture holder. Although the redemption in that question was made at par, it is also possible for a company to redeem its debentures either at a discount from nominal value, or at a premium. If the debentures have a stock market value, the company may take the opportunity to purchase its own debentures at times when they stand at a discount from the normal redemption price.

Example 3

A company has £100,000 8% debenture stock. Show the journal entries which would be necessary to record

(a) Their redemption at a discount of 4%
(b) Their redemption at a premium of 5%

Solution:

			£	£
(a)	DR	8% debenture stock	100,000	
	CR	Cash		96,000
		Discount on redemption of debentures		4,000

– Redemption of £100,000 8% debenture stock at a discount of 4%.

	DR	Profit and loss account	96,000	
	CR	Debenture redemption reserve		96,000

– Transfer of amount equal to cash paid on redemption of debentures.

(b)	DR	8% debenture stock	105,000	
	CR	Cash		105,000

– Cash paid on redemption of £100,000 8% debenture stock at a premium of 5%.

	DR	Premium on redemption of debentures	5,000	
		(or share premium account, if any)		
	CR	8% debenture stock		5,000

– Premium on redemption of debentures transferred against capital reserve.

	DR	Profit and loss account	105,000	
	CR	Debenture redemption reserve		105,000

– Transfer of amount equal to cash paid on redemption of debentures.

COMMENTARY

In both cases a transfer has been made to a debenture redemption reserve for reasons outlined in the commentary to Example 2. The discount on redemption is a capital reserve, unavailable for distribution, whilst the premium payable by the company is either debited to its own account or can be offset against any existing share premium account.

Some companies operate a sinking fund for the purpose of ensuring that sufficient funds exist for the purpose of the redemption, but a detailed consideration of this topic is outside the scope of this book.

The Companies Act of 1981 (now consolidated in the 1985 Companies Act) gave companies the power to *purchase* their own shares subject to certain restrictions. This was a significant departure from previous practice, and had the effect of bringing British practice into line with that operating within the United States and Europe. The conditions that must be satisfied before a company can purchase its own shares include the following:

1. The company's articles of association must authorise it to do so.
2. The company must, after the purchase, have other shares in issue, some of which at least are not redeemable. (This is designed to prevent a situation arising whereby the company redeems its entire share capital and thus ceases to have any shareholders.)
3. The company must have, after the purchase, at least two members.

In addition, certain conditions applicable to the redemption of shares also apply to a company's purchase of its own shares. These include:

(a) The shares must be fully paid.
(b) The payment for the shares must be made at the time that the shares are redeemed or purchased.
(c) Shares may be redeemed or purchased either out of distributable profits or out of the proceeds of a new issue of shares made for the purpose of the redemption or purchase. In addition a *private* company may make a payment out of capital to redeem or purchase its shares provided that its articles or association authorise it to do so.

Note that the terms of redemption of a company's capital must be stated in the articles of association, but there is no requirement for the terms of a share purchase to be stated.

REASONS FOR THE REDEMPTION OF SHARES

These include:

(a) A desire by the company to reduce its level of gearing by redeeming preference shares.
(b) The possibility of raising fresh capital at a lower dividend percentage rate than the capital being redeemed.
(c) A reduction in the level of the company's activities requiring less capital funding.

REASONS FOR THE PURCHASE BY A COMPANY OF ITS OWN SHARES

These include:

(a) A minority shareholder wishes to dispose of his shares and the other shareholders either cannot or do not wish to purchase the shares.
(b) A shareholder dies and there are no persons available to purchase the shareholding.
(c) There is a dispute between major shareholders, and one or more of them cannot afford to purchase the other's shares.
(d) There is a reduction in the level of the company's activities requiring less capital funding.

ACCOUNTING PROCEDURES

1. *Redemption of shares*
(a) DR   Share capital a/c
     CR   Redemption of capital a/c
     – Transfer nominal value of redeemed capital.

(b) DR   Redemption of capital a/c
     CR   Cash
     – Cash paid to shareholders on redemption.

(c) DR   Share premium a/c (or premium on redemption of capital a/c)
     CR   Redemption of capital a/c
     – Premium (if any) payable on redemption.

(d) DR   Profit and loss a/c
     CR   Capital redemption reserve a/c
     – Amount of capital redeemed other than from the proceeds of the issue of new share capital.

2. *Purchase by a company of its own shares*

(a) DR   Share capital a/c
     CR   Purchase of own shares a/c
     – Transfer nominal value of purchased capital.

(b) DR   Purchase of own shares a/c
     CR   Cash
     – Cash paid to shareholders.

(c) DR   Share premium a/c (or premium on purchase of own shares a/c)
     CR   Purchase of own shares a/c
     – Premium (if any) payable on purchase.

(d) DR   Profit and loss a/c
     CR   Capital purchase reserve a/c
     – Amount of capital purchased other than from the proceeds of the issue of new share capital*.

Example 4

The following balances are in the books of Worthing plc at 31 August 1987.

	£
Ordinary share capital (50p shares)	180,000
Preference share capital (£1 shares)	150,000
Share premium account	15,000
General reserve	27,000
Profit and loss account	118,000
Cash at bank	137,500

On 1 September 1987, 60,000 preference shares are to be redeemed at a premium of 6%. It was decided to make a bonus issue of one ordinary share for every twelve held, and to help finance the redemption a new issue of 40,000 ordinary shares was to be made at a price of 80p per share.

   Show by journal entries how the above transactions would be recorded in the company's books assuming that all amounts due were paid or received on 1 September 1987.

Solution:

Worthing plc

Journal

		DR £	CR £
(a)	DR Preference share capital	60,000	
	CR Redemption of preference shares		60,000
	– Transfer of nominal value of preference shares redeemed.		
(b)	DR Redemption of preference shares	63,600	
	CR Cash		63,600
	– Cash paid to preference shareholders on redemption of 60,000 shares at a 6% premium.		
(c)	DR Share premium account	3,600	
	CR Redemption of preference shares		3,600

*If a private company, it may reduce its capital provided that all available distributable profits and the proceeds of new shares issued in connection with the purchase are set against the amount of the capital reduction.

      – Premium on redemption of preference shares offset against share premium a/c.

(d)   DR   General reserve   15,000
      CR   Ordinary share capital   15,000
      – Utilisation of reserve for the purpose of issuing bonus shares on a 1 for 12 basis.

(e)   DR   Cash   32,000
      CR   Ordinary share capital   20,000
             Share premium account   12,000
      – Issue of 40,000 ordinary shares of 50p at a price of 80p per share.

(f)   DR   Profit and loss account   16,600
      CR   Capital redemption reserve   16,600
      – Transfer to capital reserve of an amount equal to the capital redeemed other than from the proceeds of the issue of new share capital*.

*Workings:

	£	£
Cash repaid to preference shareholders		63,600
Less: General reserves capitalised	15,000	
Proceeds of new share issue	32,000	47,000
Amount to be transferred to capital redemption reserve		£16,600

COMMENTARY

A comparison of the balance sheet extracts before and after the share transactions reveals the reason why the transfer to capital redemption reserve is required.

	'Before' £	'After' £
Capital and capital reserves		
Ordinary share capital	180,000	215,000
Preference share capital	150,000	90,000
Share premium account	15,000	23,400
Capital redemption reserve	—	16,600
	345,000	345,000
Revenue reserves		
General reserve	27,000	12,000
Profit and loss account	118,000	101,400
	490,000	458,400

As can be seen, the capital and non-distributable reserves are kept at the same level by reason of the transfer from profit and loss account to the capital redemption reserve. If the transfer had not been made, the capital base of the company would have been reduced by £16,600.

Example 5

Using the figures of the previous example after the transactions of 1 September 1987 had been completed, show the journal entries required to record the purchase by Worthing plc of 100,000 of its own ordinary shares at par value.

Solution:

		DR £	CR £
(a)	DR Ordinary share capital	50,000	
	CR Purchase of own shares		50,000
	– Transfer nominal value of shares to be purchased £100,000 × 50p).		
(b)	DR Purchase of own shares	50,000	
	CR Cash		50,000
	– Cash paid to shareholders by the company.		
(c)	DR Profit and loss account	50,000	
	CR Capital purchase reserve		50,000

– Transfer to capital reserve of an amount equivalent to the ordinary shares purchased by the company.

COMMENTARY

The revised balance sheet would be:

	£
Capital and capital reserves	
Ordinary share capital	165,000
Preference share capital	90,000
Share premium account	23,400
Capital redemption reserve	16,600
Capital purchase reserve	50,000
	345,000
Revenue reserves	
General reserve	12,000
Profit and loss account	51,400
	408,400

Although the balance sheet total has decreased by £50,000, the capital base is maintained by the transfer to the capital purchase reserve.

7.6 Capital reorganisation

After having studied the previous sections of the chapter, it should be apparent that share capital need not be a static feature of a company, but can be subject to certain changes. To summarise the position, we have seen that share capital can be:

(a) Increased by means of (i) a fresh issue of shares; (ii) a rights issue to existing share-holders; (iii) a bonus issue to existing shareholders.
(b) Decreased by means of (i) the redemption of capital; (ii) the purchase of the company's own shares.
(c) Made more 'marketable' by means of a share split.

In addition to (b) above, there could be a situation where a company may seek to decrease its share capital, without the necessity of compensating for the decrease by a transfer from revenue to capital reserves. This is known as a capital reduction scheme, and is generally undertaken by companies which have suffered substantial losses, causing 'negative reserves' to appear on the balance sheet, i.e. there is a debit balance on the profit and loss acount.

By reducing the nominal value of its share capital, the company is acknowledging that there has been a decline in the value of its shares. However, the shareholders may well agree to such a reduction if it is felt that the company is 'getting back on its feet', and would be able to pay dividends out of (albeit modest) future profits. Any capital reorganisation scheme which results in a reduction in the company's share capital must be within the company's powers as stated in its articles, and must also be approved by the court. The company's shareholders must also approve the scheme at a general meeting.

Example 6

The balance sheet of GHK Ltd at today's date is as follows:

	£000		£000	£000
Authorised and issued		Goodwill		12
Share capital:		Freehold property		130
Ordinary shares				
of 50p full paid	100	Machinery at cost	148	
5% cum. pref. shares of £1	50	*Less:* Depreciation	79	69
	150			
10% debentures 1985		Investments		32
(secured on property)	100	Preliminary expenses		3

Creditors	43	Profit and loss a/c		68
Bank overdraft	81	Stock		37
Accrued debenture interest	5	Debtors		28
	379			379

The company has suffered heavy losses in recent years and the dividends on the preference shares are now two years in arrear.

The necessary approval has just been given for the following capital reduction scheme:

1. The profit and loss account and all intangible assets are to be written off completely.
2. Debts of £3,000 and stock with a book value of £11,000 are to be written off.
3. The machinery is to be written down to £48,000.
4. The debenture holder is to take over the property at a valuation of £200,000 and to pay the company the balance in cash, after deducting the amount due to him.
5. All investments are to be sold for £36,000.
6. The existing ordinary shares are to be written down to a nominal value of 20p each.
7. The nominal value of the preference shares is to be reduced to 80p per share. The holders are to receive two ordinary 20p shares for every £1 of dividends in arrears. Future preference dividends are to be at 8% per annum.
8. The authorised share capital is to be changed to 250,000 ordinary 20p shares and 100,000 8% preference 80p shares.

Required:

(a) The capital reduction account in the books of GHK Ltd, giving effect to the provisions of the scheme.

Note: Journal entries are *not* required.

(b) i What are the main objectives of a capital reduction scheme?

ii Briefly discuss whether they have been achieved in this case.

(LCCI – Higher)

Solution:

(a)

GHK Ltd

Capital reduction account

	£000		£000
Profit and loss account	68	Freehold property	70
Goodwill	12	Investments	4
Preliminary expenses	3	Ordinary share capital	60
Debtors	3	Preference share capital	10
Stock	11		
Provision for depreciation on machinery	21		
Transfer to capital reserve	26		
	144		144

(b) i The main objectives of a capital reduction scheme are to eliminate the negative reserves which have accumulated owing to past losses, and to create the correct environment for the company to be able to resume dividend payments if and when profits can be earned. Although a capital reduction scheme may involve certain sacrifices on the part of the shareholders and lenders, this might be a reasonable price to pay for the restoration of confidence in the company and its ability to survive in future years.

ii The objectives of the scheme can be demonstrated to have been successful by drawing up the balance sheet following the completion of the reorganisation:

	£000		£000	£000
Share capital		*Fixed assets*		
Authorised:		Machinery at cost	148	
Ordinary 20p shares	50	*Less:* Depreciation	100	48
8% preference 80p shares	80			
	130			

Issued:			Current assets		
Ordinary 20p shares,			Stock	26	
fully paid	40		Debtors	25	
8% preference 80p shares	40		Cash	50	
	80				101
Capital reserve	26				
	106				
Current liabilities					
Creditors	43				
	149				149

COMMENTARY

The company has achieved not only the elimination of the debit balance on the profit and loss account, but also a strengthening of its liquid position. It now stands able to utilise fully any profits it makes from future trading activities.

Exercises

7.1 Distinguish between a rights issue and a bonus issue.

7.2 Under what circumstances might a company wish to purchase its own shares?

7.3 The balance sheets of Mayflower Ltd included the following items as at 31 May 1984 and 1985:

	31 May 1984 £	31 May 1985 £
Share capital:		
Ordinary shares of £1 each	40,000	60,000
6% Redeemable preference shares	10,000	—
Share premium account	—	10,000
Capital redemption reserve	—	10,000

You are required to:

(a) Explain the probable reasons for the changes during the year ended 31 May 1985 in each of the items stated above.

(b) Comment on the effects on a company and its shareholders of a bonus issue of shares.

(ULSEB)

7.4 Beet and Root plc has an authorised capital of 500,000 ordinary shares of £1 each and an issued and paid-up capital of £300,000. It has also issued £200,000 12% debentures.

The directors decided to:

1. Issue the remaining 200,000 ordinary shares at £1.40 per share.
2. Redeem the 12% debentures at a discount of 10%.

The payment for the shares was received as follows: 50p on application, 50p on allotment and the balance on first and final call. Applications were received for exactly 200,000 shares and all monies due on application, allotment and call were received by the due dates. The cash due on allotment included the amount of the premium.

The debentures were subsequently redeemed.

Required:

(a) Show by means of journal entries the recording of the issue of shares and the redemption of the debentures.

(b) After the above transactions have taken place show the part of the balance sheet which gives details of the shareholders' interest.

Notes:

1. All cash receipts are to be journalised.
2. Narrations are *not* required.

(LCCI – Intermediate)

7.5 At 31 March, Year 4 the summarised balance sheet of Marrow Ltd was as follows:

	£		£
Ordinary £1 shares,		Goodwill	21,000
fully paid	150,000	Freehold land at cost	90,000
10% Preference £1 shares,		Other fixed assets	65,000
fully paid	80,000	Net current assets	147,000
Profit and loss account	43,000		
12% debentures			
year 4 to year 8	50,000		
	323,000		323,000

The following occurred during the next three months.

1. On 1 April the directors decided that the land should be restated at an expert's valuation of £130,000.
2. On 15 April some machinery, which originally cost £12,000 and had a book value of £3,000, was sold for £2,000.
3. On 1 June the preference shares were redeemed at par. In order to provide part of the necessary funds the company made a 'one for three' rights issue of ordinary shares at £1.20 per share payable 80p on application on 20 April, and the balance (including the premium) payable on 20 May. All of these additional shares were taken up and were paid for when due with the exception of 4,000 shares for which the full amount was paid on 20 April.
4. On 15 June one-fifth of the debentures were redeemed at a premium of 5%.
5. On 30 June the directors decided to write off one-third of the goodwill.

Required:

i Journal entries to record the above, including cash. *Note:* Narrations are not required.
ii Assuming that, in addition to the other transactions, the company made a net trading profit in the three months of £45,000 (after deducting depreciation of other fixed assets of £7,000), prepare its balance sheet as at 30 June Year 4. *Note:* Ignore dividends, debenture interest and taxation.

(LCCI – Higher)

7.6 The Gravelea Haulage Company plc is an established company which intends to expand its activities from 1982 onwards.

In the opinion of the directors, the only feasible means of financing the expansion programme is by obtaining funds from outside sources.

Over a period of weeks, the directors have been considering alternative ways of raising the £500,000 needed.

They have now narrowed down the choice to one of three possibilities:

Scheme:

A. An issue of £500,000 7% redeemable debentures 1990/1997 at par.
B. An issue of 500,000 10% redeemable preference shares of £1.00 per share, at par.
C. An issue of 400,000 ordinary shares of £1.00 per share, at a premium of £0.25 per share, on which it is hoped to pay an annual dividend of 15% currently paid on existing ordinary shares.

Currently, the company's issued share capital consists of 3 million ordinary shares at £1.00 per share, fully paid.

The chief accountant has estimated that the company's profit before interest and tax (without taking account of the additional profit from the expansion programme) is likely to remain static at £574,000 for the next five years. Interest payable on bank overdraft for each of these years has been estimated at £4,000.

It has also been estimated that, after it has been implemented, the programme will produce an annual amount of £130,000 profit before interest and tax, additional to the figure shown above.

Corporation tax has been estimated as an effective rate of 40% on the company's total profit after interest and before tax.

Without taking the expansion programme into account, the company's earning per share is estimated to be 11.4p, arrived at as follows:

	£
Profit before interest and tax	574,000
Less: Interest	4,000
Profit after interest before tax	570,000
Less: Corporation tax (40% × £570,000)	228,000
Profit after tax	342,000
Less: Preference dividends	Nil
Earnings (attributable to ordinary shareholders)	£342,000
Number of ordinary shares in issue and ranking for dividend	3,000,000
Earnings per share (eps) (as above)	11.4p

$((342,000 \times 100)/3,000,000)$

Required:
Write notes, or produce calculations as appropriate, to answer the following questions which have been raised:

(a) In schemes A and B, what is the significance of the term 'redeemable'?

(b) For what reasons might the company wish to redeem its shares or debentures?

(c) What is the significance of the date 1990/1997 in scheme A?

(d) In scheme C will the dividend of 15% be calculated on the nominal value (£400,000) of the additional ordinary shares or on the issue value (£500,000)? What is an alternative way in which the dividend could be expressed?

(e) What will be the company's annual earnings per share on the basis that:
  i   Scheme A is adopted?
  ii Scheme B is adopted?
  iii Scheme C is adopted?

(Eps is defined as the profit in pence attributable to each ordinary share after tax and before taking extraordinary items into account. No extraordinary items have been forecast for the next five years.)

(f) What will be the company's capital gearing in a full year after implementation, separately for each of the schemes?

(ACCA – Level 1)

7.7 What are the main objectives of a capital reduction scheme?

7.8 Why does company law insist on the maintenance of capital following the redemption of shares by a company?

CHAPTER 8

Accounting for Limited Liability Companies (3): groups of companies

8.1 Why have groups?

When a business reaches a certain size, it may find that opportunities for further increasing its profits are restricted by a number of factors, including:

(a) difficulty in developing new products due to the costs involved;
(b) the emergence of strong competitors;
(c) restrictions on the geographical area which the business can satisfactorily cover;
(d) limitations to the expertise of existing employees;
(e) insufficient funding resulting in under-utilisation of assets;
(f) over-dependence on suppliers of raw materials and/or services resulting in events such as stoppages caused by stock shortages or machine breakdowns.

There are a number of ways to circumvent these problems, the most obvious being to 'take over' competing companies, supplier companies or, so as to diversify the range of activities, companies which make products or provide services which are dissimilar from those presently being made or offered.

Most large business organisations are comprised of a *holding* company and numerous *subsidiary* companies, the definitions of each being given in SSAP 14 as follows:

'*Holding company*
'A company is a holding company of another if but only if that other is its subsidiary as defined (below).
'*Subsidiary company*
'A company shall be deemed to be a subsidiary of another if but only if,
   '(a) that other either:
      '(i) is a member of it and controls the composition of its board of directors; or
      '(ii) holds more than half in nominal value of its equity share capital; or
   '(b) the first mentioned company is a subsidiary of any company which is that other's subsidiary.'

As can be seen from the above, a company does not necessarily require a 51% shareholding in another company to be classed as its holding company. The fact that the company is a member (i.e. shareholder) and controls the way in which the other company's directors are selected would also create a holding company/subsidiary relationship.

There is no limitation on the number of subsidiaries that a holding company might have. For example, The Distillers Company plc had seventy-nine subsidiaries on 31 March 1985 whilst the British Petroleum Company plc had fifty-six.

In addition to subsidiaries, many companies also have associated companies. The definition of an associated company, as contained in SSAP 1, is as follows:

'An *associated company* is a company not being a subsidiary of the investing group or company in which:

'(a) the interest of the investing group or company is effectively that of a partner in a joint venture or consortium and the investing group or company is in a position to exercise a significant influence over the company in which the investment is made; or

'(b) the interest of the investing group or company is for the long term and is substantial and, having regard to the disposition of the other shareholdings, the investing group or company is in a position to exercise a significant influence over the company in which the investment is made'.

The term 'investing group or company' simply means the business entity which is considering whether another company is an associated company. In the case of (b) above, a 'significant influence' is presumed to be in existence where the investing group or company holds in excess of 20% of the equity voting rights (i.e. shares which give an entitlement to vote at company general meetings).

BASIS OF ACCOUNTING FOR ASSOCIATED COMPANIES

If a company has one or more 'associated companies' as per the above definition, then any income received from investments in those associated companies should be accounted for as follows:

(a) in the investing company's profit and loss account: dividends received and receivable are credited;

(b) in the investing company's balance sheet: the cost of the investment is shown, less any amounts written off.

The major part of the standard deals with the way in which the results of associated companies are included in the *consolidated* accounts of a group of companies (i.e. the 'combined' financial statements of a holding company and its subsidiaries). A simplified summary of the provisions are:

(a) in the consolidated profit and loss acount: the investing group's share of the profits or losses of the associated company is included;

(b) in the consolidated balance sheet: the investing group's share of the net assets of the associated company is included.

8.2 Accounting for groups of companies

Although a detailed consideration of group accounting is outside the scope of this textbook, readers should be aware of the general nature and significance of this topic.

When a company has a subsidiary, it is obliged by law to present *consolidated* accounts to its members, i.e. financial statements showing the combined position of all the group companies. These comprise mainly a consolidated balance sheet and a consolidated profit and loss account.

8.3 The consolidated balance sheet

This is compiled from the individual company balance sheets, with the exceptions of the following.

'UNREALISED' PROFIT ON STOCK MUST BE ELIMINATED

Where a group company has sold goods to another group company at a price above cost, and some or all of those goods remain in stock at the end of the financial year, then the 'profit' arising from those goods left in stock must be eliminated when consolidating the balance sheet. For example, H plc sells goods which cost £7,000 to S Ltd (its subsidiary) for £10,000. At the date of the consolidated balance sheet, the 'profit' of £3,000 must be eliminated if S Ltd has not sold the goods to a purchaser who is 'outside' the group of companies. This is achieved by reducing H plc's profit and loss account balance by £3,000 and similarly reducing the value of S Ltd's stock.

The purpose of this adjustment is to eliminate the risk of over-stating profit by means of artificial inter-group transactions. If no such adjustment were needed, then there would, in theory, be no limit to the amount of profit which could be recorded, despite the fact that sales might never have been made to 'real' customers outside the group!

Consolidated profit and loss account
(for the year ended 30 June 1985)

	1985 £m
Turnover	1,412.1
Operating costs	1,050.7
Trading profit	361.4
Share of profits of associated companies	15.0
Investment income less interest payable	26.5
Profit on ordinary activities before taxation	402.9

Consolidated balance sheet (extract)
(at 30 June 1985)

	£m	£m
Fixed assets		
Tangible assets		413.2
Investments in associated companies		43.0
		456.2

Notes to the accounts

Investments in associated companies

The investment represents the group's share of associated companies' net tangible assets at dates of acquisition and their post acquisition retained profits.

	£m
At 1 July 1984	41.0
Exchange adjustments on opening net assets	(2.1)
Additions	1.2
Retained profits for the year	2.9
At 30 June 1985	43.0

Fig. 8.1 Glaxo Holdings plc – treatment of the result of associated companies.

INTER-COMPANY INDEBTEDNESS MUST BE ELIMINATED

As the consolidated balance sheet shows the combined position of the group, it would be misleading to show assets and liabilities which have arisen solely by virtue of the creation of loans between companies within the group. If this adjustment were not made, both consolidated asset and liability totals would be overstated because of the existence of purely internal financing arrangements. For example, H plc is owed £12,000 by S A Ltd and owes £7,000 to S B Ltd, both being subsidiaries of H plc. Although the loans would appear either as assets or liabilities in the individual balance sheets of the three companies, they would be cancelled out when the figures were consolidated. Any loans shown on the consolidated balance sheet will thus represent monies owed or owing by persons or companies who are outside the group.

Dividends owed by one group company to another must similarly be cancelled out, unless there is a 'minority interest' (see below) in the subsidiary company, in which case that proportion of the dividend belonging to the minority is included in the consolidated balance sheet as part of the minority interest.

'INVESTMENT IN SUBSIDIARIES' IS ELIMINATED

Although the balance sheet of the holding company includes 'investment in subsidiary' as a fixed asset, when preparing the consolidated balance sheet this is cancelled against the share capital and reserves of the subsidiary as shown in the subsidiary's balance sheet. However, it often happens that the amount paid for the investment differs from the combined total of the subsidiary's share capital and reserves. The reasons for this might be:

1. The price paid for the shares was greater than the balance sheet value of those shares at the time of purchase. The surplus price represents *goodwill*, and should be treated in accordance with SSAP 22 (see section 8.6).
2. The price paid for the shares was less than the balance sheet value of those shares at the time of purchase. This difference is treated as a *capital reserve*, and is included as such in the consolidated balance sheet.
3. The reserves of the subsidiary have changed since the date of acquisition by the holding company. Increases are known as 'post-acquisition' profits and decreases are referred to as 'post-acquisition' losses. Such changes are added to or deducted from the group reserves on the consolidated balance sheet, after which such reserves are available for distribution. This position should be contrasted with that of 'pre-acquisition' profits, which represent part of the net assets in existence at the time of the purchase by the holding company. Such profits are *not* available for distribution to the holding company's shareholders, as it would be prejudicial to the interests of creditors and financiers if part of the price paid for the subsidiary were to be used for the purpose of paying dividends.

'MINORITY INTERESTS' MUST BE COMPUTED

In many cases, a holding company does not own the entire share capital of its subsidiary. The proportion of shares which it does not own is referred to as 'the minority', and a calculation must be made of the value of the minority's stake in the subsidiary. This calculation is made as follows:

Minority % of subsidiary capital and reserves at date of consolidated balance sheet	x
Minority % of subsidiary's proposed dividend*	x
Total minority interest	x

Example 2

Maxi Ltd purchased the shares in its subsidiary Mini Ltd on 1 April year 3 for £340,000. The draft (summarised) consolidated balance sheet of Maxi Ltd at 31 March year 4 is as follows:

*Alternatively, this may be shown as a current liability in the consolidated balance sheet.

	£000		£000
Ordinary share capital		Freehold property (at cost)	150
£1 shares	500	Plant and machinery (at cost	
Profit and loss*	160	less depreciation)	400
Creditors	270	Goodwill on consolidation	80
		Stock	170
		Debtors	120
		Bank	10
	930		930

Mini Ltd has no preference capital, has no reserves other than the profit and loss account and has paid no dividend since 1 April year 3.

The following additional information has now become available.

1. The book-keeper who drafted the above balance sheet assumed that Maxi Ltd had acquired all Mini Ltd's shares. In fact only 75% have been acquired.
2. Mini Ltd's plant and machinery was overvalued by £20,000 on 1 April year 3; depreciation of 20% of this has also been charged in Mini Ltd's profit and loss account for the year to 31 March year 4.
3. Maxi Ltd's stock at 31 March year 4 includes £12,000 in respect of goods purchased from Mini Ltd, which originally cost Mini Ltd only £8,000. Maxi Ltd still owed Mini Ltd £12,000 at 31 March year 4.

Required:

(a) Journal entries indicating the adjustments made necessary to Maxi Ltd's consolidated balance sheet at 31 March year 4 in respect of *each of the items* (1) to (3) above.
   Note: Narrations are not required but all calculations should be shown.
(b) Prepare Maxi Ltd's consolidated balance sheet at 31 March year 4 in accordance with your journal entries.

(LCCI – Higher)

Solution
(*Note:* narrations have been given for the benefit of the reader.)

(a) *Journal* (for purposes of consolidation only)

1. DR Goodwill   80,000
    CR Reserves   80,000
    – Increase in goodwill valuation (see working 1).
2. DR Reserves   75,000
    CR Minority interests   75,000
    – Creation of minority interests previously omitted (see working 2).
3. DR Reserves   20,000
    CR Plant and machinery   20,000
    – Adjustment in respect of the over-valuation of Mini Ltd's plant and machinery.
4. DR Plant and machinery   4,000
    CR Reserves   4,000
    – Adjustments in respect of the depreciation charged on over-valued assets.
5. DR Reserves   4,000
    CR Stock   4,000
    – Elimination of unrealised profit on stock.
6. DR Creditors   12,000
    CR Debtors   12,000
    – Elimination of inter-company indebtedness.

(b)

Maxi Ltd
Consolidated Balance Sheet
at 31 March Year 4

	£000		£000
Share capital	500	Freehold property (at cost)	150
Reserves (see Working 3)	145	Plant and machinery (at cost	
Minority interests	75	less depreciation)	384
		Goodwill	160

*Including the £60,000 profit of Mini Ltd earned since acquisition.

166

Creditors	258				
		Stock			166
		Debtors			108
		Bank			10
	978				978

Workings: £   £

1. Goodwill: Purchase price of Mini Ltd   340,000
      Less: Value of Mini Ltd at acquisition date
             (purchase price – 'original' figure of goodwill)
                    340,000 – 80,000 =   260,000
    Overvaluation of plant and machinery   20,000
                                                                 £340,000

            Proportion of shares purchased   75%
            75% × £240,000   180,000

                 Goodwill on consolidation   160,000

2. Minority interests: £
       Value of share capital and reserves of Mini Ltd, after adjustment
       for over-valuation of plant and machinery, on date of acquisition   240,000
       Add: Profit for year   60,000
          Unrealised profit on stock   (4,000)
          Depreciation adjustment   4,000   —   60,000
                                                                                300,000

            Minority proportion (25%)   =   75,000

3. Reserves: £
       Maxi Ltd's reserves at 31 March year 4
                 160,000 – 60,000   =   100,000
    Mini Ltd's reserves (adjusted) at 31 March year 4   =   60,000

       Proportion owned by Maxi Ltd (75%)   =   =   45,000

                                                               Total   145,000

COMMENTARY

The consolidated balance sheet shows the combined position of both Maxi Ltd and Mini Ltd and recognises that 25% of Mini Ltd's value is owned by an outside minority. This minority interest is thus a liability of the group as a whole.

8.4   The consolidated profit and loss account

When producing the consolidated balance sheet, it was seen how various adjustments had to be made to the aggregated company balance sheets so as to present a true and fair view of the state of the group as a whole at the balance sheet date. Similar considerations apply when preparing the consolidated profit and loss account, as the aggregated profit and loss accounts of the holding and subsidiary companies are adjusted for:

(a) *'Unrealised' profit on stock*, whereby profit occasioned solely by virtue of one group company selling goods to another group company at a price greater than cost to the group as a whole, is eliminated from the combined stock value on consolidation.

(b) *Inter-company sales*, whereby the group's turnover is reduced by the value of sales between group companies.

(c) *Minority interests*, whereby the proportion of the profits or losses attributable to outside interests is calculated by applying the appropriate percentage to the subsidiary company's reserves, and showing the total minority interest in the consolidated profit or losses separately in the consolidated profit and loss account.

(d) *Pre-acquisition profits*, whereby profits of a subsidiary which were earned prior to its acquisition in the financial year are excluded from the consolidated profit and loss account.

Note that a holding company need not publish its own profit and loss account separately from the group's consolidated profit and loss account, but it must publish its balance sheet in addition to that of the group.

8.5 Drawbacks of consolidated financial statements

Although the consolidated statements are drawn up to give a financial picture of the group as a whole, there is a danger that the end result will reveal a misleading situation for the following reasons:

(a) The profit of one group company may conceal the losses of another.

(b) A group company's insolvency may be hidden by the solvency (i.e. liquidity) of the other group members.

(c) Ratios (see Chapter 10) used to determine the trends of the group may be distorted if inconsistent accounting methods have been used by group companies.

(d) The preparation of consolidated statements may imply that creditors of weak group companies are offered some protection by virtue of the strength of the group as a whole. As the idea of a 'group of companies' is only an artificial accounting concept, without specific legal backing, it follows that individual group companies may fail, notwithstanding the financial strength of other group members. In practice, however, the group may step in and provide some assistance to preserve its reputation.

8.6 Accounting for goodwill

The topic of goodwill has been covered in the chapter on partnership, and it has also been seen how goodwill may arise on the consolidation of financial statements. In January 1985, the Accounting Standards Committee published SSAP 22 'Accounting for Goodwill' which applies to all financial statements relating to accounting periods beginning on or after 1 January 1985. It is worthwhile to reproduce the first five paragraphs of Part 1 of the Standard, which contains a highly useful summary of the character of goodwill and the differences between 'purchased' and 'non-purchased' goodwill:

'Nature and meaning of goodwill
'1. It is usual for the value of a business as a whole to differ from the value of its separable net assets. The difference, which may be positive or negative, is described as goodwill.

'2. Goodwill is therefore by definition incapable of realisation separately from the business as a whole; this characteristic of goodwill distinguishes it from all other items in the accounts. Its other characteristics are that:
   '(a) the value of goodwill has no reliable or predictable relationship to any costs which may have been incurred;
   '(b) individual intangible factors which may contribute to goodwill cannot be valued;
   '(c) the value of goodwill may fluctuate widely according to internal and external circumstances over relatively short periods of time; and
   '(d) the assessment of the value of goodwill is highly subjective.
   'Thus, any amount attributed to goodwill is unique to the valuer and to the specific point in time at which it is measured, and is valid only at that time, and in the circumstances then prevailing.

'3. 'Purchased goodwill' (positive or negative) is established when a business combination is accounted for as an acquisition; it includes goodwill arising on consolidation, and on the acquisition of an interest in an associated company or of an unincorporated business. On the purchase of a company, the shares acquired are recorded at cost, being the fair value of the consideration given. For the purposes of consolidated accounts, the cost of the shares is allocated amongst the separable net assets acquired, with purchased goodwill emerging as the difference. Similar principles apply on the acquisition of an unincorporated business.

'4. Goodwill can also be attributed to businesses which are not the subject of an acquisition (non-purchased goodwill) in that as going concerns they are worth more (positive goodwill), or less (negative goodwill), than the sum of the fair values of their separable net assets. However, except when goodwill is evidenced by a purchase transaction, it is not an accepted practice to recognise it in financial statements.

'5. There is no difference in character between purchased goodwill and non-purchased goodwill. However, the value of purchased goodwill, although arising from a subjective valuation of the business, is established as a fact at a particular point in time by a market transaction; this is not true of non-purchased goodwill.'

As can be seen from the above, 'non-purchased' goodwill is not recognised in the financial statements of companies, and the standard therefore concentrates solely on the accounting treatment of purchased goodwill.

Paragraph 31 of the standard is unequivocal:

'Purchased goodwill should not be carried in the balance sheet of a company as a permanent item'.

The ways in which goodwill can be written off are described in paragraphs 32 and 34, whereby goodwill

(para 32) '. . . should normally be eliminated from the accounts immediately on acquisition against reserves', or

(para 34) '. . . may be eliminated from the accounts by amortisation through the profit and loss account in arriving at profit or loss on ordinary activities on a systematic basis over its useful economic life'.

As can be seen, the standard expresses a preference for immediate write-off, and only a minority of companies are likely to use the alternative of amortisation.

If a company has negative goodwill, defined in paragraph 33 as 'any excess of the aggregate of the fair values of the separable net assets acquired over the fair value of the consideration given', it should be credited directly to reserves. This represents the mirror image of the preferred treatment of positive goodwill.

The accounting policy followed in respect of goodwill should be explained in the notes to the accounts.

Exercises

8.1 Explain the meaning of the following terms:

(a) Group accounts.
(b) Holding company.
(c) Subsidiary company.

8.2 Why must unrealised profit on stocks be eliminated when consolidating accounts?

8.3 What is a 'minority interest'?

8.4 The summarised balance sheet of Savoy Ltd, a subsidiary of Cabbage Ltd, as at 31 December year 3 was as follows:

	£		£
Ordinary £1 shares, fully paid	100,000	Fixed assets	88,000
Profit and loss account	24,960	Net current assets	36,960
	124,960		124,960

The profit and loss account balance includes net profit for the year 3 of £7,920. In year 2 the company made a net loss of £3,540. No dividends were paid in either year.

Required:

Calculation of the amounts, if any, to be included in the consolidated balance sheet as at 31 December year 3 in respect of the following three items:
  Goodwill arising from the purchase by Cabbage Ltd of shares in Savoy Ltd.
  Profit & loss account of Savoy Ltd.
  Minority interest.
These calculations are to be based on each of the following alternative assumptions:

(a) That Cabbage Ltd acquired 60,000 shares in Savoy Ltd on 31 December year 3 for £90,000.

(b) That Cabbage Ltd acquired 100,000 shares in Savoy Ltd on 31 December year 2 for £140,000.

(c) That Cabbage Ltd acquired 75,000 shares in Savoy Ltd on 31 December year 1 for £100,000.

(LCCI – Higher)

8.5 Although consolidated accounts are drawn up with the intention of displaying a true and fair view of a group's financial picture, certain distortions may exist which may lead to an inaccurate assessment of the state of individual companies within the group. Why is this, and what specific distortions might occur?

8.6 Differentiate between 'purchased' goodwill and 'non-purchased' goodwill.

8.7 SSAP 22 permits two methods of 'writing off' goodwill. What are they, and which of the two methods does the standard favour?

8.8 How should 'negative goodwill' be treated in company accounts?

CHAPTER 9

Statements of Source and Application of Funds

9.1 Introduction

The published accounts of all but the smallest limited companies will contain not only a profit and loss account and a balance sheet, but also a statement of source and application of funds (also called a 'funds flow' statement).

Although companies are not bound by statute to provide such a statement, SSAP 10 has recommended its inclusion in the audited financial accounts of every enterprise with an annual turnover in excess of £25,000.

Whereas the profit and loss account summarises the income position during the financial year, and the balance sheet discloses the capital position at the end of the year, the statement of source and application of funds provides a link between the two, by showing the ways in which the company generated funds during the year and, as importantly, what use it made of those funds. In other words, it explains *why* the balance sheet values at the year-end were different from those at the start of the year.

9.2 Presentation of the statement

Most companies broadly follow the example statement given in SSAP 10, which divides into three main headings, summarised as follows.

	£
1. Source of funds	x
2. Application of funds	(x)
Net source/net application of funds	x
(matched by an equivalent)	
3. Change in working capital	x

Note that if the total source of funds as computed in (1) above exceeds the total application in (2), then this 'net source' will be exactly matched by an *increase* in working capital, shown in (3). A 'net application' would be exactly matched by a *decrease* in working capital.

Other methods of presentation are acceptable, and these will be dealt with later in the chapter.

9.3 Where do funds come from?

The main source of funds in a healthy business is likely to be the net profit which is derived from its trading operations. This will rarely be the same figure as is shown in the profit and loss account, as we need to adjust 'non-cash' items such as changes in provisions, or profits and losses arising on the disposal of fixed assets. The reason for this can best be seen from Example 1.

Example 1

The trading and profit and loss accounts of Marple Ltd for the year ended 31 August 1982 are as follows:

	£		£
Opening stock	14,000	Sales	220,000
Purchases	87,000		
	101,000		
Less: Closing stock	19,000		
Cost of goods sold	82,000		
Gross profit c/d	138,000		
	£220,000		£220,000
Directors' salaries	54,000	Gross profit b/d	138,000
Wages and salaries	21,000		
Office rent and rates	9,280		
Telephone, insurance, etc.	4,050		
Advertising and stationery	2,260		
Audit fee	2,500		
Bank charges and interest	4,840		
Depreciation	7,600		
Net profit	32,470		
	£138,000		£138,000

Required:

A calculation of the total funds generated by the trading activities of the business in the year.

Solution:

The 'source of funds' which net profit represents for Marple Ltd is calculated as follows:

	£
Net profit	32,470
Adjustment for item not involving the movement of funds: Depreciation	7,600
Total generated from operations	£40,070

COMMENTARY

If you look through the list of overheads shown in the profit and loss account, you should be able to understand why 'depreciation' is singled out for special treatment. Salaries/rent/telephone/insurance/audit fee; all these and the other expenses (except depreciation) involve the outflow of funds from the business, i.e. cheques or cash must be paid. Depreciation, whilst still an overhead, does not require funds to leave the business (which company ever paid a cheque to someone named 'depreciation'?). On the contrary, the existence of a provision enables profits to be *retained* by the business by being placed in a special 'compartment' in the balance sheet, profits which might otherwise have been paid out by the company, for example by paying an increased dividend to shareholders.

9.4 Other possible adjustments to net profit

The same principle applies to increases in other types of provisions, e.g. provisions for doubtful debts. These would be adjusted in a similar manner to the depreciation 'add-back' shown previously.

Other items appearing in the profit and loss account which require adjusting include a loss on disposal of a fixed asset (treated in the same way as depreciation), a *reduction* in a provision (deducted from the net profit) and a profit on the sale of an asset (also deducted).

Example 2

Moonstone Ltd's summarised profit and loss account for the year ended 30 September 1983 is as follows:

	£		£
Administration expenses	30,800	Gross profit b/f	96,700
Selling and distribution	15,060	Profit on sale of plant	1,680
Depreciation	8,400	Provision for bad debts,	
Net profit	46,320	written back	2,200
	£100,580		£100,580

Required:

A calculation of the funds generated by the trading operations of the business in the year.

Solution:

	£	£	£
Net profit			46,320
Adjustments for items not involving the movement of funds:			
Depreciation		8,400	
Profit on sale of plant	(1,680)		
Provision for bad debts, written back	(2,200)		
		(3,880)	
			4,520
Total generated from operations			£50,840

9.5 What other sources of funds might there be?

In addition to the funds generated from trading operations, funds may be raised in a number of other ways, including the following:

(a) Selling long-term assets.
(b) Raising money through share issues.
(c) Borrowing via long-term loans and debentures.
(d) Decreasing working capital levels.

9.6 How might the funds be used?

To answer this question, we need to look at the converse of the ways in which funds are raised. For many businesses, this process unhappily starts with the opposite of a net profit, i.e. a net loss. A loss represents a drain on the resources of the enterprise and consequently 'requires funding'. The adjustments made to establish the 'total generated from operations' which we saw earlier, must also be applied when a net loss is made. (See Example 3 below.)

Other ways in which funds might be applied are:

(a) Buying long-term assets.
(b) Repaying long-term loans and debentures.
(c) Paying corporation tax.
(d) Paying dividends.
(e) Increasing working capital levels.

Example 3

Noprof Ltd's summarised profit and loss account for the year ended 28 February 1982 is as follows:

	£		£
Wages and salaries	58,900	Gross profit b/f	64,740
Administration costs	12,590		
Depreciation	5,970		
Loss on sale of assets	800	Net loss	13,520
	£78,260		£78,260

Required:

A calculation of the total loss which required funding in the year.

Solution:

			£
Net loss			
Adjustments for items not involving the movement of funds:			
Depreciation		5,970	
Loss on sale of assets		800	
			6,770
Total loss which required funding			£(6,750)

COMMENTARY

Both the adjustments reduce the net loss; contrast this with the previous illustrations where a net profit had been recorded. If a profit on a sale of a fixed asset, or a write-back of a provision had been included in the profit and loss account, then the adjustments required would be to *increase* the net loss.

SUMMARY

We said at the beginning of the chapter that the statement of source and application of funds explains the changes in the balance sheet values between the start and end of the financial year. We can now look at the detailed make-up of the statement, using a similar presentation to SSAP 10's example statement.

	Figures derived from: (see note 3)
Source of funds	
Adjusted net profit (see note 1)	Profit and loss account
Share capital (sale of shares, including any premium)	Balance sheet
Loans received	Balance sheet
Proceeds from sale of fixed assets or investments (see note 2)	Supplementary information appended to accounts
Application of funds	
Adjusted net loss (see note 1)	Profit and loss account
Redemption of shares	Balance sheet
Repayment of loans	Balance sheet
Purchases of fixed assets or investments (see note 2)	Balance sheet
Corporation tax paid	Balance sheet
Dividends paid	Balance sheet

Net source or net application matched by either an:

Increase or decrease in working capital	
Change in stock levels	Balance sheet
Change in debtors	Balance sheet
Change in creditors	Balance sheet
Movement in net liquid funds	
Change in bank and cash	Balance sheet

Notes:

1. The only changes in reserves which affect funds are the net profit or loss (adjusted in the ways previously shown) and an increase in a share premium account due to shares having been sold at a premium in the year. 'Internal' transfers such as to or from a general reserve, or the creation of an asset revaluation reserve consequent upon a revision of asset values have no effect whatsoever on the flow of funds and are therefore neither classified as a 'source' nor as an 'application'.
2. Fixed assets purchased and sold should be shown separately on the statement

and not 'netted off' to show just one figure.

3. Examination questions will give both the current balance sheet and that at the previous year-end.

4. In practice, the statement will show comparative amounts for the previous year, although examination candidates are likely to be asked to produce only the current year's figures.

We are now able to tackle a detailed illustration.

Example 4

The following are the summarised final accounts for the last two years of Xyplon Ltd:

Trading and profit and loss accounts year ended 31 December

1981 £	1981 £		1982 £	1982 £
246,000		Sales		369,000
184,500		Cost of goods sold		295,200
61,500		Gross profit		73,800
	16,400	Salaries	17,220	
	13,120	Trading expenses	14,760	
	7,380	Depreciation	13,120	
36,900				45,100
24,600		Net profit, before taxation		28,700
11,000		Less corporation tax		13,000
13,600		Net profit after taxation		15,700
	2,000	Transfer to general reserve	3,000	
	4,000	Proposed dividend	4,500	
6,000				7,500
7,600				8,200
11,200		Profit and loss account b/f		18,800
£ 18,800		Profit and loss account c/f		£27,000

Balance Sheets as at 31 December:

1981 £	1981 £	1981 £		1982 £	1982 £	1982 £
49,200			Fixed assets (A); net book value			93,480
			Current assets			
	19,680		Stock (B)		32,800	
	13,420		Trade debtors (C)		31,160	
	16,400		Bank (D)		—	
	49,500				63,960	
			Less current liabilities			
		12,900	Creditors (E)	23,940		
		11,000	Corporation tax (F)	13,000		
		4,000	Proposed dividend (G)	4,500		
		—	Bank overdraft (D)	9,000		
	27,900				50,440	
21,600			Net current assets			13,520
£70,800						£107,000
50,000			Share capital (H)			70,000
—			Share premium account (J)			5,000
18,800			Profit and loss account (K)			27,000
2,000			General Reserve (L)			5,000
£70,800						£107,000

175

Notes:
  i No fixed assets were sold in 1982.
  ii No bonus issues were made during 1982.
  iii Letter references in the balance sheet are to help locate items appearing in the solution.

Required:
A statement of source and application of funds for the year ended 31 December 1982.

Solution:

Xyplon Ltd
*Statement of source and application of funds
for the year ended 31 December 1982*

	£	£	'Step'
Source of funds			
Profit before taxation		28,700	1
Adjustment for items not involving the movement			
of funds: Depreciation		13,120	2
Total generated from operations		41,820	6
Funds from other sources			
Issue of shares for cash		25,000	4
		66,820	6
Application of funds			
Purchase of fixed assets	(57,400)		3
Corporation tax paid	(11,000)		5
Dividend paid	(4,000)		5
		(72,400)	6
Net application of funds		£(5,580)	6/8
Decrease in working capital			
Increase in stock	13,120		7
Increase in debtors	17,740		7
Increase in creditors	(11,040)		7
Movement in net liquid funds:			
Decrease in bank balance	(25,400)		7
		£(5,580)	8

Note that the 'step' column should not be reproduced in an examination answer (see Commentary below).

Workings:

We are not given balance sheet values for the cost of fixed assets or for total depreciation provisions at the start and end of the year. We therefore have to reconstruct the entries of 1982 by drawing up an account, showing how the changes in the net book values of fixed assets must have arisen. The 'balancing figure' in this account represents the cost of fixed assets purchased in the year.

Fixed Assets (at book values) Account

		£			£
1 Jan 1982	Balance b/f	49,200	31 Dec 1982	P and L a/c:	
31 Dec 1982	Additions			Depreciation for	
	(balancing			year	13,120
	figure)	57,400	31 Dec 1982	Balance c/f	93,480
		£106,600			£106,600

COMMENTARY

The following is the procedure adopted to answer the question.
Preliminary: Taking an unused page, draw up a 'skeleton' statement, with the three main headings as shown in section 9.2. Leave about eight lines between each heading.

Step 1 Identify the net profit from the 1982 profit and loss account (£28,700) and enter on statement.

Step 2 Look for 'non-cash' items in the 1982 profit and loss account (depreciation £13,120) and enter on statement.

Step 3 Scrutinise all long-term assets on 1982 balance sheet (item A). No assets were sold, but balance has increased. Assets were in fact bought for £57,400 (see working at end of solution). Enter on statement.

Step 4 Scrutinise capital and share premium account. As there were no bonus issues, all the increase in (H) must represent cash received (20,000), and the premium paid on shares (J) also reflects cash received. These amounts are combined, and entered on the statement.

Step 5 Establish how much was *paid* in 1982 in respect of corporation tax and dividends (not merely 'provided for').

The 1981 provisions were paid in 1982.

Corporation tax (F)   £11,000
Dividend (G)   £ 4,000

Enter both items on statement.

Step 6 Insert all sub-totals and totals on the statement, arriving at either a 'net source of funds' or a 'net application of funds'.

Step 7 Complete the statement by analysing the changes in the various working capital items (other than tax and dividends, which were dealt with at step 5), by comparing the respective amounts in the 1981 and 1982 balance sheets. The following matrix may be useful in this respect:

	Overall effect on working capital	
Item	*Increase*	*Decrease*
Stock	More stock	Less stock
Debtors	More debtors	Fewer debtors
Creditors	Fewer creditors	More creditors
Bank	Larger balance (or reduced o/draft)	Smaller balance (or larger o/draft)

In this question we have:

	£
Increase in stock (B)	13,120
Increase in debtors (C)	17,740
Increase in creditors (E)	(11,040)
Movement in net liquid funds:	
Decrease in bank balance (D)	(25,400)
	£(5,580)

Items (B) and (C) increase working capital, but the increased liabilities at (E) and the overall reduction in the bank balance (D) £16,400 + £9,000, have meant a decrease in the total level of working capital by £5,580.

Step 8 Ensure that the change in working capital is exactly matched by the net source/net application of funds as computed in step 6. If it is, then we can be reasonably confident that the statement has been correctly drawn up.

QUESTIONS WHERE THE 'NET PROFIT' IS NOT GIVEN

In Example 4 the additions to fixed assets had to be found by reconstructing a ledger account. This is a typical 'ploy' of examiners in order to test the ability to piece together facts from given information. Another example of this is when the net profit itself is not immediately evident from the question.

Example 5

Kobol Ltd's balance sheets as at 31 August 1987 and 1988 are given below:

	1987 £	1988 £		1987 £	1988 £
Share capital: Ordinary	20,000	20,000	Fixed assets, at cost	81,500	87,400

Preference	10,000	—	*Less:* Accumulated depreciation	14,800	17,800
				66,700	69,600
Share premium account	5,000	5,000			
Capital redemption reserve	—	10,000	Current assets		
General reserve	20,000	15,000	Stock	29,700	37,600
Profit and loss account	36,800	52,700	Debtors (net of provision)	37,200	26,400
	91,800	102,700	Bank	—	9,500
Current liabilities					
Trade creditors	18,800	16,400			
Corporation tax	12,000	13,000			
Proposed dividend	9,000	11,000			
Bank overdraft	2,000	—			
	133,600	143,100		133,600	143,100

Notes:

i   Fixed assets which had originally cost £11,000 were sold in November 1987 for £3,000. This represented a loss of £2,000 from book value.

ii   Debtors are shown net of a provision for doubtful debts. At 31 August 1987 this totalled £1,800, and a year later had been reduced to £1,300.

iii   The provisions for corporation tax and dividends shown in the 1987 balance sheet were paid during the year ended 31 August 1988.

Required:

A statement of source and application of funds for the year ended 31 August 1988.

Solution:

Kobol

Statement of Source and Application of Funds for the year ended 31 August 1988

	£	£
Source of funds		
Profit before taxation (see working 1)		44,900
Adjustments for items not involving the movement of funds: Depreciation (see working 2)	9,000	
Loss on sale of assets	2,000	
Provision for doubtful debts, written back	(500)	
		10,500
Total generated from operations		55,400
Funds from other sources		
Proceeds from sale of fixed assets		3,000
		58,400
Application of funds		
Purchase of fixed assets (see working 2)	16,900	
Redemption of preference shares	10,000	
Corporation tax paid	12,000	
Dividend paid	9,000	
		47,900
Net source of funds		£10,500
Increase in working capital		
Increase in stock	7,900	
Decrease in debtors (39,000–27,700)	(11,300)	
Decrease in creditors	2,400	
Movement in net liquid funds:		
Increase in bank balance (2,000 + 9,500)	11,500	
		10,500

Workings:

(1) *To find the net profit*

Profit and Loss Appropriation Account

	£			£
31 Aug 1988 Transfer to capital redemption reserve	10,000	1 Sept 1987 P and L b/f		36,800
Provision for corporation tax	13,000	31 Aug 1988 Transfer from general reserve		5,000
Proposed dividend	11,000	Net profit (balancing figure)		44,900
P and L c/f	52,700			
	£86,700			£86,700

(2) *To find additions to fixed assets and provision for depreciation*

Fixed Assets Account

	£			£
1 Sept 1987 Cost b/f	81,500	31 Aug 1988 Transfer cost of assets sold		11,000
31 Aug 1988 Additions (balancing figure)	16,900	31 Aug 1988 Cost c/f		87,400
	£98,400			£98,400

Provision for Depreciation of Fixed Assets Account

	£			£
31 Aug 1988 Transfer depreciaton on assets sold*	6,000	1 Sept 1987 Balance b/f		14,800
31 Aug 1988 Balance c/f	17,800	31 Aug 1988 P and L account; provision for year (balancing figure)		9,000
	£23,800			£23,800

COMMENTARY

The difficulties fall into two main areas:

1. Finding the net profit.
2. Establishing the changes in fixed assets, and the amount of depreciation charged in the year.

The net profit can be found by reconstructing the appropriation account for the year ended 31 August 1988. The 'balancing figure' must be the net profit brought down from the profit and loss account (see Working 1).

The change in fixed assets and the depreciation charge are found in a similar way to the procedure adopted in the previous illustration, i.e. by showing the entries in the fixed assets account. In this illustration things are made a little easier for us as we are given both cost and depreciated balances, thus avoiding the need to create an artificial 'book value' account as in the previous question.

9.7 Alternative presentations: the 'cash flow' statement

The solutions to Examples 4 and 5 are set out in accordance with the guide given in SSAP 10. This method of presentation is, to quote an appendix to the standard, 'illustrative only and in no way prescriptive, and other methods of presentation may equally comply with the accounting standard. The format used should be selected with a view to demonstrating clearly the manner in which the operations of the company have been financed and in which its financial resources have been utilised'. Because of this, an alternative form of presentation, known as the 'cash

---

*Found by the equation Cost − Book Value = Depreciation. Book value is found by adding the 'proceeds' of sale to the loss on sale. Therefore;

Cost of assets sold − (Proceeds of sale + Loss on sale) = Depreciation on assets sold
(11,000   −   (3,000 +   £2,000) = £6,000

flow statement' is often used. In this statement, the emphasis is shifted away from the overall change in the working capital, towards a specific explanation of the movement in the level of cash and bank balances.

Example 6

Using the information in Example 5 relating to Kobol Ltd, re-draft the statement to explain why the bank balance had changed from an overdraft of £2,000 at the start of the year to an 'in hand' balance of £9,500 at the end of the year.

Solution:

Kobol Ltd
Cash Flow Statement
for the year ended 31 August 1988

Sources of cash	£	£
Profit before taxation (adjusted for 'non-cash' items)		55,400
Proceeds from sale of fixed assets		3,000
Decrease in debtors		11,300
		69,700
Applications of cash		
Purchase of fixed assets	16,900	
Redemption of preference shares	10,000	
Payment of corporation tax	12,000	
Payment of dividend	9,000	
Increase in stock levels	7,900	
Decrease in creditors	2,400	
		58,200
Increase in cash levels in year		£11,500
Analysed as follows:		
opening bank overdraft, 1 September 1987	2,000	
closing cash at bank, 31 August 1988	9,500	
		£11,500

COMMENTARY

The working capital items (other than the bank balance) which were segregated in the source and application of funds statement are 'woven in' to the main body of the cash flow statement. The spotlight is thereby focused on the change in the level of the bank balance in the year.

Whilst the majority of items appearing in the statement are self-explanatory, the movements on debtors and creditors need further comment.

Debtors decreased in the year, i.e. sales ledger balances represented a lower total at the end of the year than at the beginning. Looked at in overall terms, this must have been due to more cash being paid into the business by credit customers than the sales debited to them in the year, hence the inclusion of the decrease as a source of cash. If debtors had increased, then credit customers would have paid less cash than the sales debited to them. The shortfall in the amount received would be shown as an application of cash on the cash flow statement, although students may find it helpful to think of the debtors 'depriving' the business of a source of cash due to their delay in paying their bills!

Similar principles can be applied to creditors. In the example, creditors (i.e. purchase ledger balances) decreased between the start and end of the year. The business must have paid out more cash than the total of invoices received in the year, hence the inclusion of the net outflow as an application of cash. If the total of creditors had increased by the year-end compared with the start of the year, then this would have resulted from less cash being paid out than the total of purchases invoices, the business thus retaining cash which it would otherwise have paid out to suppliers. This increase would be shown as a source of cash.

9.8 Statements for non-corporate enterprises

If a statement of source and application of funds is being prepared for a sole trader or a partnership, the same principles must be followed as for a limited company. However, certain items found in a corporate statement would not be applicable to a non-corporate business, and vice-versa.

Items unique to limited company statements are:

(a) changes in share capital and share premium;
(b) issue and redemption of debentures;
(c) payment of corporation tax and dividends.

Item unique to 'non-corporate' statements;

proprietor's drawings (show as an application of funds).

9.9 Interpretation of the statement

A statement of source and application of funds can help the user of accounting information to gain additional knowledge of the company's progress in the year. This can be demonstrated by looking back at Kobol Ltd in Example 5. Below is shown not only the statement for the year ended 31 August 1988, but also the comparative figures for the year ended 31 August 1987.

Kobol Ltd
Statement of Source and Application of Funds
for the years ended 31 August

	1988 £	1988 £	1987 £	1987 £
Source of funds				
Profit before taxation		44,900		21,200
Adjustments for items not involving the movement of funds: Depreciation	9,000		8,400	
Loss on sale of assets	2,000		—	
Provision for doubtful debts				
written back	(500)		—	
written off	—		1,200	
		10,500		9,600
Total generated from operations		55,400		30,800
Funds from other sources				
Proceeds from sale of fixed assets	3,000		—	
Proceeds from sale of shares	—		15,000	
		3,000		15,000
		58,400		45,800
Application of funds				
Purchase of fixed assets	16,900		23,100	
Redemption of preference shares	10,000		—	
Corporation tax paid	12,000		4,000	
Dividend paid	9,000		6,000	
		47,900		33,100
Net source of funds		£10,500		£12,700
Increase in working capital				
Increase in stock	7,900		13,000	
Decrease in debtors (1987: Increase)	(11,300)		5,100	

Decrease in creditors (1987: Increase)	2,400	(7,000)
Movement in net liquid funds		
Increase in bank balance	11,500	1,600
	£10,500	£12,700

In overall terms, the company's performance in 1988 seems to be similar to that of 1987. However, on closer analysis we can see that 95% of the 1988 total source of funds has been generated internally (£55,400 as a percentage of £58,400) compared with only 67% (£30,800 as a percentage of £45,800) in 1987. Reliance on outside funding has therefore diminished in the year. The proportions of total sources applied in the strengthening of the fixed asset base dropped to 29% (£16,900 as a percentage of £58,400) in 1988, compared with 50% (£23,100 as a percentage of £45,800) in the previous year.

Despite a near doubling of the net profit in 1988, other factors can be seen operating which caused a decline (albeit marginal) in the net source of funds between the two years. A company chairman, faced with disgruntled shareholders who had hoped for a doubling of their dividends, can use the statement of source and application of funds to explain exactly where the doubled profits 'ended up'. However, he may still be faced with any of the following questions:

(a) Was it necessary to increase stock levels again in 1988?
(b) Although the reduction in debtors seems, *prima facie*, to be beneficial, could excessive zeal on behalf of credit controllers be driving customers away? Are discounts for prompt payment too generous?
(c) Are creditors being paid 'too quickly'? Is full advantage being taken of interest-free credit offered by suppliers?
(d) Is too much money tied up in the bank balance? Although the company has achieved a creditable turn-around from the position two years previously (it can be calculated that there was an overdraft of £3,600 on 1 September 1986), are liquid funds now available to be 'ploughed back' into the business in the form of fixed assets?

Obviously, it is only the company's management who can comment upon these matters, but the statement of source and application of funds is the financial statement which provides the 'prompts' to the shareholders for the questions to be asked.

Exercises

9.1 From the following summarised profit and loss accounts, calculate the total funds generated from or absorbed by trading operations.

	(a)	(b)	(c)	(d)
Gross profit	126,300	120,470	151,950	77,900
Administration expenses	(61,460)	(88,100)	(14,060)	(28,600)
Selling expenses	(38,750)	(45,700)	(27,100)	(21,900)
Depreciation	(10,200)	(16,600)	(31,000)	(22,500)
Provision for doubtful debts written off	(2,000)	—	(5,000)	(4,000)
Bank charges	(600)	—	(1,000)	—
Profit (loss) on sale of fixed assets	1,500	(2,000)	—	(6,000)
Net profit (loss)	14,790	(31,930)	73,790	(5,100)

9.2 State whether the following increase or decrease working capital levels:

(a) An increase in stock.
(b) A decrease in creditors.
(c) A change from an overdrawn bank balance to a balance in hand.
(d) An increase in prepayments.

(e) A decrease in accruals.
(f) A decrease in debtors.

9.3 The opening and closing balance sheets of a sports and leisure club, together with the linking income and expenditure account, have been summarised and are shown below:

	Opening £	Closing £
Tangible fixed assets at cost	18,000	27,000
Depreciation provided	(10,000)	(12,500)
Net book amount	8,000	14,500
Current assets		
Stock	4,000	6,000
Subscriptions due	3,500	5,000
Cash	2,500	500
	£18,000	£26,000
Retained surpluses	6,000	9,500
Creditors due after one year		
Loan from bank	2,500	10,000
Creditors due within one year		
Trade creditors	4,500	3,500
Subscriptions in advance	5,000	3,000
	£18,000	£26,000

	£
Subscriptions	24,000
Sundry expenses	(18,000)
Depreciation	(2,500)
Retained	£3,500

Required:

(a) Prepare a statement of source and application of funds, showing clearly the reasons for the decline in the cash balance.
(b) Explain why it is considered desirable that a statement of source and application of funds should be published.
(c) State and comment upon two different definitions of 'funds'.

(CDAF)

9.4 The balance sheets of a company on 31 December 1983 and 31 December 1984 were as follows:

	1983 £	1983 £	1984 £	1984 £
Share capital		100,000		120,000
Retained profit		44,010		49,735
		144,010		169,735
Debentures		10,000		—
Current liabilities		47,620		58,970
		201,630		228,705
Fixed assets:				
Machinery at cost	169,710		173,507	
Less depreciation	28,400	141,310	34,000	139,507
Vehicles at cost	34,500		37,960	
Less depreciation	24,100	10,400	31,000	6,960
		151,710		146,467

Current assets:

Stock	18,770		35,900	
Debtors	21,450		28,210	
Bank	9,700	49,920	18,128	82,238
		£201,630		£228,705

(a) Prepare a statement of source and application of funds (funds flow) for the year ended 31 December 1984.

(b) Explain, with the use of appropriate accounting ratios (see Chapter 10), the change in the company's working capital during the same period.

(ULSEB)

9.5 The balance sheets of a company for two years are as follows:

As at 31 Dec 1983 £		As at 31 Dec 1984 £	As at 31 Dec 1983 £		As at 31 Dec 1984 £
30,000	Issued share capital	35,000		Fixed assets, after depreciation	
—	Share premium account	2,000	34,000	(Note 2)	36,000
21,400	Profit and loss account	26,800			
20,000	10% debentures	5,000			
	Current liabilities			*Current assets*	
12,000	Creditors	8,000	17,000	Stock	35,000
6,500	Proposed dividend	7,000	42,000	Debtors	9,800
3,100	Bank overdraft	—	—	Bank balance	3,000
93,000		83,800	93,000		83,800

A summary of the profit and loss accounts is as follows:

	Year to 31 Dec 1984 £	Year to 31 Dec 1983 £
Gross profit	98,200	106,300
Profit on sale of assets	1,000	—
	99,200	106,300
Less: Expenses	86,800	87,700
Net profit	12,400	18,600
Proposed dividend	7,000	6,500
	5,400	12,100
Profit and loss balance b/f	21,400	9,300
Profit and loss balance c/f	26,800	21,400

Notes:

1. Stock valued at cost £5,000 was omitted from the stock valuation at 31 December 1984.

2. Fixed assets appeared in the nominal ledger as follows:

	£		£
1 Jan 1984 Cost b/f	46,000	31 Dec 1984 Transfer to disposals	
31 Dec 1984 Additions	12,400	account	6,000
		31 Dec 1984 Cost c/f	52,400
	58,400		58,400

The assets sold realised £4,000 which represented a profit of £1,000 over their book value at the date of sale.

3. There were no bonus (scrip) issues made during the year.

(a) You are required to draw up a sources and applications of funds statement (flow of funds statement) for the year ended 31 December 1984.

(b) By using appropriate ratios (see Chapter 10), comment on changes in the working capital structure of the company during the two years. (ULSEB)

9.6 The latest balance sheet of Telrad (UK) Ltd prepared for internal use is as shown below.

Balance Sheet as at 30 June 1984

	Cost	Depreciation	
	£	£	£
Fixed assets			
Premises	15,000	6,000	9,000
Tools and equipment	10,000	5,450	4,550
Vehicles	8,000	6,800	1,200
	33,000	18,250	14,750

	£	£	
Current assets			
Stocks		4,109	
Debtors and prepayments		3,381	
Bank balance		1,208	
Cash		83	
		8,781	
Less: Current liabilities			
Creditors and accruals	3,534		
Corporation tax	2,257		
Proposed dividends	200		
		5,991	
Working capital			2,790
Net assets employed			£17,540

Financed by:			
Issued share capital			
Ordinary shares of £0.50 per share		4,000	
6% preference shares of £1.00 per share		3,000	
			7,000
Reserves			
General reserve		5,000	
Profit and loss		2,540	
			7,540
			14,540
Loan capital			
8% debentures			3,000
			£17,540

The directors are in process of making certain forecasts for the year ended 30 June 1985 and have been considering the following statement from the chief accountant.

Forecast Statement of Source and Application of Funds
for year ended 30 June 1985

	£	£
Profit before tax		33,470
Adjustments for items not involving movement of funds		
Depreciation	6,750	
Loss on disposal of equipment	360	
Profit on disposal of vehicles	(780)	
		6,330
Total funds generated from operations		39,800
Funds from other sources		
Issue of ordinary shares for cash	2,000	
Issue of 8% debentures	5,000	
Proceeds of sale of fixed assets:		
equipment	1,440	
vehicles	1,980	
		10,420
		50,220
Application of funds		
Cost of acquisition of		
premises	30,000	
equipment	6,000	
vehicles	11,000	
Tax paid (see Note 5)	2,205	
Dividends paid (see Note 6)	540	
		49,745
		475
Increase/(decrease) in working capital		
Increase/(decrease) in stocks	1,167	
in debtors/prepayments	273	
(Increase)/decrease in creditors and accruals	(551)	
Movement in net liquid funds		
Increase/(decrease) in bank balance	(448)	
in cash	34	
		475

Notes:

The above statement has been prepared on the following assumptions:

(1) Fixed assets will be sold as follows during the year:

	Original cost	Aggregate depreciation
	£	£
Tools and equipment	4,000	2,200
Vehicles	8,000	6,800

(2) Fixed assets will be acquired as follows:

	Cost
	£
Premises (at end of year)	30,000
Tools and equipment (during year)	6,000
Vehicles (during year)	11,000

(3) The charge for depreciation comprises:

	£
Premises	1,500
Tools and equipment	3,050
Vehicles	2,200
	£6,750

(4) Additional ordinary shares will be issued at the end of the year, but will not rank for dividend until 1986, as follows:

	£
Bonus issue (3 for 4)	3,000
For cash	2,000
	£5,000

The bonus issue will be appropriated from the credit balance on general reserve after a further £1,000 has been transferred to that account from profit and loss account.

(5) Tax paid is corporation tax after adjustment of an overprovision of £52 in 1984. Corporation tax liability at 30 June 1985 is forecast at £819.

(6) Dividends paid comprise:

	£
Ordinary share final dividend proposed at 30 June 1984 but since paid during current year	200
6% preference share dividend paid	180
Ordinary share interim dividend paid (4%)	160
	£540

An ordinary share final dividend of 6% will be proposed at 30 June 1985 on those ordinary shares in issue excluding the new share issues (see *Note 4* above).

(7) The additional 8% debentures will be issued on 1 January 1985.

The directors now require a forecast profit and loss account for the period and a forecast balance sheet at 30 June 1985.

Required:

(a) Comment briefly on the apparent plans of Telrad (UK) Ltd for the year ended 30 June 1985, as far as they can be deduced from the forecast statement of source and application of funds.

(b) Prepare, from the information and data given, a forecast profit and loss account for the year ended 30 June 1985 in the following format:

	£	£
Profit before items listed below		
Add: Profit on disposal of vehicles		____
Less: Loss on disposal of equipment		
Depreciation		
Debenture interest	____	
Profit before tax		33,470
Less: Corporation tax		____
Profit after tax		
Less:		
Transfer to general reserve		
Dividends—paid:		
6% preference		
ordinary interim (4%)		
—proposed		
ordinary final (6%)	____	
Retained profits for		
current year		
previous years b/f		____
c/f		£

(c)   Prepare a forecast balance sheet as at 30 June 1985 in the same format as that given for 30 June 1984.

All workings must be shown.   (ACCA)

9.7   A friend of yours who owns a newsagent's and confectionery business has asked for your help. He is very worried because he suspects that a shop assistant is stealing money from his till. He comments as follows:

'For the year to 31 March 1982 my shop made a profit of £8,600 and yet I have had to ask the bank for an overdraft', then adds 'Will you check the figures for me, please?' You agree to help and he supplies the following information.

Nick's Newsmart
Balance Sheet as at 31 March

1981			1982	
£	£	*Fixed assets*	£	£
16,000		Premises, at cost	16,000	
3,600		*Less:* Depreciation	3,900	
3,000	12,400			12,100
1,000		Fixtures and fittings, at cost	8,200	
	2,000	*Less:* Depreciation	1,300	6,900
	14,400			19,000
		Current assets		
5,400		Stocks – magazines, periodicals, etc.	8,060	
1,480		– sweets, tobacco, etc.	3,240	
2,200		Debtors – trade	4,900	
140		– other	420	
6,400		Bank	—	
280		Cash	500	
15,900			17,120	
		Less:		
		Current liabilities		
4,200		Creditors – trade	3,600	
100		– other	120	
—		Bank overdraft	4,000	
4,300			7,720	
	11,600	*Working capital*		9,400
	26,000	*Net assets employed*		28,400
24,600		Opening capital	26,000	
6,800		*Add:* Net profit	8,600	
31,400			34,600	
5,400		*Less:* Drawings	6,200	
	£26,000	Closing capital		£28,400

You confirm that he has not disposed of any fixed assets during the year.

Required:

Prepare a statement of source and application of funds (funds flow statement) to show Nick where his profit has gone.

(ACCA)

9.8 The Balance Sheet of BHA Ltd at 31 December 1981 was as follows:

	£000		£000	£000
Issued ordinary £1				
shares fully paid	3,000	Freehold land at cost		1,458
Retained profits	580	Freehold buildings at cost	700	
Trade creditors	214	less depreciation	28	672
Bank overdraft	32	Machinery at cost	1,240	
Proposed dividends	60	less depreciation	360	880
		Stocks		368
		Trade debtors		283
		Short-term investments at cost		225
	3,886			3,886

The company's Statement of Sources and Applications of Funds for the year ended 31 December 1982 was as follows:

	£000	£000
Sources of funds:		
Net profit		474
Depreciation of freehold buildings	14	
Depreciation of machinery	192	
Depreciation of vehicles	56	262
Loss on sale of machinery		17
		753
Total generated from operations		
Funds from other sources:		
Issue of 400,000 ordinary £1 shares	480	
Sale of machinery	205	685
		1,438
Applications of funds:		
Dividends paid	60	
Purchase of machinery	338	
Purchase of vehicles	280	678
		760
Increase/(decrease) in working capital:		
Stocks	283	
Debtors	(17)	
Creditors	84	
Short-term investments	312	
	662	
Increase in net liquid funds	98	760

Notes:

1. The machinery sold had originally cost £310,000.
2. The market value of all investments held at 31 December 1982 was £650,000.
3. The directors have recommended a dividend of 4% on all shares held at 31 December 1982.

Required:

 i The balance sheet of BHA Ltd at 31 December 1982, in good style.
    Note: Ignore taxation.
 ii Calculate two liquidity ratios for both 31 December 1981 and 31 December 1982, and comment briefly, in the light of your results, on the company's decision to issue the additional shares.*

(LCCI – Higher)

*See Chapter 10.

CHAPTER 10

Interpretation of Financial Accounting Information

10.1 Introduction

Although the final accounts of an unincorporated business might consist of only two pages, containing trading and profit and loss accounts on one and a balance sheet on the other, a limited company must produce more detailed information to satisfy the requirements of the Companies Act, Accounting Standards and possibly the Stock Exchange if the company has a market 'quotation'. The factor which is common to all business organisations is that these accounting statements are not produced solely for the purpose of providing information for the owner or owners of the business, but are also likely to be used by other interested parties for various purposes. These include the following:

Banks, who need to know whether a business is capable of repaying loans, or is in a sound financial position if loans are being requested.

Potential investors, who may use the accounting information to decide whether or not to invest money in the business.

The Government, which must ensure that tax is paid on profits, where applicable, and that there is compliance with relevant Acts of Parliament.

Customers and suppliers, both actual and potential, who may wish to ensure that a business is solvent prior to entering a trading relationship.

Employees who have a direct interest in the financial affairs of the business for which they work.

The local community, which may be concerned about the effects of redundancies, factory closures, etc.

Business competitors, who can measure their own performance against that of their rivals.

Economic analysts, who can attempt to establish trends by an analysis of the results of particular businesses.

Members of the general public, who may require information relating to environmental, ecological or other attitudes revealed in company annual reports.

The amount of information which is made available depends primarily upon the type of business entity.

One of the features of sole trading or partnership is the absence of any statutory requirement to *publish* accounts.

In practice, only a handful of 'sets' of final accounts are produced (usually by a qualified accountant), their likely destination being to the owner or partners, a bank manager, and the taxation authorities. Any wider distribution is entirely at the discretion of the owner(s).

For a limited company, however, not only does each shareholder and debenture holder have a right to receive a copy of the final accounts, but also a copy must be placed on public record (in the United Kingdom by being sent to a Registrar of Companies). Members of the public may obtain copies of a particular company's accounting information on payment of a fee.

A private limited company will include in its published accounts the following statements, in addition to the profit and loss account and balance sheet in the prescribed Companies Act format:

A directors' report, which contains a brief review of the company's results and trading activities, and certain statutory information not necessarily found in the accounting statements.

Notes to the accounts, which give additional information required by statute or accounting standards to aid the fuller understanding of the company's financial position.

Statement of source and application of funds, in accordance with SSAP 10 (see Chapter 9).

An auditor's report, which is a statement from an independent qualified accountant as to whether the accounts show a true and fair view of the state of the company's affairs and comply with the various requirements of the Companies Act.

A public limited company subject to Stock Exchange regulations will provide additionally:

A chairman's report, which is a comprehensive survey of the state of the company's business, its past performance and future prospects.

A summary of statistics, which gives certain key financial figures for a five-year period (or longer). (See Figure 10.1.)

10.2 Interpretation of the accounts

As previously explained, the amount of information contained within the accounting statements will vary considerably according, primarily, to the type of business entity and secondly, the attitude of the business owners regarding the provision of additional, 'non-statutory' information.

Regardless of the quantity of information provided, the users of accounting statements must adopt a methodical and analytical approach if they are to gain the best possible understanding of the business's performance. This can best be demonstrated by using data from a fictitious company, Ace plc, for the two years

---

Fitch Lovell PLC

Five Year Summary

		1981	1982	1983	1984	1985
Sales	£m	651.4	739.5	804.2	471.4	463.2
Profit before tax	£m	9.2	10.3	14.6	16.1	16.3
Earnings attributable to ordinary shareholders	£m	8.6	8.6	10.8	11.5	12.0
Earnings per ordinary share	pence	13.61	13.14	16.01	16.84	17.13
Dividends per ordinary share						
– gross	pence	7.43	7.80	11.43	13.14	13.86
– net	pence	5.20	5.46	8.00	9.20	9.70
Ordinary shareholders' funds						
– total	£m	54.9	58.3	62.8	70.8	64.9
– per share	pence	84	87	93	103	90

Fig. 10.1 Fitch Lovell plc – five-year summary.

ended 31 December 1986. For this purpose, it has been assumed that the analyst has access to the detailed, unpublished accounting statements, as well as to the published version. (See Figures 10.2(a), 10.2(b) and 10.2(c).)

The accounting statements given in Figure 10.2 contain a mass of statistical information, and in practice this would be supplemented by other information

Ace plc

Trading and Profit and Loss Accounts

for the years ended 31 December 1985 and 1986

(All figures in £000)

	1986		1985	
Sales		4,500		3,600
Less: Cost of sales				
Opening stock	200		160	
Purchases	1,850		1,670	
	2,050		1,830	
Less: Closing stock	250		200	
		1,800		1,630
Gross profit		2,700		1,970
Less: Expenses				
Directors' salaries	148		127	
Wages and staff salaries	915		836	
Printing, stationery and advertising	275		223	
Postages, wrappings and sundries	61		57	
Discount (net)	18		-	
Rent and rates	31		26	
Light and heat	42		60	
Motor expenses	95		90	
Telephone and insurance	25		26	
Repairs and renewals	49		45	
Interest on loans and overdraft	74		50	
Depreciation	180		170	
Audit and accountancy	19		18	
Provision for doubtful debts	18	1,950	2	1,730
Net profit		750		240
Less taxation		200		60
Net profit after taxation		550		180
Proposed dividends		150		60
		400		120
Profit and loss b/f		300		180
Profit and loss c/f		700		300

Fig. 10.2(a)   Specimen accounts for analysis.

including the directors' report and the various 'notes to the accounts'. A logical approach must be adopted to ensure that the correct conclusions are drawn from the analysis, and this is best achieved by dividing the process into three distinct parts: preliminary, calculations and interpretation.

10.3 The first stage: preliminary analysis

This consists of obtaining sufficient background knowledge to make the user aware of the environment in which the business operates. It includes such matters as the following, with the likely source of the information in brackets:

1. Type of trade (directors' report, chairman's report, advertising).
2. Geographical trading areas (directors' report, chairman's report).
3. Financial history (five-year summary, previous years' accounts, company information services, e.g. Extel).
4. Management (directors' report).
5. Competition (trade newspapers, stock market sector analyses).
6. Quality of products (visual inspection, advertising).

The amount of information which can be gleaned will obviously depend upon many factors, but *any* preliminary research is useful if it helps to place the company

---

Ace plc

Balance Sheets as at 31 December 1985 and 1986

(All figures in £000)

	1986		1985	
Fixed assets		1,114		322
Current assets				
Stock	250		200	
Debtors	434		476	
Cash in hand	22		20	
	706		696	
Current liabilities				
Creditors	128		101	
Taxation	200		60	
Dividend	150		60	
Bank overdraft	350		285	
	828		506	
Net current assets (liabilities)		(122)		190
Net assets		992		512
Share capital				
Ordinary shares of 50p each		200		200
Reserves (P & L account)		700		300
		900		500
Long-term loans		92		12
Capital employed		992		512

Fig. 10.2(b) Specimen accounts for analysis.

Ace plc
Source and Application of Funds Statement
for the year ended 31 December 1986

(All figures in £000)

Sources of funds

Net profit before tax		750
Add items not involving the movement of funds:		
Depreciation	180	
Provision for doubtful debts	18	198
Total generated from operations		948

Other sources:

Long-term loans received	80	
Proceeds from sales of fixed assets	12	92
		1,040

Application of funds

Purchase of fixed assets	984	
Taxation paid	60	
Dividend paid	60	
		1,104
Net application of funds		(64)

Decrease in working capital:

Increase in stock	50	
Decrease in debtors	(24)	
Increase in creditors	(27)	
Increase in cash in hand	2	
Increase in bank overdraft	(65)	
		(64)

Notes:
1. The company is a retailer, with eight shops selling a wide range of household goods.
2. During 1986 the company purchased an existing supermarket from a competitor. This accounted for the large increase in fixed assets in the year.

Fig. 10.2(c) Specimen accounts for analysis.

and its business in an appropriate context prior to the detailed calculation of ratios and percentages.

Having obtained a general impression of the scope and nature of the business, the analyst should then take the current year's accounts and read through each statement, making careful notes of any unusual or interesting items, changes in accounting policies, qualifications in auditors' reports, etc. By looking at the 'bottom lines' of the profit and loss account and balance sheet, i.e. the net profit and total capital employed, an immediate impression can be gained of the progress of the business in the year. For Ace plc, the net profit has increased from £240,000 to £750,000, whilst total capital employed has also increased, from £512,000 to

£992,000. This seems to indicate that the company had a 'good year', which may or may not be borne out by the detailed calculations to be made in the second stage of the analytical process.

10.4 The second stage: calculations

The task of extracting meaningful statistics is usually broken down into three sections:

1. A *horizontal* analysis, which is a comparison of the current year's figures with those of the previous year.
2. A *vertical* analysis, whereby each profit and loss account item is expressed as a percentage of the sales total, and each balance sheet item is expressed as a percentage of the total capital employed.
3. *Ratio analysis*, whereby strengths and weaknesses are revealed by comparisons between various items appearing in the balance sheet or profit and loss account.

The process of horizontal and vertical analysis can be demonstrated by reference to the accounts of Ace plc as shown in Figs 10.3(a) and 10.3(b).

INTERPRETATION OF THE ANALYSIS

The horizontal analysis shows the percentage changes from the preceding year to the current year. Major movements within the revenue statement have occurred in such areas as sales, gross profit, loan interest, provision for doubtful debts, net profit, taxation and dividends. Within the balance sheet, fixed assets have more than doubled whilst the value of net current assets has reduced by 164%. Long-term loans have increased six fold.

If the business's performance in 1986 were to be summarised in one sentence, it could be said that whilst both net profit and fixed assets doubled in the year, the working capital deteriorated. The extent of these changes is emphasised further by the vertical analysis which, *inter alia*, shows that in 1986 the business's net profit was 16.7% of sales revenue, compared with only 6.7% in 1985. The balance sheets for the two years disclose an even stronger contrast, whereby the total net assets are made up as follows:

	1986 (%)	1985 (%)
Fixed assets	112.3	62.9
Net current assets (liabilities)	(12.3)	37.1
Total net assets	100.0	100.0

Within the net current assets, it can be seen that stocks and debtors were proportionately more dominant in the 1985 balance sheet than in 1986 (132% of the balance sheet total in 1985, compared with 80% in 1986). Although the bank overdraft increased in monetary terms in the year, it actually declined from 55.7% to 35.3% of the balance sheet total.

RATIO ANALYSIS

Having established the percentage movements between the two years, and assessed the relative strengths of the component parts of the revenue and capital statements, the next step is to calculate ratios which reveal specific aspects of the financial picture of the business as a whole.

These ratios are usually grouped into three categories:

1. Operating ratios.
2. Financial ratios.
3. Investment ratios.

Operating ratios

These are extracted primarily from the trading and profit and loss accounts and also

Ace plc

Trading and Profit and Loss Accounts

for the years ended 31 December 1985 and 1986

	1986 £000	1985 £000	'Horizontal' analysis % change in year	'Vertical' analysis 1986(%)	1985(%)
Sales	4,500	3,600	+ 25.0	100	100
Less: Cost of sales					
Opening stock	200	160	+ 25.0	4.4	4.4
Purchases	1,850	1,670	+ 10.8	41.1	46.4
	2,050	1,830	+ 12.0	45.5	50.8
Less: Closing stock	250	200	+ 25.0	5.5	5.5
	1,800	1,630	+ 10.4	40.0	45.3
Gross profit	2,700	1,970	+ 37.1	60.0	54.7
Less: Expenses					
Directors' salaries	148	127	+ 16.5	3.3	3.5
Wages and salaries	915	836	+ 9.4	20.3	23.2
Printing, etc.	275	223	+ 23.3	6.1	6.2
Postages, etc.	61	57	+ 7.0	1.4	1.6
Discount (net)	18	-	+ ∞	0.4	-
Rent and rates	31	26	+ 19.2	0.7	0.7
Light and heat	42	60	− 30.0	0.9	1.7
Motor expenses	95	90	+ 5.6	2.1	2.5
Telephone, etc.	25	26	− 3.8	0.5	0.7
Repairs	49	45	+ 8.9	1.1	1.2
Interest	74	50	+ 48.0	1.7	1.4
Depreciation	180	170	+ 5.9	4.0	4.7
Audit, etc.	19	18	+ 5.6	0.4	0.5
Provis. for doubtful debts	18	2	+800.0	0.4	0.1
	1,950	1,730	+ 12.7	43.3	48.0
Net profit	750	240	+212.5	16.7	6.7
Taxation	200	60	+233.3	4.4	1.7
Net profit after tax	550	180	+2,065.6	12.3	5.0
Prop. dividends	150	60	+150.0	3.3	1.7
	400	120	+233.3	9.0	3.3
P & L b/f	300	180	+ 66.7	6.6	5.0
P & L c/f	700	300	+133.3	15.6	8.3

Fig. 10.3(a)   Horizontal and vertical analysis of Ace plc trading and profit and loss accounts.

from within the working capital section of the balance sheet. All figures used are taken from Figure 10.2 (Ace plc).

1. Gross profit margin $\dfrac{\text{Gross profit}}{\text{Sales}} \times 100$

$$1986 \quad \frac{2,700}{4,500} \times 100 = 60\%$$

$$1985 \quad \frac{1,970}{3,600} \times 100 = 54.7\%$$

This shows the proportion of the sales revenue which resulted in a gross profit to the company. It is affected by various factors including changing price levels and altered sales mix. The margin might be reduced by companies that wish to increase their share of a particular market. For Ace plc, however, the position strengthened in 1986 as compared with 1985.

Ace plc

Balance Sheets as at 31 December 1985 and 1986

	1986 £000	1985 £000	'Horizontal' analysis % change in year	'Vertical' analysis 1986(%)	1985(%)
Fixed assets	1,114	322	+246.0	112.3	62.9
Current assets					
Stock	250	200	+ 25.0	25.2	39.0
Debtors	434	476	− 8.8	43.8	93.0
Cash in hand	22	20	+ 10.0	2.2	3.9
	706	696	+ 1.4	71.2	135.9
Current liabilities					
Creditors	128	101	+ 26.7	12.9	19.7
Taxation	200	60	+233.3	20.2	11.7
Dividend	150	60	+150.0	15.1	11.7
Bank overdraft	350	285	+ 22.8	35.3	55.7
	828	506	+ 63.6	83.5	98.8
Net current assets (liabilities)	(122)	190	−164.2	(12.3)	37.1
Net assets	992	512	+ 93.7	100.0	100.0
Ordinary share capital	200	200	-	20.2	39.1
Reserves (P & L)	700	300	+133.3	70.5	58.6
	900	500	+ 80.0	90.7	97.7
Long-term loans	92	12	+666.7	9.3	2.3
Capital employed	992	512	+ 93.7	100.0	100.0

Fig. 10.3(b)   Horizontal and vertical analysis of Ace plc balance sheets.

2. Net profit margin $\dfrac{\text{Net profit}}{\text{Sales}} \times 100$

$$1986 \quad \frac{750}{4{,}500} \times 100 = 16.7\%$$

$$1985 \quad \frac{240}{3{,}600} \times 100 = 6.7\%$$

The net profit margin shows the efficiency with which expenses are controlled, and it is clear that 1986 was a far better year than 1985 in this respect. However, the figure can become distorted by factors such as the company imposing rigid 'wage freezes' on employees' pay, or by drastic although temporary cut-backs in overheads, which may be storing up trouble for future years.

3. 'Mark-up' $\dfrac{\text{Gross profit}}{\text{Cost of goods sold}} \times 100$

$$1986 \quad \frac{2{,}700}{1{,}800} \times 100 = 150\%$$

$$1985 \quad \frac{1{,}970}{1{,}630} \times 100 = 120.9\%$$

Directly linked to the gross profit margin, the 'mark-up' indicates the pricing policy of the business, as it shows the percentage addition made to cost prices to arrive at selling prices.

In 1986, every £100 of goods bought in by Ace plc was being sold at an average of £250. Similarly priced goods bought in 1985 were being sold at just over £220.

4. Return on capital employed
    (ROCE) $\dfrac{\text{Net profit before interest and tax}}{\text{Average capital employed}} \times 100$

$$1986 \quad \frac{750 + 74}{992} \times 100 = 83.1\%$$

$$1985 \quad \frac{240 + 50}{512} \times 100 = 56.7\%$$

This is a measure of overall profitability, showing the percentage return from the capital employed within the company. In both years, the ROCE was exceptionally high, which might indicate that the time will come soon when new competitors emerge. The denominator used in the formula is the capital employed at the balance sheet date, but the average of capital between the start and end of the year could also be used. The ROCE can be distorted if significant loans and overdrafts have been 'netted off' when arriving at the balance sheet totals. In Ace plc's case, the revised formulae would be (adding back the overdraft):

$$1986 \quad \frac{750 + 74}{992 + 350} \times 100 = 61.4\%$$

$$1985 \quad \frac{240 + 50}{512 + 285} \times 100 = 36.4\%$$

Although the ROCE percentages are reduced, the returns are still high, and the revised formulae do little to change the original comment on the figures.

5. Fixed assets turnover $\dfrac{\text{Sales}}{\text{Fixed assets (net value)}}$

$$1986 \quad \frac{4{,}500}{1{,}114} = 4.0{:}1$$

$$1985 \quad \frac{3{,}600}{322} = 11.2{:}1$$

The fixed assets turnover ratio measures the sales generated by each £1 of fixed assets: £11.20 in 1985 but only £4 in 1986. The purchase of the supermarket referred to in the notes to the accounts appears to have been completed in the latter part of 1986, which would seem to indicate that the sharp decline in the ratio is only temporary. When the 1987 accounts are available analysts would expect to see a reversal of the downward trend as the sales from the new premises would be recorded for the full year.

6. Rate of stock turnover ('stock turn') $\dfrac{\text{Average stockholding}}{\text{Cost of goods sold}} \times 365$

$$1986 \quad \frac{2(200 + 250)}{1,800} \times 365 = 45.6 \text{ days}$$

$$1985 \quad \frac{2(160 + 200)}{1,630} \times 365 = 40.3 \text{ days}$$

If a company can increase the speed at which it sells its stocks, then it can generate more profit in the process, provided that the increase in turnover is not obtained by simply slashing the gross profit margin. In 1985, the business took an average of 40.3 days to sell its stock, but this had increased to 45.6 days in 1986. The drawback of this calculation is that accurate average stock figures need to be used, but those appearing in the balance sheets are likely to be at an unrealistically low level owing to the fact that most businesses choose the end of their financial year so that it coincides with their period of least activity.

7. Debtors' collection period $\dfrac{\text{Debtors}}{\text{Sales}} \times 365$

$$1986 \quad \frac{434}{4,500} \times 365 = 35.2 \text{ days}$$

$$1985 \quad \frac{476}{3,600} \times 365 = 48.3 \text{ days}$$

The efficiency of the business's credit control department is measured here by calculating the average length of time that money is owed by debtors. The department was more efficient in 1986 than 1985, and a collection period of five weeks is considered to be a very good average.

8. Creditors' payment period $\dfrac{\text{Creditors}}{\text{Cost of goods sold}} \times 365$

$$1986 \quad \frac{128}{1,800} \times 365 = 26 \text{ days}$$

$$1985 \quad \frac{101}{1,630} \times 365 = 22.6 \text{ days}$$

In 1986, creditors were paid, on average, twenty-six days after the supplies were made. This appears to indicate that attractive discount terms were being offered in return for payment within one calendar month of the invoice date. If no such discount were available then the company might delay payment (within reason), thus taking advantage of the interest-free credit provided by its suppliers. However, great care should be taken not to alienate suppliers through undue delays in the settling debts.

9. Cash operating cycle

	1986 (days)	1985 (days)
Stock turn	45.6	40.3
Debtors' collection period	35.2	48.3
	80.8	88.6

Less: Creditors' payment period	26.0	22.6
	54.8	66.0

By using the results of the three previous ratios, it is possible to assess the period of time which elapses between the payment for stock received and the collection of cash from customers in respect of the sale of that stock. The shorter the length of time between the initial outlay and the ultimate receipt of cash, the less working capital needs to be financed by. the company. Ways of 'speeding up' the cycle include selling stock faster by reducing margins or increasing advertising, tightening up the collection of debtors' balances, and delaying payments to creditors.

Financial ratios

These are extracted exclusively from the balance sheet, and concentrate on the liquidity, solvency and financial structure of the business.

1. Working capital ratio $\dfrac{\text{Current assets}}{\text{Current liabilities}}$
   (or current ratio)

$$1986 \quad \frac{706}{828} = 0.85:1$$

$$1985 \quad \frac{696}{506} = 1.4:1$$

This measures the overall adequacy of the working capital. The 'ideal' ratio is often quoted as 2:1 but this depends upon the type of business, and many thriving companies continue successfully, despite having a negative ratio. However, it is apparent that Ace plc's position has deteriorated markedly in the year, which is of concern if the company is having, or is likely to have, difficulty in meeting its debts as they fall due. This aspect is further explored by the acid test ratio (see below).

2. Acid test ratio $\dfrac{\text{'Quick' assets}}{\text{Current liabilities}}$
   (or 'quick assets' or 'liquidity' ratio)

$$1986 \quad \frac{456}{828} = 0.6:1$$

$$1985 \quad \frac{496}{506} = 1.0:1$$

It is of obvious importance that a company should be able to meet its debts as they fall due. 'Quick assets' are those which can be converted quickly into cash as the need arises, and stocks and work-in-progress are excluded as being, generally, slow-moving assets. The 'ideal' ratio is 1:1, as recorded in 1985 by Ace plc. By 1986, the company has only 60p of quickly realisable assets to meet each £1 of its current liabilities which indicates that it might be unable to withstand a crisis whereby the majority of its creditors demand payment at about the same time. Analysts consider the acid test to be of fundamental importance when assessing the ability of a business to survive; a fact which must cause great anxiety to the directors of Ace plc.

3. Gearing ratio $\dfrac{\text{Fixed return funding}}{\text{Total long-term capital}} \times 100$

$$1986 \quad \frac{92}{992} \times 100 = 9.3\%$$

$$1985 \quad \frac{12}{512} \times 100 = 2.3\%$$

The importance of gearing was explained in Chapter 6, and it is clear that, using the formula quoted, Ace plc was 'low geared' in both of the years under review. The directors may feel that this gives them scope for further borrowing so as to alleviate their liquidity problems (cf. acid test ratio). Note, however, that there are other ways of calculating a company's gearing; for example, the level of bank borrowing is sometimes included in the numerator. For Ace plc, this would increase the gearing levels to the following percentages:

$$1986 \quad \frac{92 + 350}{992} \times 100 = 44.6\%$$

$$1985 \quad \frac{12 + 285}{512} \times 100 = 58\%$$

The analyst will use the formula which he feels gives him the greatest insight into the position and trends of the company; there are no hard and fast rules as to the composition of the gearing calculation.

The first formula showed that long-term borrowing had increased in 1986 as compared to 1985, whilst the second formula shows that when the overdraft is included in the definition of 'long-term borrowing', the proportion of borrowing to total capital actually decreased in 1986.

Investment ratios

These are used primarily by potential investors when assessing the shares and dividends of publicly listed companies. For the purpose of calculating ratios 2 and 3 below it is assumed that Ace plc's current stock market price is 412p (1985 370p).

1. Earnings per share (eps)

$$\frac{\text{Net profit before extraordinary items} - (\text{Tax} + \text{pref divs})}{\text{Number of ordinary shares in issue}}$$

$$1986 \quad \frac{(750 - 200)}{400} = 137p$$

$$1985 \quad \frac{(240 - 60)}{400} = 45p$$

There were neither extraordinary items nor preference dividends in either of the two years, the formula thus becoming 'net profit after tax' divided by the number of ordinary shares in issue. The progress made in 1986 reflects the increased profitability obtained despite a weakening in the liquidity position. For further discussion of eps, see Chapter 5.

2. Price/earnings ratio $\qquad\qquad\qquad \dfrac{\text{Stock market price}}{\text{eps}}$

$$1986 \quad \frac{412p}{137p} = 3$$

$$1985 \quad \frac{370p}{45p} = 8$$

The p/e ratio, as explained in Chapter 5, is a reflection of the way in which the stock market views the prospects of a particular company. The higher the p/e, the more optimistic are investors' views concerning future profits and dividends. The decline in Ace possibly indicates concern that the company has over-reached itself with the acquisition of the supermarket, and that the liquidity problems might force the company to cut back its operations.

3. Dividend yield $\qquad\qquad\qquad \dfrac{\text{Dividend per share}}{\text{Market price per share}} \times 100$

$$1986 \quad \frac{(150 \div 400)}{£4.12} \times 100 = 9.1\%$$

$$1985 \quad \frac{(60 \div 400)}{£3.70} \times 100 = 4.05\%$$

This measures the actual rate of return obtained by way of dividends, assuming that the shares are purchased at the current stock market price. Although the yield from Ace has doubled in 1986 this indicates the higher risk which is associated with the investment, due to factors explained previously.

4. Dividend cover $$\frac{\text{Profit available for dividend}}{\text{Dividend}}$$

$$1986 \quad \frac{550}{150} = 3.7 \text{ times}$$

$$1985 \quad \frac{180}{60} = 3 \text{ times}$$

This reveals the proportion which the dividend bears to profit available for dividend, thus giving an indication as to how secure future dividend payments may be. As has been seen throughout the analysis, however, profit does not equal liquidity, and whilst Ace's profits are three times greater than the proposed dividend payments, the poor state of the company's liquid resources may well jeopardise future dividend payments.

Summary of the ratios

Operating ratios		1986	1985	*Trend* (A = Adverse) (F = Favourable)
(a)	GP margin	60%	54.7%	F
(b)	NP margin	16.7%	6.7%	F
(c)	Mark-up	150%	120.9%	F
(d)	ROCE	83.1%	56.7%	F
(e)	Fixed assets turnover	4:1	11.2:1	A
(f)	Rate of stock turnover	45.6 days	40.3 days	A
(g)	Debtors' collection period	35.2 days	48.3 days	F
(h)	Creditors' payment period	26 days	22.6 days	F
(i)	Cash operating cycle	54.8 days	66 days	F
Financial ratios				
(j)	Working capital ratio	0.85:1	1.4:1	A
(k)	Acid test ratio	0.6:1	1:1	A
(l)	Gearing ratio	9.3%	2.3%	—
Investment ratios				
(m)	Earnings per share	137p	45p	F
(n)	Price/earnings ratio	3	8	A
(o)	Dividend yield	9.1%	4.05%	—
(p)	Dividend cover	3.7	3	F

'Pyramids of ratios'

Although the above represents the major ratios required for analysis purposes, it is possible to produce a far more detailed breakdown, whereby ratios are subdivided into their various components. This enables an analyst to make an assessment of the strengths and weaknesses of all areas within the business. One way of illustrating the inter-connection between ratios is by means of a 'pyramid', whereby the apex is progressively broken down into its supporting components (see Figure 10.4). The wider the base of the pyramid, the more detailed becomes the analysis, and specific 'problem areas' can be identified when compared with the ratios of previous years and those of other companies.

10.5 The third stage: interpretation

The summary of the ratios reveals a stark contrast between the operating ratios and the financial ratios, clearly showing that the increased profits of the company were

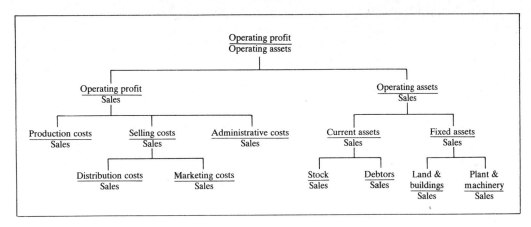

Fig. 10.4   A pyramid of ratios.

gained at the cost of a weakened working capital position. For example, whilst the net profit margin increased from 6.7% to 16.7%, the acid test declined from 1:1 to 0.6:1. In addition, the decline in the price/earnings ratio appears to reflect stock market anxieties that the company is over-trading, i.e. expanding its turnover and profits without sufficient working capital to meet its debts as they fall due. However, there are unanswered questions regarding the future returns from the new supermarket, and this may well prove crucial for the company in 1987. Only time will tell whether conditions will be sufficiently favourable to bring the business back on to an 'even keel'.

Although this chapter has concentrated on the use of ratios and percentages to highlight various aspects of the business's performance, another useful aid to analysis is a cash flow statement. As explained in Chapter 9, this is prepared by redrafting the source and application of funds statement to explain the reasons for the change in the cash and bank balances from the start to the end of the financial year (see Figure 10.5).

	£000	£000
Ace plc		
Cash Flow Statement		
for the year to 31 December 1986		
Opening cash and bank balances		(265) overdrawn
Add: Sources of cash:		
Net profit (after 'non-cash' items added back)	948	
Long-term loans received	80	
Proceeds from sales of fixed assets	12	
Decrease in debtors	24	
Increase in creditors	27	
		1,091
		826
Less: Applications of cash:		
Purchase of fixed assets	984	
Taxation paid	60	
Dividends paid	60	
Increase in stock levels	50	1,154
Closing cash and bank balances		(328) overdrawn

Fig. 10.5   Cash flow statement for Ace plc.

For a truly objective assessment of a company's results, comparisons should be made not only with the performance of previous years, but also with the performance of competitors. In many business sectors, trade organisations exist which collate data from member companies and publish key statistics which enable companies to measure their own efficiency against that of their rivals. In addition, The *Financial Times* publishes daily, in conjunction with the Institute of Actuaries and Faculty of Actuaries, a list of share indices which, *inter alia*, show average yields and p/e ratios for companies divided between various equity groups, e.g. 'building materials', 'leisure', 'stores', etc.

10.6   The validity of accounting statements

In the analysis of company statements, it is assumed that the financial information as presented is accurate and reliable and provides a suitable database for study. However, in this section it will be seen that the traditional method of accounting may well prove to be unreliable for reasons connected with the incidence of *inflation* upon the reported results.

SSAP2 'Disclosure of Accounting Policies' requires companies to disclose the specific policies adopted when preparing the accounts. These policies are listed within a 'note to the accounts' and usually commence with a statement that the accounts are drawn up 'under the historical cost convention as modified by the revaluation of certain fixed assets'.

Historical cost accounting (HCA) is the traditional method of accounting whereby all items are recorded at their purchase price at the date of acquisition. HCA has a number of advantages including:

(a)   it provides a fair degree of objectivity, as measurements are based on actual costs;

(b)   it lends itself to the application of double entry book-keeping;

(c)   verification by auditors is relatively straightforward;

(d)   it is the only system of accounting recognised for the purpose of taxation assessment;

(e)   it is easy to understand by both accountants and non-accountants.

However, the disadvantages of HCA are hinted at in part by the addition of the words 'as modified by the revaluation of certain fixed assets' in the notes explaining accounting policies, previously mentioned. If HCA is such a reliable system, then why does it need to be 'modified'? The answer is that despite its advantages the use of HCA can seriously distort the results of a business owing to its inability to reflect the impact of inflation.

In times of inflation, the purchasing power of the currency is falling, which means that fixed assets and stock cost more to replace than their original (historical) cost and assets such as debtors lose value, as debtors are able to use 'devalued' currency to pay their debts. Liabilities such as creditors lose value for the same reason.

Additionally, any attempt to compare the accounts of one year with those of another will be hampered because of the different values of the monetary units used at the different dates. HCA may, therefore, result in:

(a)   Overstated profits due to inadequate provisions being made for the *future replacement* prices of fixed assets.

(b)   Overstated profits due to the failure to adjust for the increased replacement cost of stock.

(c)   Understatement of assets due to their inclusion at their *historical* value rather than their current value at the balance sheet date; although HCA can, as we have seen, be modified to incorporate revaluations of certain fixed assets, notably land and buildings. This may further lead to:

i   Excessive dividend payments based on inflated profits, and over-generous pay settlements being reached with employees, which the business cannot afford.

ii   Inaccurate and misleading analysis of the company's performance.
iii   Inadequate retention of profits causing difficulty when fixed assets require replacement.

If it is acknowledged that HCA is an imperfect system, one would suppose that suitable alternative accounting systems exist to remedy the deficiencies. The accountancy profession has, for nearly two decades, been debating the pros and cons of 'current purchasing power' accounting (CPP) and 'current cost' accounting (CCA) but has not, at the time of writing, been able to persuade the majority of those who prepare and use accounts that their advantages outweigh their disadvantages, and there is at present no compulsion on companies to present accounts in any form other than HCA. However, a brief explanation of CPP and CCA follows.

CURRENT PURCHASING POWER ACCOUNTING

This is based upon the translation of 'historical cost' amounts appearing in the profit and loss account and balance sheet into inflation-adjusted values by the use of 'CPP-units', which represent stable monetary units calculated by reference to general price indices. This conversion would not apply to debtors and creditors, which represent definite amounts payable or receivable at the balance sheet date, nor to cash and bank balances.

Advantages claimed for CPP are that it provides a 'real' measure of profit and allows meaningful comparisons to be made from one year to the next. The system is based on HCA, and therefore retains the advantages of that system as previously listed. Disadvantages are that the application of 'CPP-units' based on general price indices could cause distortions when applied to specific companies, particularly those operating in highly specialised areas. Additionally, there are uncertainties over the public's perception of items expressed in terms of an artificial 'accounting currency'.

An attempt was made in 1974 in the United Kingdom to introduce CPP accounting, to be presented as supplementary statements to the HCA accounts. An SSAP was issued, but was withdrawn in the following year when a Government-appointed committee produced a report (known as 'The Sandilands Report') which favoured *current cost accounting*. A new SSAP No 16 was issued in 1980, but it ceased to have mandatory status in 1985.

CURRENT COST ACCOUNTING

The Sandilands Report proposed that companies should present CCA accounts which would include a current cost profit and loss account and current cost balance sheet. These are detailed below.

Current cost profit and loss account

This is where the net profit as calculated under the historical cost convention would be subject to adjustments which show the increased costs required to maintain the *operating capability* of the business, i.e. the ability of the business to maintain the output of goods and services from its existing resources. Specifically, four adjustments are applied to the HC profit to arrive at the CC profit:

1.   *The depreciation adjustment*, which reflects the extra depreciation that is required to provide for the replacement cost of fixed assets rather than the historical cost.
2.   *The cost of sales adjustment*, which represents the difference between the historical cost of stock sold and the replacement value of that stock.
3.   *The monetary working capital adjustment*, which is a calculation of the extra finance required to fund the increased net debtors (debtors less creditors) which are likely to result when inflation raises invoice prices.
4.   *The gearing adjustment*, which is applied as a percentage reduction to the total of the previous three adjustments, recognises that for many companies, the

'burden' of inflation is carried in part by external providers of finance to the company (e.g. debenture holders) rather than by its shareholders.

Current cost balance sheet

As CCA accounting is concerned with the business's ability to maintain its operating capability, it follows that balance sheet values should reflect the value to the business of its assets and liabilities at the balance sheet date rather than using historical cost data which do not relate values to current conditions as affected by inflation. Consequently the CCA balance sheet shows fixed assets and stock at replacement prices (which may be calculated by reference to price indices) and a current cost reserve is opened to record the surpluses (or deficits) caused by the revaluations from the HC figures. The reserve also carries the adjustments made in the CC profit and loss account. No amendments would be made to actual amounts owing by, or to, third parties, e.g. trade debtors and creditors, cash and bank balances, shareholders' capital and debentures.

Advantages claimed for CCA are that the accounts present a more realistic picture of the business by, on the one hand, showing the effects of inflation on HC profit, and on the other, showing the current values of assets rather than outdated ones. Proponents of CCA believe that evaluation of business performance can be made only from accounting information which is both accurate and relevant, and management are more likely to obtain relevant data from CCA statements.

Disadvantages of CCA include the difficulty of making reliable estimates of replacement values of assets, particularly when price indices are used. The inclusion of separate CC accounting statements in a company's annual report may lead to confusion for the non-expert user of the information. A survey conducted amongst major bankers published in *Accountancy* in April 1985 revealed the following attitudes to the use of CCA accounts rather than to the 'traditional' HCA statements, in the responses to the question 'why not use CCA'?

		(%)
1.	The banker adjusts HCA figures intuitively to take account of inflation	22
2.	CCA is not fully understood/HCA is better understood	22
3.	CCA is subjective/biased/unreliable	14
4.	CCA is not comparable as between companies	14
5.	CCA is not used in the United States	14
6.	Lack of consensus in United Kingdom	14
		100

Of the twenty-six banks surveyed, fifteen said they used CCA in their corporate lending decisions, whilst *all* respondents used audited historical cost accounts.

Exercises

10.1 From the following figures calculate the gross profit margin, the stock turn, in days, and the mark-up.

	(a)	*(b)*	*(c)*	*(d)*
Sales	48,000	126,000	59,000	68,000
Purchases	21,000	58,000	30,000	45,000
Opening stock	6,000	12,000	20,000	30,000
Closing stock	7,000	6,000	24,000	25,000

10.2 From the following figures calculate the current ratio, acid test ratio and gearing ratio.

	(a)	*(b)*	*(c)*	*(d)*
Stock	72,000	16,000	30,000	50,000
Debtors	26,000	60,000	50,000	20,000
Bank	11,000	(30,000)O/D	30,000	20,000
Creditors (short-term)	35,000	65,000	10,000	20,000

Debentures	40,000	—	60,000	50,000
Capital employed	240,000	190,000	100,000	200,000

10.3 Colin Black is considering investing a substantial sum in the ordinary shares of Jacks Ltd. Having some accounting knowledge he has extracted the following information from the accounts for the last two financial years:

	As at 31 March 1984 £	As at 31 March 1985 £
Issued share capital		
£1 ordinary shares, fully paid	100,000	150,000
Reserves		
Share premium	10,000	60,000
Retained earnings	140,000	160,000
Loan capital		
10% debentures 1987–89	40,000	40,000

	For year ended 31 March 1984 £	For year ended 31 March 1985 £
Net profit after tax	60,000	70,000

Because he was disappointed with the result he obtained when he calculated the return on the equity capital employed, Colin Black has asked for your advice.

Required:

(a) Calculate the figures which prompted Colin Black's reaction.
(b) Prepare a memorandum to Colin Black pointing out other information to be considered when comparing the return on equity capital employed over two years as a basis for his investment decision.
(c) Explain why a company builds up and maintains reserves.

(AEB)

10.4 The following are extracts from the balance sheets as at 31 March 1984 and 31 March 1985 of Glebe Ltd:

	31 March 1984		31 March 1985	
Current assets	£	£	£	£
Stocks	20,000		25,000	
Trade debtors	10,000		17,000	
Cash	5,000		3,000	
		35,000		45,000
Less:				
Current liabilities				
Trade creditors	12,000		16,000	
Proposed dividends	6,000		5,000	
Bank overdraft	7,000		29,000	
		25,000		50,000
		10,000		(5,000)

Required:

(a) Calculate for each of the two years *two* ratios that indicate the liquidity position of the company.
(b) (i) From the information given, give reasons for the changes which have occurred in the working capital.
(ii) What other information regarding the current assets and current liabilities would you consider necessary to assess the ability of the business to continue in operation?

(c)   Discuss any other information available from a balance sheet that may affect an assessment of the liquidity of a business.

(AEB)

10.5   Lemon Ltd and Pear Ltd are retailers trading in similar goods, and situated in the same area. Their summarised revenue accounts and balance sheets relating to the last financial year are as follows:

Revenue Accounts

	Lemon £000	Pear £000		Lemon £000	Pear £000
Opening stock	30	10	Sales	200	200
Purchases	144	152	Closing stock	36	8
Overhead costs	46	31			
Net profit	16	15			
	236	208		236	208

Balance Sheets

	Lemon £000	Pear £000		Lemon £000	Pear £000
Issued share capital	100	100	Fixed assets	128	120
Retained profits	80	20	Stock	36	8
Bank overdraft	—	2	Debtors	30	19
Trade creditors	26	25	Bank	12	—
	206	147		206	147

Required:

(a)   Calculate the following accounting ratios for both companies.
  i   Current ratio
 ii   Liquidity (acid test) ratio
iii   Rate of stock turnover
 iv   Gross profit percentage of sales
  v   Net profit percentage of sales
 vi   Return on capital employed
(b)   As a customer using these two shops what differences would you expect to find between them?

(LCCI – Higher)

10.6   The following forecasts are provided in respect of Grassington Ltd, a company trading in a single product, for 1984:

	£000
Sales	2,700
Purchases	1,800
Cost of goods sold	1,830
Average trade debtors outstanding	300
Average trade creditors outstanding	160
Average stocks held	305

All purchases and sales are made on credit, and trading transactions are expected to occur at an even rate throughout the year.

Required:

(a)   Calculations of the rate of payment of creditors, the rate of collection of debtors and the rate of stock turnover.
(b)   A calculation of the expected cash operating cycle (i.e. the time lag between making payment to suppliers and collecting cash from customers in respect of goods purchased and sold) for 1984.

(c)   Using the information provided, explain any one method by which the directors might achieve a reduction of £20,000 in the company's bank overdraft requirement at 31 December 1984, and demonstrate the effect on the cash operating cycle.

Note: Assume a 360-day year for the purpose of your calculations.

(IOB)

10.7   The following balance sheet, profit and loss account and statement of source and application of funds are those of a group of manufacturing companies. Also shown are some statistics prepared by the appropriate trade association.

Balance Sheet as at 31 October

	1982		1983	
	£000	£000	£000	£000
Fixed assets				
Tangible assets				
Cost	540		680	
Depreciation	120		188	
Net book amount		420		492
Current assets				
Stock	300		356	
Trade debtors	200		300	
Cash	4		5	
		504		661
Total assets		924		1,153
Capital and reserves:				
Share capital paid up		200		300
Share premium account		100		200
Profit and loss account		246		275
Shareholders' funds		546		775
Creditors due after more than one year:				
Debentures, 1995		200		150
Creditors due within one year:				
Trade creditors	150		175	
Taxation	15		30	
Bank overdraft	13		23	
		178		228
		924		1,153

Profit and Loss Account year ended 31 October

	1982	1983
	£000	£000
Sales turnover	826	1,043
Cost of sales, after charging depreciation £54,000 and £68,000	(734)	(896)
Gross profit	92	147
Interest payable:		
Debenture interest paid £20,000 and £15,000		
Bank interest paid £2,000 and £3,000	(22)	(18)
Profit before tax	(70)	129
Tax	(15)	(30)
Profit for the financial year	55	99
Dividend paid	(35)	(70)
Surplus transferred to reserves	20	29

Statement of Source and Application of Funds year ended 31 October

	1982 £000	1983 £000
Cash flow from operations	124	197
Shares issued	—	200
	124	397
Fixed assets purchased	—	(140)
Debentures repaid	—	(50)
Dividends paid	(35)	(70)
Tax paid	—	(15)
	89	122

Analysis of change in working capital:

	1982	1983
Increase in stock	60	56
Increase in debtors	30	100
Increase in cash	(5)	1
(Increase) in creditors	(20)	(25)
(Increase) in overdraft	24	(10)
	89	122

Statistics prepared by the Trade Association – industry averages.

			1982	1983
1.	Return on all assets employed	(%)	12	14
2.	Return on shareholders funds	(%)	15	16
3.	Return on long-term funds	(%)	14	15
4.	Profit margin	(%)	9	10
5.	Sales turnover ratio	(times)	1.5	1.5
6.	Fixed assets ratio	(%)	30	40
7.	Debt equity ratio		0.4:1	0.45:1
8.	Current ratio		2:1	2.1:1
9.	Liquid ratio (sometimes called acid ratio)		0.9:1	1.1:1
10.	Debtors (day sales)		70	75

Required:

(a) Calculate the corresponding statistics for the company for 1983 from the financial statements provided in respect of 31 October 1982 and 1983 and the years ended on those dates (to two significant figures).

(b) Comment on the performance of the company, with appropriate statistics, from the viewpoint of:

i the management,

ii the shareholders,

iii the debenture holders,

iv the trade creditors.

(CDAF)

APPENDIX 1

Supplementary Topics

The following areas of financial accounting, whilst being of considerable importance to specific businesses, are considered peripheral to the central core of study contained within this textbook. Readers who are preparing for examinations should check against an up-to-date syllabus to see whether any of these topics are likely to be included in the examinations for which they are preparing. In each case, only the main features of the subject area are given, and a specialist text should be consulted if more detailed study is required.

1. Branch accounts

Where a business is divided into a head office and one or more branches, a system of book-keeping should exist which enables the management to control the finances and, where appropriate, determine the profit or loss made by each branch. The system used will vary from company to company, often dependent upon the level of expertise available within the branch. The two most common forms are (a) where the branch keeps only rudimentary cash records, with the head office keeping control within its own books, and (b) where the branch has a full set of double entry records and prepares final accounts which are incorporated with those of the head office.

(A) INCOMPLETE BRANCH BOOK-KEEPING SYSTEM

In the books of the head office, an account is opened for the branch, which is debited with goods supplied and expenses incurred on the branch's behalf. The account is credited with the sales and the volume of closing stock, any balance remaining on the account representing profit (credit balance) or loss (debit balance), which is then transferred to the profit and loss account of the whole business. Care must be taken where goods are transferred at selling prices (or 'cost plus') to eliminate the profit element from stocks figures.

(B) COMPLETE BRANCH BOOK-KEEPING SYSTEM

The 'branch account' in the head office's books will be matched by a 'head office account' in the branch's books. These accounts are complementary, and the balance on one should always be matched by an equal and opposite balance on the other. The 'branch account' balance represents the net assets of the branch, whilst the 'head office account' in the branch's books becomes the equivalent of capital when the branch's balance sheet is prepared. In practice, the accounts are often divided between 'goods to branch' account, 'remittances' account, etc. Closing entries are made by transferring the profit (or loss) made by the branch from the branch profit and loss account to the credit (or debit) of the head office account. In the head office books, the profit or loss is entered in the branch account and is then transferred to the profit and loss account of the whole business.

Should there be goods or cash in transit at the balance sheet date, a discrepancy will be shown between the head office and branch. In the case of goods in transit from head office, an adjusting entry is made, debiting 'goods in transit' account and crediting branch account, whilst in the case of cash in transit from the branch, a 'remittance in transit' account is debited in the branch books and 'remittances' account credited.

2. Consignment accounts

A consignment refers to the transfer of goods, usually from one country to another, for the purpose of sale by an agent, who is remunerated by means of a percentage commission on the sale value. The legal ownership of the goods remains with the consignor until sold. The book-keeping entries are as follows:

Consignor's books

DR   Consignment a/c
CR   Goods sent on consignment a/c
   – cost of goods sent to agent.
DR   Consignment a/c
CR   Cash (or suppliers' personal accounts)
   – expenses (e.g. freight costs).
DR   Consignee's personal a/c
CR   Consignment a/c
   – sales proceeds (gross).
DR   Consignment a/c
CR   Consignee's personal a/c
   – expenses and commission deducted by consignee.
DR   Cash
CR   Consignee's personal a/c
   – cash remitted by consignee.
DR   Goods sent on consignment a/c
CR   Trading a/c
   – transfer of balance on goods sent on consignment a/c.
either DR   Profit and loss a/c   or   DR   Consignment a/c
      CR   Consignment a/c   CR   Profit and loss a/c
   – loss on consignment or profit on consignment.

Any goods remaining unsold at the balance sheet date are carried down at cost price on the consignment account, and appear as an asset in the balance sheet.

Consignee's books

DR   Consignor's personal a/c
CR   Cash (or suppliers' personal accounts)
   – expenses (e.g. advertising).
DR   Cash (or customers' accounts)
CR   Consignor's personal a/c
   – sale of the consigned goods.
DR   Consignor's personal a/c
CR   Commission
   – commission charged on sales.
DR   Consignor's personal a/c
CR   Cash
   – cash remitted to consignor.

3. Joint ventures

Where two or more parties decide to form a temporary partnership for a specific business venture, it is usual for each party to open a 'joint venture' account to which all payments for goods and expenses are debited and receipts are credited. At the conclusion of the venture, parties exchange copies of their account and a combined profit and loss account is prepared. The accounts are closed by a transfer of cash between the parties to the venture. Alternatively, one of the parties is appointed as the 'manager and book-keeper' of the venture, opening a joint venture account in his books alone. All expenses are debited to the account, the other parties remitting their share of the cost, with their personal accounts being credited. The profit or loss on the venture is then transferred from the joint venture account to the personal accounts, with the accounts being closed by cash transfers.

Permitted Formats under Companies Act 1985

Balance sheet

FORMAT 1

A Called up share capital not paid

B Fixed assets
    I   Intangible assets
        1. Development costs
        2. Concessions, patents, licences, trade marks and similar rights and assets
        3. Goodwill
        4. Payments on account
    II   Tangible assets
        1. Land and buildings
        2. Plant and machinery
        3. Fixtures, fittings, tools and equipment
        4. Payments on account and assets in course of construction
    III Investments
        1. Shares in group companies
        2. Loans to group companies
        3. Shares in related companies
        4. Loans to related companies
        5. Other investments other than loans
        6. Other loans
        7. Own shares

C Current assets
    I   Stocks
        1. Raw materials and consumables
        2. Work-in-progress
        3. Finished goods and goods for resale
        4. Payments on account
    II   Debtors
        1. Trade debtors
        2. Amounts owed by group companies
        3. Amounts owed by related companies
        4. Other debtors
        5. Called up share capital not paid
        6. Prepayments and accrued income
    III Investments
        1. Shares in group companies
        2. Own shares
        3. Other investments
    IV Cash at bank and in hand

D Prepayments and accrued income

E Creditors: amounts falling due within one year
        1. Debenture loans
        2. Bank loans and overdrafts
        3. Payments received on account
        4. Trade creditors
        5. Bills of exchange payable
        6. Amounts owed to group companies
        7. Amounts owed to related companies
        8. Other creditors including taxation and social security
        9. Accruals and deferred income

F Net current assets (liabilities)

G Total assets less current liabilities

H Creditors: amounts falling due after more than one year

1. Debenture loans
2. Bank loans and overdrafts
3. Payments received on account
4. Trade creditors
5. Bills of exchange payable
6. Amounts owed to group companies
7. Amounts owed to related companies
8. Other creditors including taxation and social security
9. Accruals and deferred income

I Provisions for liabilities and charges
    1. Pensions and similar obligations
    2. Taxation, including deferred taxation
    3. Other provisions

J Accruals and deferred income

K Capital reserves
    I Called up share capital
    II Share premium account
    III Revaluation reserve
    IV Other reserves
        1. Capital redemption reserve
        2. Reserve for own shares
        3. Reserves provided for by the articles of association
        4. Other reserves
    V Profit and loss account

FORMAT 2

Assets

A Called up share capital not paid

B Fixed assets
    I Intangible assets
        1. Development costs
        2. Concessions, patents, licences, trade marks and similar rights and assets
        3. Goodwill
        4. Payments on account
    II Tangible assets
        1. Land and buildings
        2. Plant and machinery
        3. Fixtures, fittings, tools and equipment
        4. Payments on account and assets in course of construction
    III Investments
        1. Shares in group companies
        2. Loans to group companies
        3. Shares in related companies
        4. Loans to related companies
        5. Other investments other than loans
        6. Other loans
        7. Own shares

C Current assets
    I Stocks
        1. Raw materials and consumables
        2. Work-in-progress
        3. Finished goods and goods for resale
        4. Payments on account
    II Debtors
        1. Trade debtors
        2. Amounts owed by group companies
        3. Amounts owed by related companies
        4. Other debtors
        5. Called up share capital not paid
        6. Prepayments and accrued income
    III Investments
        1. Shares in group companies
        2. Own shares
        3. Other investments
    IV Cash at bank and in hand

D Prepayments and accrued income

Liabilities

A Capital and reserves
    I Called up share capital
    II Share premium account
    III Revaluation reserve
    IV Other reserves
        1. Capital redemption reserve
        2. Reserve for own shares
        3. Reserves provided for by the articles of association
        4. Other reserves

V   Profit and loss account

B   Provisions for liabilities and charges
    1.   Pensions and similar obligations
    2.   Taxation, including deferred taxation
    3.   Other provisions

C   Creditors (13)
    1.   Debenture loans
    2.   Bank loans and overdrafts
    3.   Prepayments received
       on account
    4.   Trade creditors
    5.   Bills of exchange payable
    6.   Amounts owed to group companies
    7.   Amounts owed to related companies
    8.   Other creditors including taxation and social security
    9.   Accruals and deferred income

D   Accruals and deferred income

Profit and loss account

FORMAT 1

1.   Turnover
2.   Cost of sales
3.   Gross profit or loss
4.   Distribution costs
5.   Administration expenses
6.   Other operating income
7.   Income from shares in group companies
8.   Income from shares in related companies
9.   Income from other fixed asset investments
10. Other interest receivable and similar income
11. Amounts written off investments
12. Interest payable and similar charges
13. Tax on profit or loss on ordinary activities
14. Profit or loss on ordinary activities after taxation
15. Extraordinary income
16. Extraordinary charges
17. Extraordinary profit or loss
18. Tax on extraordinary profit or loss
19. Other taxes not shown under the above items
20. Profit or loss for the financial year

FORMAT 2

1.   Turnover
2.   Change in stocks of finished goods and work-in-progress
3.   Own work capitalised
4.   Other operating income
5.   (a) Raw materials and consumables
    (b) Other external charges
6.   Staff costs:
    (a) wages and salaries
    (b) social security costs
    (c) other pension costs
7.   (a) Depreciation and other amounts written off tangible and intangible fixed assets
    (b) Exceptional amounts written off current assets
8.   Other operating charges
9.   Income from shares in group companies
10. Income from shares in related companies
11. Income from other fixed asset investments
12. Other interest receivable and similar income
13. Amounts written off investments
14. Interest payable and similar charges
15. Tax on profit or loss on ordinary activities
16. Profit or loss on ordinary activities after taxation
17. Extraordinary income
18. Extraordinary charges
19. Extraordinary profit or loss
20. Tax on extraordinary profit or loss

21. Other taxes not shown under the above items
22. Profit or loss for the financial year

FORMAT 3

A Charges
1. Cost of sales
2. Distribution costs
3. Administrative expenses
4. Amounts written off investments
5. Interest payable and similar charges
6. Tax on profit or loss on ordinary activities
7. Profit or loss on ordinary activities after taxation
8. Extraordinary charges
9. Tax on extraordinary profit or loss
10. Other taxes not shown under the above items
11. Profit or loss for the financial year

B Income
1. Turnover
2. Other operating income
3. Income from shares in group companies
4. Income from shares in related companies
5. Income from other fixed asset investments
6. Other interest receivable and similar income
7. Profit or loss on ordinary activities after taxation
8. Extraordinary income
9. Profit or loss for the financial year

FORMAT 4

A Charges
1. Reduction in stocks of finished goods and work-in-progress
2. (a) Raw materials and consumables

(b) Other external charges
3. Staff costs:
(a) wages and salaries
(b) social security costs
(c) other pension costs
4. (a) Depreciation and other amounts written off tangible and intangible fixed assets
(b) Exceptional amounts written off current assets
5. Other operating charges
6. Amounts written off investments
7. Interest payable and similar charges
8. Tax on profit or loss on ordinary activities
9. Profit or loss on ordinary activities after taxation
10. Extraordinary charges
11. Tax on extraordinary profit or loss
12. Other taxes not shown under the above items
13. Profit or loss for the financial year

B Income
1. Turnover
2. Increase in stocks of finished goods and in work-in-progress
3. Own work capitalised
4. Other operating income
5. Income from shares in group companies
6. Income from shares in related companies
7. Income from other fixed asset investments
8. Other interest receivable and similar income
9. Profit or loss on ordinary activities after taxation
10. Extraordinary income
11. Profit or loss for the financial year

Summarised Answers to Exercises

Chapter 1

1.1 Gross profit 64,100; Net profit 10,862; FA 15,160; CA 60,462; CL 37,760; Cap 37,862.

1.2 (a) 1-1-81 B/F 475 + 31-12-81 P + L 195 = 670 − 31-12-82 P + L
16 = 654 − 31-12-83 P + L 154 = 500 CR balance at 31-12-83

(b) P + L: y/e 31-12-81 Bad debts 807 Increase in prov. 195
y/e 31-12-82 Bad debts 400 Decrease in prov. (16)
y/e 31-12-83 Bad debts 433 Decrease in prov. (154)

Balance sheets (1981) Debtors 25,373 − Provis 670 = 24,703
(1982) Debtors 32,700 − Provis 654 = 32,054
(1983) Debtors 27,767 − Provis 500 = 27,267

1.3 (a) Journal: DR Rent 310, CR Sales 310
DR Rent 540, CR Accruals 540
DR Prepayments 449, CR Rates 449
DR Prepayments 38, CR Insurance 38

(b) Rent a/c: DR 31-12-84, Cash 1,380, Sales 310, Accrual c/f 540
CR 1-1-84, Accrual b/f 420, 31-12-84 P + L 1810
Rates a/c: DR 1-1-84, Prepayment b/f 390, 1-4-84 Cash 898, 1-10-84
Cash 898
CR 31-12-84, Prepayment c/f 449 (³⁄₆ × 898), P + L 1,737
Insurance a/c: DR 1-1-84, Prepayment b/f (31-10-84 Cash 228
CR 31-12-84, Prepayment c/f (¹⁄₆ × 228), 38, P + L 384

1.4 Rent and rates a/c
DR 1-4-89 Cheque (Rates) 1,200; 1-10-89 Cheque (Rates) 600, Jan–July
Cheques (Rent) 10 × 250 = 2,500; 31-12-89 Rent in arrears (5 × 250) c/f
1,250.
CR 1-1-89 Rent in arrears b/f (3 × 250) 750, Rates accrual b/f (½ × 600)300;
31-12-89 P + L Rent 3,000, Rates 1,200; Prepayments (Rates) ½ × 600 = 300

1.5 (a) DR 12 May, Cash 887; Discount 23; 18 May, Credit note 47, 31 May,
balance c/f 2,261.
CR 1 May b/f 1,697*; 1–25 May, Goods
(114 + 97 + 268 + 172 + 356 + 213 + 87 + 214) 1,521.

(b) Balance in James' Bros books 2,261 + Invoice not yet entered
386 = 2,647 − Invoice omitted by Hardware 213 = 2,434 − Goods not
contr'd 52 = 2,382 (balance in Hardware's books).

1.6 (a) Machinery cost 100,000 − 3 years at £15,000 = 55,000.
Fittings and equip cost 50,000 − 3 years at £5,000 = 35,000

(b) Depreciation adjustments:
1979 Machinery (25,000 − 15,000) 10,000
Fittings (10,000 − 5,000) 5,000
15,000

*Balance per Hardware's statement 1,916 − Invoices entered in April 114 + 97 = 1,705 − Debit note
entered in 28 April = 1,677 + Understated invoice 20 = 1,697

1980 Machinery (18,750 − 15,000) 3,750
Fittings (8,000 − 5,000) 3,000

————
6,750
————

1981 Machinery (14,062 − 15,000) (938)
Fittings (6,400 − 5,000) 1,400

————
462
————

Revised profit 1979, 64,120; 1980–81, 512; 1981, 105,071.

1.7 (i) Motor vehicles disposals a/c DR: 30-4-81 Transfer cost of van and car £6,500; CR 1-1-81 Proceeds of sale of van £2,200; 3-81 Compensation for car £1,800; 4-81 Transfer depreciation on vehicles sold (450 + 1,575) 2,025 P + L a/c (underprovision) 475

(ii) Provision for depreciation of vehicles a/c DR: Transfer disposals (450 + 1,575) 2,025, c/f 15,050

CR: b/f 14,000 P + L a/c (15% × 20,500) 3,075

(iii) Fixed assets: Motor vehicles cost b/f 23,000 + additions 4,000 − disposals 6,500 = 20,500. Depreciation b/f 14,000 + provision for year 3,075 − Provided on Disposals 2,025 = 15,050 net book value 5,450.

Chapter 2

2.2 (a) (i) DR Cash book 5,000 CR Disposal of assets 5,000.

(ii) DR Disposal of assets 100,000 CR Machinery 100,000.

(iii) DR Depreciation 90,000 CR Disposal of assets 90,000.

(iv) DR P + L 5,000 CR Disposal of assets 5,000.

(v) DR Machinery 240,000 CR Cash book 240,000.

2.3 *Motor vans*

(1981) DR A 2,750; B 2,800; C 2,800; CR c/f 8,350.

(1982) DR b/f 8,350; CR Transfer A 2,750; c/f 5,600.

(1983) DR b/f 5,600; Canopy C 400 CR c/f 6,000.

Depreciation

(1981) DR c/f 840 CR P + L a/c 840.

(1982) DR Transfer disposals (A) 650 c/f 1,540, CR b/f 840 P + L a/c 1,350.

(1983) DR c/f 2,720, CR b/f 1,540 P + L a/c 1,180.

Disposal of vans

(1982) DR Transfer cost of A 2,750; CR Insurance Co 2,000; Depreciation 650; P + L a/c (underprovision) 100

2.4 Factory cost 521,000; profit on Manfg 26,050; Gross profit on trading 92,630; net profit 47,670. Interest: Roberts 18,000; Davies 12,000. Salary; Davies 5,000; profit shared, Roberts 7,602; Davies 5,068. Balance sheet: Fixed assets 127,197; current assets 297,224; current liabilities 81,741. Capital; Roberts 180,000; Davies 120,000; Current a/cs Roberts 20,392; Davies 22,288.

2.5 Prime cost 458,400; Factory cost 572,150 + 10% Profit = 629,365. Trading a/c Sales 728,800 (net); Cost of goods sold 614,515; Gross profit 114,285.

2.6 Gross profit (N) 36,000 (S) 22,500.
Net profit (N) 4,200 (S) 600.

2.7 Bar trading a/c 245 profit.
I + E a/c excess of income 235.
Balance sheet: Furniture 1,664 (net); stock 1,431; bar debtors 23; Subs owing 168; Cash at bank 4,323; Cash in hand 99. Acc. fund 3,484; Prize fund 500; Creditors (2,628 + 266 + 330 + 500) = 3,724.

2.8 Restaurant trading a/c gross profit 15,130; net profit 4,070.
I + E a/c excess of income 3,016.
Balance sheet: Fixed assets 82,040 net; investments 11,000; current assets (1,640 + 990 + 480 + 4,030) = 7,140.
Acc. fund 96,772; Current liabilities (3,320 + 88) = 3,408.

Chapter 3

3.1 Missing figures: (b) 27,783; (c) 36,960; (d) 50,083.

3.2 Missing figures: (b) 71,391; (c) 10,206; (d) 80,998.

3.3 Gross profit 581.63; Net profit 3.54.
Balance sheet fixed assets 989.28 (net);
Current assets $(1197.36 + 48.80 + 80.00 + 10.00) = 1336.16$;
Current liabilities $(1034.18 + 21.50 + 870.25) = 1925.93$.
Capital a/c $(500.00 + 3.54 - 104.03) = 399.51$.

3.4 Sales $94,860 -$ cost of goods sold $83,200 = 11,660$ gross profit $- 13,685$ expenses $= 2,025$ net loss.
Balance sheet: Fixed assets 17,000; Current assets $5,720 -$ current liabilities 4,185. Capital $18,160 + 5,000 - (2,025 + 2,600) = 18,535$.

3.6 (i) Fixed assets (1982) 37,000, (1983) 34,250; Current assets (1982) 33,670, (1983) 38,540; Current liabilities (1982) 10,060, (1983) 8,960; Capital (1982) 60,610, (1983) 63,830.

    (ii) Op. capital $60,610 -$ Closing capital $63,830 = 3,220 +$ Drawings 12,000 $= 15,220 -$ Cap. introduced $10,000 =$ Net profit 5,220.

    (iii) Machinery cost $20,000 - 4$ years at $10\% = 12,000 - (1,500 - 600) = 11,100 - 1983$ Depreciation $(10\% \times 18,500)$ $1,850 = 9,250$ net book value at 31-12-83.

3.7 (i) Gross profit 13,896; Net profit 9,936.
       Balance sheet: Fixed assets 6,320; current assets 10,950; current liabilities 1,900; capital a/c $(10,004 + 30 + 9,936 - 4,600)$ 15,370.

3.8 (i) Cash missing $=$ £7,500.

    (ii) Sales $(1,980 + 4,326 + 648 + 1,750) = 8,704$ Less cost of goods sold $3,519 =$ gross profit 5,185.

Chapter 4

4.2 Sales (net) $43,760 -$ cost of sales $31,160 =$ gross profit $12,600 + 200$ discount $- 6,640$ expenses $= 6,160$ net profit $-$ partners' salaries, R.S. 1,500, L.P. $1,500 = 3,160$, shared equally R.S. 1,580, L.P. 1,580.

4.3 (a) Gross profit (shop) 88,500; (workshop) 56,650.
       Net profit before commission (shop) 11,000; (workshop) 20,000.
       Commission $(1/(9 + 1))$ (shop) 1,100; (workshop) 2,000.
       Net profit (shop) 9,900; (workshop) 18,000. Total $= 27,900$.
       Add interest on drawings D 70; U 30; V 20; less salary V 4,000, less interest on capital D 2,000; U 2,000; V $1,000 = 19,020$ profit shared D 9,510; U 6,340 and V 3,170.
       Balance sheets fixed assets (net) 80,730; current assets 95,360; current liabilities 21,520.
       Capital D 40,000; U 40,000; V $20,000 = 100,000$.
       Current D 11,240; U 9,410; V $8,920 = 29,570$.
       Long-term loans bank 15,000; U $10,000 = 25,000$.

4.3 (b) Current accounts.
       Debit: b/f D 290.
       interest on drawings D 70; U 30; V 20.
       deficiency V 150.
       c/f D 11,240; U 9,410; V 8,920.
       Credit: b/f U1,040; V 920.
           salary V 4,000.
           interest on capital D 2,000; U 2,000; V 1,000.
           profit D 9,510; U 6,340; V 3,170.
           deficiency D 90; U 60.

4.6 (a) (i) Fixed assets 45,000; current assets $(6,000 + 12,000 + 6,000) = 24,000$ current liabilities 23,000.
           Capital accounts A $22,000 + 9,000 - 4,500 = 26,500$.

B   18,000 + 6,000 − 4,500 = 19,500.
C   6,000 + 3,000 − 4,500 = 4,500.
D   − 4,500   = (4,500) DR.

(ii) Fixed assets 45,000; current assets (8,000 + 10,000) = 18,000; current liabilities (22,000 + 3,000) = 25,000 loan account (A) 23,750*.
Capital accounts B   19,500 + 5,250 − 7,000 = 17,750.
C   4,500 + 5,250 − 7,000 = 2,750.
D   (4,500) + 5,250 − 7,000 = (6,250) DR.

(c) (i) Reduction of £500 (¼ × 2,000).
(ii) Prudence.

4.7 Realisation account: Loss on sale 4,450 transferred to capital accounts.
Capital accounts: Debit: transfer loss (C) 2,670; (T) 890; (H) 890. Bank account (C) 77,330; (T) 35,110; (H) 11,110.
Credit: b/f (C) 80,000; (T) 36,000; (H) 12,000.
Singapore Stores Co a/c Debit: realisation a/c 114,000; Credit: bank 114,000.
Bank account debit b/f 6,130. Sundry debtors 7,960; Singapore Stores Co a/c 114,000.
Credit sundry creditors 4,100. Realisation a/c (expenses) 440. Capital a/cs (C) 77,330; (T) 35,110; (H) 11,110.

Chapter 5

5.1 (b) Turnover 17,500 − cost of sales 10,585 = G.P. 6,915 − admin expenses 3,660, distribution costs 1,200 = NP 2,055 less tax (1,180 − 375) 805 = 1,250 less extraordinary items 760 − 170 tax = 660 N.P. after tax and extraordinary items − 100 Dividend = 560 + 7,625 P + L a/c (adjusted) b/f = 8,185 P + L c/f.
(N.B. Exceptional item 750 shown as note. All figures in 000s.)

5.8 (a) Capitalise; (b) and (c) write off; (d) capitalise if desired, amortise from three years' hence.

5.9 (a) Contingent liability.
(b) Adjusting post-balance sheet event.
(c) Non-adjusting post-balance sheet event.
(d) Disclosure by note if considered probable.

Chapter 6

6.4 (b) (i) 22,984 ÷ (45,667 + 22,984) × 100% = 33%
(ii) 22,984 ÷ 45,667 × 100% = 50%.

6.5 (b) X (150 + 300) ÷ (200 + 150 + 300 + 350) × 100% = 45%
Y 150 ÷ (300 + 150 + 350) × 100% = 18.75%.

6.6 Gross profit on trading 186,800 + gross profit on manufacturing 23,200 = 210,000; expenses (net) 138,600; net profit 71,400.
Appropriations: transfer to fixed asset replacement reserve 16,000 dividends; preference 6,400 ordinary (15,000 + 25,000) 40,000; retained profit for year 9,000 + b/f 8,000 = 17,000 c/f.

6.7 Gross profit 221,912; expenses (net) 166,398† net profit 55,514; dividend 40,000; profits b/f 27,233, c/f 52,947.
Balance sheet: Fixed assets (net) 160,000; current assets (107,561 + 167,543 − provis 4,679 + 120,150 + 1,200) = 391,775; current liabilities (58,618 + 210 + 40,000) = 98,828.
Issued capital (320,000 − 1,000) = 319,000 share premium account 30,000.
General reserve 51,000 P + L a/c 52,947.

6.8 Fixed assets: intangible 48; tangible 1,191 (property 1,050, fixtures 141).
Current assets:

*b/f 26,500+5,250 goodwill − 8,000 cheque

†N.B. Decrease in provision for bad debts 2,131.

Stocks 436, debtors 404, cash 99.
Creditors falling due within one year: 270.
Total assets less current liabilities 1,908.
Creditors falling due after one year 140.
Capital and reserves:
Called up capital 800.
Revaluation reserve 270.
P + L 698*.

Chapter 7

7.4 (a)

DR Cash 100,000	CR A + A 100,000 (application)
DR A + A 100,000	CR Share capital 100,000
DR Cash 100,000	CR A + A 100,000 (allotment)
DR A + A 100,000	CR Share capital 20,000
	Share premium 80,000
DR Cash 80,000	CR Call 80,000 (first and final call)
DR Call 80,000	CR Share capital 80,000
DR 12% debts 200,000	CR Redemption of debs 200,000
DR Red-debs 200,000	CR Discount on red-of-debs 20,000
	Cash 180,000

(b) Share capital, authorised and issued:
500,000 ordinary shares of £1 each, fully paid £500,000.
Reserves (include) share premium account 80,000.
Discount on redemption of debentures account *20,000* £100,000.

7.5 (i)

DR Freehold land	40,000	CR Asset revaluation reserve	
		40,000	
DR Depreciation of machinery	9,000		
Disposal of machinery	3,000	CR Machinery	12,000
DR Cash	2,000	CR Disposal of machinery	2,000
DR P + L %	1,000	CR Disposal of machinery	1,000
DR Cash	41,600	CR A + A	41,600
DR A + A	41,600	CR Share capital	40,800
		Share premium	800
DR Cash	18,400	CR A + A	18,400
DR A + A	18,400	CR Share capital	9,200
		Share premium	
DR Pref shares	80,000		9,200
		CR Red of pref shares	80,000
DR Red of pref shares	80,000	CR Cash	80,000
DR P + L a/c	20,000	CR Capital redemption reserve	20,000
DR Debentures	10,000	CR Red of debentures	10,000
DR Red of debentures share premium	10,000 500	CR Cash	10,500
DR P + L	7,000	CR Goodwill	7,000

(ii) Fixed assets; goodwill 14,000 land 130,000 others 55,000 = 199,000
Net current assets = 170,500.
Capital + reserves; Ordinary shares = 200,000 share premium.
9,500 capital redemption reserve 20,000, asset reval'n reserve 40,000;
P + L a/c 60,000; 12% debentures 40,000.

*Net profit 229 less stock adjustment 28 = 201 less goodwill 12 = 189 less dividend
64 = 125 + b/f 573 = 698 c/f

7.6 (e) Profit before interest + tax

		(A) 704,000	(B) 704,000	(C) 704,000
Less: Interest		4,000	4,000	4,000
Debenture interest		35,000	—	—
Profit after interest, before tax		665,000	700,000	700,000
Less: Corporation tax		266,000	280,000	280,000
Profit after tax		399,000	420,000	420,000
Less: Pref dividends		—	50,000	—
Earnings		399,000	370,000	420,000
No. of ordinary shares in issue		3m	3m	3.4m
Earnings per share		13.3p	12.3p	12.4p

(f)

	(A)	(B)	(C)
Fixed interest loans or pref. shares	500,000	500,000	—
Ordinary share capital	3m	3m	3.4m
Gearing	14.3%	14.3%	nil

Chapter 8

8.4 Goodwill (a) 90,000 − 74,976 = 15,024.
(b) 140,000 − 117,040 = 22,960.
(c) 100,000 − 90,435 = 9,565.

P + L a/c (a) Nil.
(b) 7,920 (100%).
(c) 75% × (7,920 − 3,540) = 3,285

Minority interest (a) 40% × 124,960 = 49,984.
(b) Nil.
(c) 25% × 124,960 = 31,240.

Chapter 9

9.1

	(a)	(b)	(c)	(d)
NP (loss)	14,790	(31,930)	73,790	(5,100)
Dep'n	10,200	16,600	31,000	22,500
Doubtful debts	2,000	—	5,000	4,000
	26,990	(15,330)	109,790	21,400
Sale of assets:	(1,500)	2,000	—	6,000
Funds generated from (absorbed by) operations	25,490	(13,330)	109,790	27,400

9.2 Increases; (a) (b) (c) (d) (e).
Decreases: (f).

9.3 Op-Cash 2,500 + Sources 3,500 + 2,500 + 7,500 = 16,000.
Applications (9,000 + 2,000 + 1,500 + 1,000 + 2,000) = 15,500.
Closing cash 500.

9.4 (a) NP 5,725 + Dep'n 12,500 = 18,225 + share issue 20,000 = 38,225.
Less: Applications (10,000 + 3,797 + 3,460) = 17,257 net source 20,968.
Inc in Stock 17,130, inc in debtors 6,760, inc in creditors (11,350), inc in bank balance 8,428.
(b) Current ratios 1983 1.05:1 1984 1.39:1
Acid test 1983 0.65:1 1984 0.79:1

9.5 (a) NP 17,400 + Dep'n 7,400 − Profit on sale of asset 1,000 = 23,800.
Other sources shares 7,000, assets 4,000.
applications debs 15,000; dividend paid 6,500; purchase of assets 12,400;
net source = 900.
Working capital changes: stock 23,000; debtors (32,200); creditors 4,000; bank 6,100.

   (b)   Current ratios   1983 2.7:1   1984 3.5:1
          Acid test   1983 1.9:1   1984 0.85:1

9.6 (b) P + L a/c: gross profit (derived) 40,240 + profit on vehicles 780 = 41,020.

        Less: Loss on equipment 360, depreciation 6,750, deb. interest 440 = 33,470 net profit

        Less: Tax 767, transfer to reserve 1,000, dividends (180 + 160 + 240) = 580

        Retained profit 31,123 b/f 2,540, c/f 33,663.

   (c)   Balance sheet: fixed assets: premises 45,000 − 7,500 = 37,500, tools and equipment 12,000 − 6,300 = 5,700, vehicles 11,000 − 2,200 = 8,800

        Currents assets; stock 5,276, debtors and prepayments 3,654, bank 760, cash 117. Current liabilities; creditors 4,085, tax 819, dividends 240

        Share capital and reserves: ordinary 9,000 preference 3,000, general reserve 3,000. P + L 33,663 = 48,663, plus debentures, 8,000 = 56,663.

9.7   Sources: profit 8,600 + dep'n 600 = 9,200.

      Applications: fittings 5,200, drawings 6,200.

      Net applications = 2,200.

      Working capital changes: stock 4,420; debtors 2,980; creditors 580.

      Bank (10,400) cash 220.

Chapter 10

10.1 GP margin (a)70%; (b) 49%; (c) 56%; (d) 26%.

       Stock turn (a) 119 days, (b) 51 days, (c) 308 days, (d) 200 days.

       Mark up (a) 140%, (b) 97%, (c) 127%, (d) 36%.

10.2 Current ratio (a) 3.1:1; (b) 0.8:1; (c) 11:1; (d) 4.5:1.

       Acid test (a) 1.05:1; (b) 0.6:1; (c) 8:1; (d) 2:1.

       Gearing (a) 16.7%; (b)–(c) 60%; (d) 25%.

10.3 (a) Return on equity capital (1984) 24%, (1985) 19%.

10.4 (a) Current ratio 1984 1.4:1 1985 0.9:1.

          Acid test   1984 0.6:1 1985 0.4:1.

10.5 (a)   (i)   L 3:1 P1:1.

          (ii)   L 1.6:1 P0.7:1.

         (iii)   L 4.2 times; P 17 times.

         (iv)   L 31%; P 23%.

          (v)   L 8%; P 7.5%.

         (vi)   L 8.9%; P 12.5%.

10.6 (a) Creditors payment period 32 days, rate of collection of debtors 40 days, rate of stock turnover 60 days.

   (b)   68 days (60 + 40 − 32)

10.7 1. 16%; 2. 18%; 3. 19%; 4. 14%; 5. 1.4 times; 6. (Fixed assets: total assets) 43%; 7. 0.19:1 (150:775); 8. 2.9:1; 9. 1.3:1; 10. 100 days.

Index